THEOLOGICAL HERMENEUTICS AND
1 THESSALONIANS

This book proposes a theological reading of 1 Thessalonians, making an important response to the increasing demand within Biblical scholarship to relate more closely to theological concerns. Paddison's interpretation adheres very closely to the text and is divided into three parts. Part I offers a theological critique of dominant historical-critical readings of 1 Thessalonians. Part II examines the history of interpretation of 1 Thessalonians, focusing on the pre-modern exegesis of Thomas Aquinas and John Calvin. Paddison explores what theological exegetes can learn from Thomas Aquinas' *Lectura* and John Calvin's commentary on 1 Thessalonians. Aided by the insights of these neglected pre-modern commentators, Part III presents a theologically driven interpretation of the letter. Theological exegesis is practised as a dialogue with Paul, the canon and a plethora of theological voices to elucidate Paddison's central argument that the astonishing subject matter of 1 Thessalonians is God's all-powerful hold over death.

ANGUS PADDISON is Postdoctoral Research Assistant in New Testament Studies at the University of Gloucestershire.

SOCIETY FOR NEW TESTAMENT STUDIES

MONOGRAPH SERIES

General Editor: John Court

133

THEOLOGICAL HERMENEUTICS AND 1 THESSALONIANS

SOCIETY FOR NEW TESTAMENT STUDIES

MONOGRAPH SERIES

Recent titles in the series

Theological Hermeneutics and 1 Thessalonians

ANGUS PADDISON

CAMBRIDGE UNIVERSITY PRESS
Cambridge, New York, Melbourne, Madrid, Cape Town, Singapore, São Paulo

Cambridge University Press
The Edinburgh Building, Cambridge CB2 2RU, UK

Published in the United States of America by Cambridge University Press, New York

www.cambridge.org
Information on this title: www.cambridge.org/9780521849837

© Angus Paddison 2005

BS
2725.52
.P34
2005

First published 2005

Printed in the United Kingdom at the University Press, Cambridge

A catalogue record for this book is available from the British Library

Library of Congress Cataloguing in Publication data
Paddison, Angus, 1979–
Theological hermeneutics and 1 Thessalonians / Angus Paddison.
    p.   cm. – (Monograph series / Society for New Testament Studies; 133)
Revision of the author's thesis (Ph.D.) – University of Glasgow, 2004.
Includes bibliographical references (p. 197) and index.
ISBN 0 521 84983 7
1. Bible. N. T. Thessalonians, 1st – Criticism, interpretation, etc. – History.   2. Bible.
N. T. Thessalonians, 1st – Theology.   3. Thomas, Aquinas, Saint, 1225?–1274.
4. Calvin, Jean, 1509–1564.   I. Title.   II. Series: Monograph series (Society for New
Testament Studies); 133.
BS2725.52.P34   2005
227'.8106 – dc22   2004061768

ISBN 0 521 84983 7 hardback

To R. P. and L. A. P.

CONTENTS

FOREWORD

It is as great a pleasure to introduce this important monograph to the reader as it was to watch, advise and encourage the research which forms its basis. In the diversifying world of New Testament scholarship, Dr Angus Paddison is positioned at the cutting edge of one of its most exciting developments – the rediscovery of the dialogue with theology about the *subject matter* of the New Testament. Several voices in recent years have called for this dialogue to be reopened, but there are still too few scholars able or willing to immerse themselves as deeply in theology as in exegesis, or vice versa. With freshness, boldness and prodigious industry, Paddison here explores not only why but also how such a dialogue should take place, and makes a distinct contribution in at least three areas.

In the first place, this volume analyses and critiques current historical criticism, as practised on 1 Thessalonians, for its failure to take sufficiently seriously the meaning-potential of the text, and for its focus on 'archaeological' features of the text to the exclusion of engagement with its subject matter. Not all readers will accept every element of this critique, but any reader with an ounce of theological interest in the New Testament will recognise the problem here exposed and the challenge here issued. Drawing on Barth's reaction to the historical critics of his day, Paddison asks us to focus attention again on what the text is talking about and pointing towards. If a contemporary philosopher (for instance, Martha Nussbaum) can wrestle with the works of Plato or Seneca, not as historical curiosities but as serious contributors to our own philosophical problems, why does New Testament scholarship so rarely get beyond historical contextualisation of its texts to constructive engagement with their theological content? And why is this so rare even among those who believe that the New Testament is in some sense revelatory? Thus simply formulated (and Paddison's formulation is far more sophisticated), the point may sound obvious; but it is extraordinary how rarely it is heard or heeded in mainstream New Testament scholarship, and Paddison's challenge is truly welcome.

Secondly, Paddison here shows, through two fine case-studies, the value of the history of interpretation in exploring the meanings of a New Testament text. In line with trends across the humanities, Biblical scholars are waking up to the significance of the Bible's extraordinarily rich history of effects. What historical criticism brackets out – in the pretence that we are the first readers of these texts – is here shown to be not only historically interesting, but also theologically vital, if we are to appreciate the power of these texts to generate new meanings in the process of interpretation. Eschewing a 'stamp-collecting' approach, which would catalogue every usage of his text, Paddison chooses to examine just two influential and indicative readings of 1 Thessalonians – by Thomas Aquinas and John Calvin. The depth and perceptiveness with which he analyses this material are, to my mind, a model of research in the history of interpretation, and should inspire and encourage other New Testament researchers to undertake similar ventures.

Finally, in the third part of this volume, Paddison puts his method into practice, in a theologically engaged reading of the eschatology of 1 Thessalonians. In a deliberately eclectic conversation across the ages (from the third to the twenty-first century) and inclusive of diverse theological traditions, the text of 1 Thessalonians is here plumbed for its theological potential in ways which greatly illumine Pauline theology and its contribution to Christian thought. Readers will notice the dynamic metaphors Paddison chooses (he aims to 'explore', 'unfold' and 'plumb' the truths which the text 'points towards'), since he regards the text not as a static repository of a single meaning, but as a ceaselessly productive source of meaning in the continuing process of interpretation. And for this purpose 1 Thessalonians and its eschatology are not just a conveniently circumscribed case-study: in its subject matter this text is also a paradigm of the process of interpretation, as it offers a present grace which is always incomplete, stretching towards the future in the mystery of God.

This monograph is thus in every respect timely, instructive and provocative. I hope that it will provoke New Testament scholars to further reflection on the nature and aims of our discipline, and lead some to develop similarly passionate dialogues with the text, with our theological heritage and with contemporary theologians – and with equally fruitful results.

JOHN M. G. BARCLAY
University of Durham

PREFACE

An earlier version of this work was produced as a Ph.D. thesis for the University of Glasgow. I appreciate greatly the rigorous questioning of my examiners, Professors John Riches and John Webster, and indeed their subsequent support. As this work moved to its present format Dr John Court was of great assistance, and Dr Katharina Brett a source of much patience.

Over the course of my studies I received financial support from the University of Glasgow, the Cross Trust (Perth) and my parents, Ronan and Lesley Paddison. To all these individuals and committees I am very grateful. My current post at the University of Gloucestershire has afforded me much-appreciated time to prepare this monograph and continue thinking about theological hermeneutics.

A host of people, far too many to mention, have been willing to talk theology and hermeneutics with me, and have been a constant source of provocation. Postgraduate friends – especially Marije Altorf, Mark Brummitt and Karen Wenell – broadened my reading and knowledge immeasurably, and assuaged the isolation of Ph.D. research. My supervisor, Professor John M. G. Barclay, was an endlessly generous source of scholarship, patience, guidance and enthusiasm. It is very fitting that he should be writing the foreword to this monograph.

There are, thankfully, people outside the ranks of New Testament studies and hermeneutics. Three in particular – Lesley Paddison, Dimitri Vastardis and Ben Leney – proved themselves to be superbly diligent and interested readers of the typescript, for which I am extremely thankful.

ABBREVIATIONS AND NOTES ABOUT CITATION

AB	Anchor Bible
AJT	*Asia Journal of Theology*
ATR	*Anglican Theological Review*
BJRL	*Bulletin of the John Rylands Library*
BNTC	Black's New Testament Commentaries
BTB	*Biblical Theology Bulletin*
CBQ	*Catholic Biblical Quarterly*
CD	Karl Barth, *Church Dogmatics*
CH	*Church History*
CO	*Calvini Opera*
Comm. Ex.	Calvin's *Commentary on Exodus*
Comm. Gal.	Calvin's *Commentary on Galatians*
Comm. Gen.	Calvin's *Commentary on Genesis*
Comm. Heb.	Calvin's *Commentary on Hebrews*
Comm. Isa.	Calvin's *Commentary on Isaiah*
Comm. Jer.	Calvin's *Commentary on Jeremiah*
Comm. Jn.	Calvin's *Commentary on John*
Comm. 1 Peter	Calvin's *Commentary on 1 Peter*
Comm. 2 Peter	Calvin's *Commentary on 2 Peter*
Comm. Phil.	Calvin's *Commentary on Philippians*
Comm. Psalms	Calvin's *Commentary on the Psalms*
Comm. Rom.	Calvin's *Commentary on Romans*
Comm. 1 Cor.	Calvin's *Commentary on 1 Corinthians*
Comm. 2 Cor.	Calvin's *Commentary on 2 Corinthians*
Comm. 1 Thess.	Calvin's *Commentary on 1 Thessalonians*
Comm. 2 Tim.	Calvin's *Commentary on 2 Timothy*
Comp. Theol.	*Compendium of Theology*
CTJ	*Calvin Theological Journal*
ELR	*English Literary Renaissance*
EQ	*Evangelical Quarterly*
FOC	Fathers of the Church Series

GOTR	*Greek Orthodox Theological Review*
HBT	*Horizons in Biblical Theology*
HTR	*Harvard Theological Review*
ICC	International Critical Commentary
JBL	*Journal of Biblical Literature*
JECH	*Journal of Ecclesiastical History*
JETS	*Journal of the Evangelical Theological Society*
JPT	*Journal of Pentecostal Theology*
JR	*Journal of Religion*
JSNT	*Journal for the Study of the New Testament*
JSNTSup	*Journal for the Study of the New Testament, Supplement Series*
JSOT	*Journal for the Study of the Old Testament*
JSOTSup	*Journal for the Study of the Old Testament, Supplement Series*
JTS NS	*Journal of Theological Studies*, New Series
LCL	Loeb Classical Library
MT	*Modern Theology*
NICNT	New International Commentary on the New Testament
NIGTC	New International Greek Testament Commentary
NLH	*New Literary History*
NovT	*Novum Testamentum*
NPNF²	*A Select Library of Nicene and Post-Nicene Fathers of the Christian Church.* Ed. P. Schaff and H. Wace, second series.
NTS	*New Testament Studies*
PG	*Patrologia Graeca.* Ed. J.-P. Migne.
RS	*Religious Studies*
RTR	*Reformed Theological Review*
SBL	Society of Biblical Literature
SBLDS	Society of Biblical Literature Dissertation Series
SCG	*Summa Contra Gentiles*
SJT	*Scottish Journal of Theology*
SP	*Studia Patristica*
SP	Sacra Pagina (commentary series)
ST	Thomas Aquinas, *Summa Theologiae*
SVSQ	*Saint Vladimir's Seminary Quarterly*
SVTQ	*Saint Vladimir's Theological Quarterly*
TB	*Tyndale Bulletin*
TI	*Theological Investigations*

TS	*Theological Studies*
USQR	*Union Seminary Quarterly Review*
WBC	Word Biblical Commentary
WTJ	*Westminster Theological Journal*

Where I cite the Biblical text in Greek, the translation supplied is my own; other Biblical quotations are from the NRSV. Quotations and citations from 1 Thessalonians usually lack '1 Thess.' before the chapter and verse number, except where this might cause confusion.

In the course of chapter 2, the study on Thomas Aquinas, we shall be reading from both the critical edition of the text, as found in the Marietti edition of 1953, and Michael Duffy's 1969 translation of the Thessalonians *Lectura* in the Aquinas Scripture Series. Citations will take the form of *Lectio* chapter number, lecture number and lecture division, followed by references to the translation.

In the course of chapter 3, the study on John Calvin, we shall be substantially reading from Ross Mackenzie's translation, published in 1961 (and republished in 1972) in the Calvin's Commentaries series (hereafter cited as *Comm. 1 Thess.*, followed by chapter and verse). References to Calvin's other commentaries published in this Calvin's Commentaries series and by the Calvin Translation Society also follow this format. Occasional reference will also be made to the critical text of the commentary as found in *Ioannis Calvini Opera quae Supersunt Omnia*, volume 52 of the Corpus Reformatorum series. Citations will follow the form *CO*, followed by volume and column.

INTRODUCTION

1   Recent scholarship on 1 Thessalonians

Like all Paul's letters, 1 Thessalonians has received much scholarly attention in recent decades. Since historical-critical interests drive much of this scholarly exertion, the question of origins remains the pervasive concern. Karl Donfried, a prominent Thessalonians scholar, articulates well the question motivating much contemporary scholarship on 1 Thessalonians: 'What was Thessalonica like when Paul first visited and established a Christian community there and what impact does this information have for understanding 1 and 2 Thessalonians?'[1]

There have been a variety of answers to this question. To anchor ourselves somewhere within the sea of conference papers, arguments, counter-arguments and monographs provoked by 1 Thessalonians we shall focus on three seminal and prominent essays. When each of these essays appeared it moved the argument on significantly and inspired other scholars to adopt new lines of approach in understanding the original context of delivery and reception of 1 Thessalonians. As we shall see, the three essays – by Karl Donfried,[2] John Barclay[3] and Abraham Malherbe[4] – have come to act as nodal points within 1 Thessalonians scholarship.

Karl Donfried's signal essay of 1985, 'The Cults of Thessalonica and the Thessalonian Correspondence', did not of course arise from a scholarly vacuum. Donfried's argument, that attention to the religious and civic cults prominent in first-century Thessalonica assists in understanding the letter's ethical and eschatological admonitions, is substantiated only

---

[1] K. P. Donfried, 'The Cults of Thessalonica and the Thessalonian Correspondence', *NTS* 31 (1985), 336.

[2] *Ibid.*, 336–56.

[3] J. M. G. Barclay, 'Conflict in Thessalonica', *CBQ* 55 (1993), 512–30.

[4] A. J. Malherbe, '"Gentle as a Nurse": The Cynic Background to 1 Thess ii', *NovT* 12 (1970), 203–17.

with the help of archaeological discoveries made earlier in the century.[5] Straining hard to hear the 'definite connotations' for the first-century Thessalonians,[6] Donfried attempts to place exhortations such as those in 1 Thess. 4:3–8 within the sexual excesses associated with the cult of Dionysus.[7] For Donfried these ethical exhortations represent Paul's attempt to mark out the distinctive behaviour expected of the Thessalonian church, in marked contrast to their former way of life, still evident in the numerous cults of Thessalonica.[8] So too, if we are equipped with an awareness of Thessalonica's religio-political climate, is it possible to understand the politically unsettling nature of Paul's visit, testified not least in Acts 17:6–7. The Thessalonian Christians' proclamation of another 'kingdom' (2:12) and 'Lord' (2:19) would have violated the Paphlagonian loyalty oath to Augustus and his successors.[9] Political opposition to Paul's gospel thus provides the context for the Thessalonian Christians' frequently mentioned affliction and suffering,[10] a persecution Donfried extends as far as possible martyrdom.[11]

Donfried's call to pay attention to the religio-political climate of 1 Thessalonians has been enthusiastically endorsed by subsequent interpreters. Holland Lee Hendrix, consolidating the arguments of various scholars,[12] reads the 'peace and security' slogan of 1 Thess. 5:3 as a direct riposte and critique of prominent *Pax Romana* propaganda.[13] Relying upon epigraphic and numismatic evidence and recent archaeological discoveries, Hendrix argues that between the first century BCE and the first century CE there was a significant shift in the political affiliations of Thessalonica towards Rome.[14] Paul's apocalyptic prediction of what would happen to those who trust the Roman assurance of *pax et securitas* is thus to be understood from this political context, for it is those who rely upon the might of the Roman Empire who will 'be the first to fall victim to the sudden wrath of God'.[15]

These counter-Imperial readings of 1 Thessalonians have found themselves congenial company within broader political readings of Paul's

---

[5] See, e.g., M. J. Vickers, 'Hellenistic Thessaloniki', *Journal of Hellenic Studies* 92 (1972), 156–70, and C. Edson, 'Cults of Thessalonica', *HTR* 41 (1948), 153–204.

[6] Donfried, 'Cults', 340.   [7] *Ibid.*, 337.   [8] *Ibid.*, 342.

[9] *Ibid.*, 342–4.   [10] *Ibid.*, 347–52.   [11] *Ibid.*, 349–50.

[12] E.g. H. Koester, 'From Paul's Eschatology to the Apocalyptic Schemata of 2 Thessalonians', in R. F. Collins, ed., *The Thessalonian Correspondence* (Leuven: Leuven University Press, 1990), pp. 449–50.

[13] H. L. Hendrix, 'Archaeology and Eschatology at Thessalonica', in B. A. Pearson, ed., *The Future of Early Christianity: Essays in Honor of Helmut Koester* (Minneapolis: Fortress Press, 1991), pp. 441–58.

[14] *Ibid.*, pp. 114–18.   [15] *Ibid.*, p. 118.

proclamation that have come into vogue. Central to the argument that Paul is an irritant of the Imperial system is the insistence that the background of Paul's use of 'gospel' (εὐαγγέλιον) is that the same word was associated with Imperial proclamations of victory and conquest. This is especially relevant for a letter in which the term 'gospel' has a proportionately high occurrence.[16] Political readings of Paul have found expression in 1 Thessalonians scholarship most recently in J. R. Harrison's attempt to place the eschatological imagery of 1 Thess. 4:13–5:11 in an anti-Imperial, counter-cultural framework.[17] Like the work of Donfried, which can be understood as its forefather, J. R. Harrison's article reconstructs the allusions and connotations as the letter's original audience would have heard them. Just as for Donfried, Harrison's driving concern is to understand the hostile response of the Romans, as evidenced in Acts 17:7.[18] Harrison argues that Paul's chosen words and phrases throughout 1 Thessalonians, with their constant Imperial allusions, are 'a radical subversion of Roman eschatological imagery and terminology'.[19] Sensitivity to the letter's Imperial context persuades us of Paul's intention: to demonstrate the superiority of the risen and returning Christ to worldly, yet dominant, Imperial eschatologies. Thus, the various other contexts that have been suggested for Paul's eschatological admonitions – Gnostics contradicting Paul by spiritualising belief in the resurrection or sheer ignorance on the part of the Thessalonians, to list just two – are displaced in favour of an image of Paul as a political subversive.

John Barclay's essay 'Conflict in Thessalonica' shares something in common with these 'political' readings of 1 Thessalonians, insofar as his prime interest is 'the conflict in Thessalonica between Christians and non-Christians'.[20] Barclay's careful analysis of the likely causes of conflict in Thessalonica steers away from Donfried's tentative suggestion that some Thessalonian Christians died for their faith.[21] Rather, the suffering frequently mentioned in 1 Thessalonians is best understood as 'social harassment',[22] emanating from fellow Gentiles angered by those who had abruptly shunned their regular civic and religious activities as a consequence of their conversion to Christianity.[23]

John Barclay's essay is important, not just because it provides a refinement of the excesses evident in Donfried's and Robert Jewett's work on

---

[16] K. P. Donfried, 'The Assembly of the Thessalonians: Reflections on the Ecclesiology of the Earliest Christian Letter', in R. Kampling and T. Soding, eds., *Ekklesiologie des Neuen Testaments: Für Karl Kertelge* (Herder: Freiburg, 1996), p. 397.

[17] J. R. Harrison, 'Paul and the Imperial Gospel at Thessaloniki', *JSNT* 25 (2002), 71–96.

[18] *Ibid.*, 78.   [19] *Ibid.*, 92.   [20] Barclay, 'Conflict', 512.

[21] *Ibid.*, 514, n. 6.   [22] *Ibid.*, 514.   [23] *Ibid.*, 515.

1 Thessalonians, but also in the overtures it makes to social-scientific study of the letter. After discussing the likely causes of the social conflict in first-century Thessalonica, Barclay examines the letter's dualist apocalyptic symbolism, and argues that if we are aware of the Thessalonians' sense of social dislocation, then it is clear that experience and symbol will become mutually reinforcing.[24] The apocalyptic contours of 1 Thessalonians are thus best understood if we are sensitive to the social implications of the Thessalonians' traumatic conversion.[25] In the conclusion, however, Barclay states explicitly what has been implicit throughout, his tentative interest in applying sociological models to the Thessalonians' conversion experience. Citing the influence of Louis Coser's *The Functions of Social Conflict*, Barclay states that 'opposition from outsiders can serve a beneficial function in defining the boundaries of a group and reinforcing its boundaries'.[26]

Barclay's overtures to applying social-scientific approaches to study of 1 Thessalonians have been eagerly taken up by Todd Still and Craig S. De Vos. The work of these two scholars, in which sociological models of conflict are applied to the study of 1 Thessalonians, demonstrates the clear influence of John Barclay.[27]

Todd Still's *Conflict at Thessalonica: A Pauline Church and its Neighbours* is explicitly concerned with recovering the nature of the suffering experienced by Paul's converts in Thessalonica, an instance of intergroup conflict which he proposes can be understood best through the lenses of social-scientific study of deviance and conflict.[28] The influence of John Barclay's work on the social situation in Thessalonica is evident throughout Still's monograph, with 'Conflict in Thessalonica' being cited some thirty-five times. For Still, the apocalyptic tone of 1 Thessalonians is Paul's polemical response to the social dislocation both he and his converts were experiencing;[29] the Thessalonian Christians would have attracted the opprobrium of non-Christian family, friends and acquaintances for identifying with an 'upstart movement';[30] and like Barclay

---

[24] *Ibid.*, 518.   [25] *Ibid.*, 519.   [26] *Ibid.*, 529.

[27] C. S. De Vos, *Church and Community Conflicts: The Relationships of the Thessalonian, Corinthian, and Philippian Churches with their Wider Civic Communities* (SBLDS 168; Atlanta: Scholars Press, 1999), p. 1, p. 156 *passim*; T. Still, *Conflict at Thessalonica: A Pauline Church and its Neighbours* (JSNTSup 183; Sheffield: Sheffield Academic Press, 1999), pp. 17, 198, 209–14, 223–5 *passim*.

[28] For Still, *Conflict*, pp. 209–17, it is very important that the suffering endured by the Thessalonian Christians is not psychological, but involves some real level of physical harassment.

[29] Still, *Conflict*, pp. 197, 206. Cf. Barclay, 'Conflict', 516–20.

[30] Still, *Conflict*, p. 214. Cf. Barclay, 'Conflict', 515.

he argues that the suffering of the Thessalonians emanated exclusively from fellow Gentiles, and not a group of townspeople that might have included Jews.[31] Likewise, in broad sympathy with Barclay's thesis, Still locates the source of this Gentile opposition in their suspicion that conversion to Christianity was 'subversive to the foundational institutions of Greco-Roman society, namely, family, religion and government'.[32] Todd Still's more obviously independent contribution lies in his awareness of social-scientific study of intergroup conflict, and his application of this to the situation of external opposition portrayed in 1 Thessalonians. The conflict endured by the Thessalonian Christians, Still argues, had three effects: it reinforced the faith of the afflicted Christians; it strengthened congregational relations; and it served to heighten their eschatological hope in Christ's return.[33]

Craig S. De Vos' *Church and Community Conflicts: The Relationships of the Thessalonian, Corinthian, and Philippian Churches with their Wider Civic Communities* demonstrates an equal indebtedness to Barclay's 1993 essay (as well as some of Barclay's earlier work). De Vos' aim is to draw on social-scientific theory to explain why some of Paul's churches experienced conflict with outsiders, whilst others did not.[34] Where Still gives a fairly broad overview of social-scientific study of intergroup conflict,[35] De Vos examines social-scientific theories of the development of conflict in Mediterranean societies, investigating why conflict might vary in intensity in different contexts. De Vos argues that Greco-Roman cities, with their high degree of socialisation, can be classified as *Gemeinschaft*-types of community,[36] those whose close internal bonds make them more predisposed to sharp conflict.[37] The differences between Greek and Roman societies in conflict response can be traced to divergent approaches and attitudes towards religion.[38] Consolidating his argument with a comparison between the social-structural composition of Greek and Roman cities,[39] De Vos proposes that Greek communities represent a higher-conflict culture than Roman communities (although both, being Mediterranean, represent a high-conflict culture). De Vos successively reconstructs the nature of first-century Thessalonica and the Christian community established by Paul before examining the 'severe

[31] Still, *Conflict*, pp. 218–27. Cf. Barclay, 'Conflict', 514.

[32] Still, *Conflict*, pp. 228–67 (esp. p. 267). Cf. Barclay, 'Conflict', 515.

[33] Still, *Conflict*, pp. 268–86.   [34] De Vos, *Church*, pp. 5–8.

[35] Still, *Conflict*, pp. 107–24.

[36] De Vos is drawing upon the sociology of F. Tönnies, *Community and Society: Gemeinschaft und Gesellschaft* (East Lansing: Michigan State University Press, 1957).

[37] De Vos, *Church*, pp. 28–42.   [38] *Ibid.*, pp. 42–86.   [39] *Ibid.*, pp. 87–116.

conflict' between the church and its civic neighbours.[40] This high level of conflict can be linked to Thessalonica's status as a *civitas libera* and a correspondingly dominant Greek mentality in terms of political structure and religious practice. Such conflict can be traced to a combination of Thessalonica's norms, values and beliefs; the lack of cross-cutting ties or ethnic integration within the Thessalonian church; and the Thessalonian Christians' impotence within the wider political structures of the city.[41]

Abraham Malherbe's essay '"Gentle as a Nurse": The Cynic Background to 1 Thess ii' decisively interrupted hitherto dominant interpretation of 1 Thess. 2:1–12. For many decades these verses had overwhelmingly been read as apologetic, though there was little agreement about whether Paul was defending himself from specific attacks by either Jewish or Gnostic opponents.[42] There had been some occasional lone voices, not least that of Martin Dibelius in 1937, who proposed that Paul was drawing on examples of wandering Cynic philosophers who held up their selfless behaviour as a paradigm.[43]

Malherbe's fuller exposition of this thesis in his 1970 essay has now come to represent an influential riposte to apologetic readings of 1 Thess. 2:1–12 and thus to reading the text always as a foil to an event lying behind it. Malherbe exposes the similarities in language and style between Paul and the Cynic philosopher Dio Chrysostom's (40–120 CE) Alexandrian oration in which he sets out the qualities of a true philosopher. Crucial for the thesis Malherbe is trying to draw out of this parallel is that in Dio's oration there is 'no question of his [Dio] having to defend himself here against *specific* charges that he was a charlatan'.[44] Rather, Dio's aim is to illustrate the kind of preacher he is, by comparing himself to other Cynic philosophers, many of whom he denigrates. Malherbe demonstrates how 'strikingly similar' are Dio's critical depiction of Cynic preachers and Paul's antithetical description of his own behaviour in Thessalonica.[45] Many of these similarities demonstrate compelling lexical parallels.[46] If these parallels convince us, it is not unreasonable to use Dio's context in helping us understand 1 Thessalonians 2:

[40] *Ibid.*, pp. 123–77 (esp. p. 176).   [41] *Ibid.*, pp. 292–300.

[42] For the former view see J. E. Frame, *A Critical and Exegetical Commentary on the Epistles of St Paul to the Thessalonians* (ICC; Edinburgh: T. & T. Clark, 1912), pp. 9–10; for the latter view see W. Schmithals, *Paul and the Gnostics*, tr. J. E. Steely (Nashville: Abingdon Press, 1972), pp. 123–218.

[43] M. Dibelius, *An die Thessalonicher I, II; An die Philipper* (Tübingen: J. C. B. Mohr, 1937), pp. 7–11.

[44] Malherbe, '"Gentle as a Nurse"', 205 (my italics).

[45] *Ibid.*, 216.   [46] *Ibid.*, 216–17.

One is not obliged to suppose that Dio was responding to specific statements that had been made about him personally. In view of the different types of Cynics who were about, it had become desirable, when describing oneself as a philosopher, to do so in negative and antithetic terms. This is the context within which Paul describes his activity in Thessalonica. We cannot determine from his description that he is making a personal apology.[47]

Malherbe's argument is that Paul is not responding to a *specific* complaint, but is drawing upon traditional motifs used in discussion of Cynic preachers. In his subsequent work Malherbe has sought to demonstrate further Paul's paraenetic intentions in providing the Thessalonian Christians with a self-depiction worthy of imitation.

Malherbe's thesis has generally been well received, and with the recent enthusiasm for rhetorical readings of Paul's letters, there has been a general shift away from 'apologetic readings' of 1 Thess. 2:1–12. With now just a few voices of dissent, most scholars are convinced that in 1 Thess. 2:1–12 Paul's intention is to present before the Thessalonian Christians his own apostolic example as one worth emulating.[48] Whereas antithetical statements were previously read as mirrors of polemical situations, Malherbe's essay signalled a scholarly shift away from the 'reconstruction of unverifiable data behind the text' towards that which is only 'explicitly offered by the text'.[49]

These three essays, by Karl Donfried, John Barclay and Abraham Malherbe, represent highly significant contributions to recent Thessalonians scholarship. They are important, not just for the new perspectives they have provided on 1 Thessalonians, but for the impetus they have given to subsequent political, social-scientific and rhetorical readings of Paul's letter. Moreover, they are contributions representative of the diverse field that is contemporary Pauline interpretation.

2 Theological interpretation of Scripture and interest in *Wirkungsgeschichte*

Despite all this scholarly exertion, which we have only glimpsed so far, there are still lacunae in the study of 1 Thessalonians. One such gap,

---

[47] *Ibid.*, 217.

[48] O. Merk, '1 Thessalonians 2:1–12: An Exegetical Study', in K. P. Donfried and J. Beutler, eds., *The Thessalonians Debate: Methodological Discord or Methodological Synthesis?* (Grand Rapids: Eerdmans, 2000), p. 112.

[49] J. S. Vos, 'On the Background of 1 Thessalonians 2:1–12: A Response to Traugott Holtz', in Donfried and Beutler, *The Thessalonians Debate*, p. 82.

which this study proposes to meet, is the epistle's theological interpretation. To be sure, there have been attempts to exposit the epistle's theology. Without presaging the critique presented in chapter 1, I shall say merely that such theological offerings have remained stubbornly tied to regnant historical-critical modes of reading.[50] There has been a notable silence in exposing theological treatments of 1 Thessalonians either to the text's history of interpretation or to (broadly) systematic categories of theological thought. This might seem unsurprising were it not both for the recent emergence of interest in the Bible's history of interpretation and use (it is worth noting that the two are slightly different), *and* the prominence and volume of those advocating a closer relationship between the disciplines of Biblical studies and systematic theology. Study of 1 Thessalonians has stood stubbornly aloof from both these academic currents.

Literature on both of these academic trends is voluminous. Within the last decade a growing band of scholars have argued for a closer relationship between theological categories of thought and Biblical studies. These appeals have emanated from both the guild of Biblical scholars and systematic theological colleagues, with the contributions of Francis Watson, John Webster and Stephen Fowl perhaps especially standing out.

Alongside this growing interest in the perceived need for systematic theology and Biblical scholarship to work more closely has been a growing awareness that one of the more interesting aspects of the Scriptural text is its life after it has left the pen of its author. As the quest for the authorial intention has waned, so examination of the Bible's history of effects has gathered momentum, with the academy gradually realising that one of the more engaging aspects of a text's history is the sheer variety of readings it has proved able to sustain. A variety of scholars have called attention to this aspect of the Biblical text's historicity,[51] as readings capable of casting new perspectives on the text's ambiguities and richness of meaning, and of providing a 'hermeneutical bridge from the world of the text to the world of the Christian reader and his or her community'.[52] Three German terms, all of them broadly within this school, are used to refer to three different areas of interest: *Wirkungsgeschichte* (history of effects); *Auslegungsgeschichte* (interpretation history); and *Rezeptionsgeschichte* (reception history).

[50] E.g. K. P. Donfried, 'The Theology of 1 Thessalonians', in K. P. Donfried and I. H. Marshall, *The Theology of the Shorter Pauline Letters* (Cambridge: Cambridge University Press, 1993), pp. 1–79.

[51] E.g. U. Luz, *Matthew in History: Interpretation, Influence, and Effects* (Minneapolis: Fortress Press, 1994).

[52] M. Bockmuehl, 'A Commentator's Approach to the "Effective History" of Philippians', *JSNT* 60 (1995), 87.

This growing interest in the Bible's meaning and significance in the light of its reading and impact throughout history manifests itself in different forms. The commentaries of Ulrich Luz on Matthew and Anthony Thiselton on 1 Corinthians have sought to incorporate insights from the text's use and influence within their comments on the text. Allied to this is the Ancient Christian Commentary on Scripture series edited by Thomas C. Oden, which has translated and made available a wide selection of Patristic exegesis. Margaret Mitchell has recently offered a monograph on Chrysostom's exegesis of Paul. A new commentary series to be published by Blackwell promises 'a genuinely new approach in . . . [its] emphasis on the way the Bible has been used and interpreted through the ages, from the church fathers through to current popular culture, and in spheres as diverse as art and politics, hymns and official church statements'.[53] Interest in the Biblical text's afterlives – whether in the medium of relatively élite literature or through more diffuse cultural representations – is undeniably in ascendancy.

3   The contribution of this study

In this broad depiction of scholarly activity where does the contribution of this book lie? First, and most importantly, the book endeavours to make a contribution towards understanding 1 Thessalonians. In this sense the constantly stable element of our labours is the eighty-nine verses that make up this earliest extant Christian text. Choosing to focus on this text we inescapably become part of its continuing interpretation, some of whose recent trends were sketched above.

If the text of 1 Thessalonians is the focus of attention throughout this study, the constant mode of interpretation is theological. This is a study that attempts to make a contribution within the growing project of relating Biblical studies more closely to theological concerns. As one commentator sympathetic to the *Auslegungsgeschichte* states, 'the widespread rejection of theological interpretation in contemporary exegesis is a most extraordinary self-inflicted wound',[54] and it is with that similar conviction that I shall offer an interpretation of 1 Thessalonians

---

[53] http://www.blackwellpublishing.com/SeriesBySeries.asp?series=BC& SearchOrd= Rank&type=series&show=Sseries&subj=RB&site=1.

[54] J. K. Riches, 'Theological Interpretation of the New Testament and the History of Religions – Some Reflections in the Light of Galatians 5:17', in A. Y. Collins and M. M. Mitchell, eds., *Antiquity and Humanity: Essays on Ancient Religion and Philosophy – Presented to Hans Dieter Betz on his 70th Birthday* (Tübingen: Mohr Siebeck, 2001), p. 261.

that constantly interacts with 'systematic' theological categories of thought. Correspondingly, one of the major themes of this book is a marked unease at the balkanisation inflicted upon the Christian theological endeavour. The fragmentation of theology – a symptom of its professionalisation within the context of post-Enlightenment universities – is a cause for regret, insofar as the various ways of thinking and exploring theologically (be they 'systematic' or 'Biblical') are directed towards the understanding of God revealed in Christ. In this sense, given its subject matter, Christian theology's tendency to fragment into a myriad of disciplines which have come to forget their mutual relations is a fateful step.

Two theological *leitmotivs* recur implicitly and explicitly throughout the interpretations of the text I successively critique (Part I), explore (Part II) and propose (Part III). These *leitmotivs* guide and direct the shape of the argument as a whole. The first *leitmotiv* is the conviction that in 1 Thessalonians we are reading the issue of an apostle, and hence words of witness pointing to a reality calling for ever deeper attention and exploration. The second *leitmotiv* is that the revelation of God in Christ is a ceaselessly profound well of meaning, a depth and potential plumbed in the church's reading of its Scripture. As this book progresses, the witness of the text will be accumulatively glimpsed, discerned and explored, as something that *emerges* from attention to the text's interpretation history, an interpretation history situated within our understanding of revelation.

The importance of 'witness' and the text as an agency within the 'process of revelation' arises from the reading of two of the most important conversation partners for this book: Karl Barth and Dumitru Stǎniloae. It is these theologians who have indicated the potential of grappling with the 'witness' character of Paul's writing and the conception of revelation, in which Scriptural exegesis plays its part, best understood as an eschatological momentum.

From the work of Karl Barth (1886–1968) we have become convinced of the importance and urgency of wrestling with the miracle of witness within the words of Scripture, that aspect of the text which radically points away from itself and wills the transformation of its readers. This hermeneutical aspect of Karl Barth's theological exegesis is receiving growing interest and inquiry, and will be enthusiastically followed through in our attempt to understand Paul's thought. For Barth, Paul was above all a witness to revelation, and if we are to understand him we must prepare to be gripped by what gripped him. It is from within this commitment to Paul as an apostle, as one who sees things that we could not see for ourselves unaided,[55] that the thorny question of authorial intention is properly placed. Understanding Paul as author is less a question of understanding his putative authorial intention, and far more a question of comprehending (if not allowing ourselves to be comprehended by) the object Paul is willing us to perceive. The climactic aim of this close reading which Barth proposes is for the witness miraculously to become the Word and for the reality indicated by the text to take root in our lives.[56]

Barth's plea that we should encounter the miraculous witness of the Bible, i.e. what the text is really pointing to, is an important theme throughout this study. An equally important theme infiltrating our encounter with the text's history of exegesis (in Thomas Aquinas, Calvin and others) is that revelation is best approached as an eschatological dynamic, a momentum discerned in the church's task of unfolding the meaning of Paul's witness. It is here that the thought of the Romanian Orthodox theologian Dumitru Stăniloae (1903–93) has been influential. The profundity of his thought is only slowly being realised in the West, although he has been compared to such theological luminaries as Karl Rahner and Karl Barth.[57] Dumitru Stăniloae's theological style, needless to say, is rather different from that of Karl Barth. Imbued with the Fathers (not least the cosmic vision of the seventh-century Byzantine theologian Maximus the Confessor), Stăniloae's thought is spiritual and doxological to its core, a reminder that 'theology is nothing else than an existential expression of the Spirit's life offered to God'.[58]

Stăniloae's theology, centred on the cosmic transfiguration manifest in the incarnation, creatively interplays God's transcendence and his involvement within the world, or the necessarily apophatic and cataphatic elements of theology, and hence it is no surprise that his thought contains much reflection on revelation within the continuing life of the church. For Stăniloae, the revelation of God in Christ is the central mystery of the world, and 'the source from which the power which continually maintains the divine life in the church unceasingly springs'.[59] The event of the incarnation is, for Stăniloae, the dynamic pulling together of the infinite

---

[55] K. Barth, 'Biblical Questions, Insights and Vistas', in *The Word of God and the Word of Man*, tr. D. Horton (New York: Harper and Row, 1957), p. 63.

[56] *Ibid.*, p. 75.

[57] I. Bria, 'The Creative Vision of D. Stăniloae: An Introduction to his Theological Thought', *Ecumenical Review* 33 (1981), 53.

[58] *Ibid.*, 59.

[59] D. Stăniloae, 'The Mystery of the Church', no tr., in G. Limouris, ed., *Church, Kingdom, World: The Church as Mystery and Prophetic Sign* (Geneva: World Council of Churches, 1986), p. 53.

God with finite humanity, a communication of God's ceaseless spiritual fecundity,[60] an encounter whose meaning is unfolded in the dynamic, progressive life of the church schooled to see the divine will within the form of the world's apparent opaqueness:

> God in himself is a mystery. Of his inner existence nothing can be said. But through creation, through providence and his work of salvation, God comes down to the level of man . . . Touching our spirit he wakens in us thoughts and words which convey the experience of his encounter with us. But at the same time we realize that our thoughts and our words do not contain him completely as he is in himself . . . Our words and thoughts of God are both cataphatic and apophatic, that is, they say something and yet at the same time they suggest the ineffable. If we remain enclosed within our formulae they become our idols; if we reject any and every formula we drown in the undefined chaos of that ocean. Our words and thoughts are a finite opening towards the infinite, transparencies for the infinite.[61]

Stăniloae's conception of theology as an unceasing exploration of the mystery of God's will in Christ, revealed in Scripture, and sustained by the church's historical reflection on 'the content lying within' Scripture,[62] provides a central insight for the shape of this book.

These conceptions of Paul's text as a witness to revelation, and revelation as an eschatological dynamic expanding through time, under-gird the book as a whole, as it moves in Part I *to critique* historical-critical readings of 1 Thessalonians, *to explore* in Part II the 'interpretation history' of the text in the specific instances of Thomas Aquinas (1224–75) and John Calvin (1509–64), and *to propose* in Part III my own theological reading of the text. In this sense, this book is an exploratory attempt to follow through with utter seriousness the witness of the text, a witness that only begins to emerge through careful reading of Thomas and Calvin. Throughout this book, it is worth emphasising, terms like 'witness', 'ultimate reality' and 'subject matter' will be deployed as virtual synonyms to indicate our interest in the substance of what the text is ultimately trying to communicate and hence what requires attention from us as theologians.

---

[60] *Ibid.*, p. 54.

[61] D. Stăniloae, 'The Holy Trinity: Structure of Supreme Love', in *Theology and the Church*, tr. R. Barringer (Crestwood: Saint Vladimir's Seminary Press, 1980), p. 73.

[62] C. Miller, *The Gift of the World: An Introduction to the Theology of Dumitru Stăniloae* (Edinburgh: T. & T. Clark, 2000), p. 46.

Part I of the book presents a theologically informed critique of dominant strands in the historical-critical interpretation of 1 Thessalonians. Whilst constantly seeking to work with models of Biblical interpretation as it is in practice deployed and defended, we shall likewise engage with the theological and hermeneutical concepts of revelation and conversation. Particularly important to the formation of the thoughts in chapter 1 is the work of Karl Barth and Dumitru Stăniloae, but also the theologians David Brown and David Tracy. Working alongside and with instances of Biblical scholarship on 1 Thessalonians, I shall propose that historical criticism can be critiqued from three perspectives: that it operates with a restricted notion of meaning and truth; that its historicist tendencies tend to limit the dynamic potential of Scripture's language; and that historical critics are vulnerable to readings which completely miss the subject matter of the very texts they are studying.

The final conclusion of Part I leads naturally on to the task of Part II, which is to explore the under-utilised commentaries of Thomas Aquinas and John Calvin. Our study of these two readers of the text is correctly viewed from the perspective set out on the process of revelation within the church (above, and in Part I in sustained detail). Responsible to the historical context and hermeneutical devices of both of these pre-modern commentators I am equally attentive to their potential in helping us explore the depth of 1 Thessalonians. My turn to the text's history of interpretation, in particular its pre-modern interpretation, is motivated both by the search for new methodological tools with which to read 1 Thessalonians (in the light of my dissatisfaction with historical criticism) and by the quest for the text's witness.

Consequently, it is argued that in Thomas' commentary the causality of Christ's resurrection forms the climax and pivotal guiding point, a Christ-driven exegesis which we shall be keen to explore and expand in our own theological reading of the text. Calvin's exegesis is, unsurprisingly, somewhat different in style, but nevertheless offers us the vision of exploring the whole of 1 Thessalonians from an eschatological perspective which works with the dialectic of the future's transcendence and salvation as a principle already at work in the world.

Taking on board the hermeneutical and interpretative insights of these pre-modern voices on the text, in Part III I move to propose my own theological reading. The distinguishing characteristic of this part of the book is a commitment to the text itself, and the understanding of the text through a historically informed vision. Consequently, the insights of Thomas and Calvin are not the only aids to the proposed reading of 1 Thessalonians. Equally important in the theologically driven (or better, Christ-driven) exegesis offered in this part are numerous Patristic voices on the meaning and significance of the union of God in Christ. The attention paid to these voices should be read as my attempt to explore alongside them the infinite depth contained within Scripture. Especially important to the conversation constructed around the depth of 1 Thessalonians are Patristic figures most associated with Eastern Orthodoxy: Origen (c. 182–251); Athanasius (c. 296–373); Gregory Nazianzen (c. 325–89); Gregory Nyssen (c. 334–95); Cyril of Alexandria (c. 376–444); Maximus the Confessor (c. 580–662); John Damascene (c. 675–749) and Gregory Palamas (c. 1296–1359).

Other voices we shall consult in proposing a reading of 1 Thessalonians' witness are the previously examined contributions of Thomas Aquinas and John Calvin, alongside contributions from Karl Rahner (1904–84), Karl Barth and a host of other theologians and Biblical scholars. These are all notably eclectic voices, and my intention in convening them is not in any way to ignore the very real differences amongst their starting points and conclusions. The aim is neither to pretend that these differences do not exist nor to blend these voices into some flavourless cocktail, but rather to listen to their disparate contributions as a richness appropriate to the infinite depth of 1 Thessalonians. This is a project whose coherence and viability are best seen in its actual practice.

After hermeneutical insights have been garnered from Karl Rahner, the central drive of this part of the book will be to explore in their infinite depth *the images of redemption* presented in 1 Thessalonians, most especially the apostolic witness that 'since we believe that Jesus died and rose again, even so, through Jesus, God will bring with him those who have died' (4:14).

By the time this monograph's theologically driven reading of 1 Thessalonians reaches its conclusion it should be clear that the structure of this project is somewhat different from still dominant historical-critical modes of reading the Bible. This is patent not just from Part I, but equally from our study of the contributions of Thomas and Calvin, voices examined to help us garner the wealth of meaning contained within 1 Thessalonians. Recalling the all-important nature of the Bible's witness, and the infinite capacity of revelation, I make a sustained attempt in this book to show the possibility that in the eighty-nine verses of our focus there resides an ultimate reference of inexhaustible depth.

PART I

The critical task

1

1 THESSALONIANS AND THE HISTORICAL-CRITICAL PROJECT IN THEOLOGICAL PERSPECTIVE

Introduction

Historical criticism's assumed control over the reading of 1 Thessalonians is best challenged as it is actually practised, deployed and defended. Throughout this chapter, therefore, we shall analyse and critique instances of historical criticism, especially as they pertain to scholarship on 1 Thessalonians. Through these critiques, I hope that my distinct theological perspectives will begin to emerge. It is these theological perspectives, only partly forged in negative reaction to historical criticism, which will be worked out practically in the readings of 1 Thessalonians that comprise the remainder of the monograph.

This chapter will be composed of the following sections. To prepare ourselves theologically and hermeneutically for the ensuing critiques and proposals, we shall initially examine three important concepts implied throughout our work: historicism, revelation and conversation (section 1). We shall then be ready to launch our theologically driven critique of historical criticism by examining the work of two distinguished historical-critical scholars, James Dunn and Karl Donfried (section 2). The burden of section 3 will be to set out three specific charges that will be made against historical criticism. These critiques will be advanced in relation to specific instances of 1 Thessalonians scholarship and should be understood as something of a triad, as each belongs closely with the others. The first charge is that historical-critical studies operate with a limited notion of meaning and truth (section 3.1). The second charge is that historical criticism is disabled by a historicism that fixes language into a restrictively reflective relationship between text and original context (section 3.2). The third charge is that the historicism within historical criticism distracts historical critics from the actual subject matter of the Biblical texts (section 3.3). The conclusion (section 4) will prepare the way for the subsequent chapters of the book.

1   Historicism, revelation and conversation

Before proceeding any further it is necessary to set out some preliminary definitions of three theological and hermeneutical terms which will be deployed (implicitly and explicitly) throughout this study. These three terms are historicism, revelation and conversation.

1.1   Historicism

One of the charges I shall frequently make against Biblical scholars is that they are often disabled by a silent, or not so silent, historicism. This is a term which needs explanation, not least because amidst the variety of ways in which this term has been and is used, my use might be read as idiosyncratic. I am aware of the variety of historiographical, philosophical and literary schools of thought that have adopted the term 'historicism'.[1] In its own complex history of interpretation, 'historicism' as a term has been consistently intermeshed within prevailing ethical, philosophical and political debates.[2]

Historicism, as I identify it within Biblical scholarship, is an assumption that the meaning of what the Bible communicates, through its diverse literary genres, is basically *recoverable* by examining the text's particular historical context. The historicism I am opposing is, above all, one that de-limits and restricts the meaning of a text by retreating to the authority of a 'neutral' historical meaning. Such a perspective militates against *both* the timeless capacity of the Biblical texts as classics (the extent to which their status now is a record of their ability to speak apart from their context of production) *and* their revelatory potential (the extent to which they continue to speak to the church). This is how James Barr has defined historicism:

> historicism is the idea that, in order to understand something, the essential mode is to get at its origins. The historicist is never satisfied with the thing as it is, he or she has to understand it by discovering the past.[3]

Barr's focus on the historicist's dissatisfaction 'with the thing as it is' is crucial. The historicist is never content to read the text as it stands. For the historicist the *only* way to understand the text is to seek its origins.

---

[1] See G. G. Iggers, 'Historicism: The History and Meaning of the Term', *Journal of the History of Ideas* 56 (1995), 129–52.

[2] D. E. Lee and R. N. Beck, 'The Meaning of "Historicism"', *American Historical Review* 59 (1954), 575.

[3] J. Barr, 'Allegory and Historicism', *JSOT* 69 (1996), 106.

Examination of a text's origins often leads the historicist to the distracting possibility that there is an authorial intention we can retrieve, no matter how distant we are from the text's origins. In the historicist mindset everything we can say about a text is based on an assumption that the meaning of a text is exhaustively enclosed by the intention of its author, an intention excavated by a process that examines every nuance of the social-cultural conditions of the time of the text's original production.[4] For the historicist, Biblical texts are to be read as sources whose origins define, control and limit any reference they have beyond their original context. Rather than reading the text as it is, the historicist is distracted by an unholy triad: origins, intention and context. The search for the text's *origins* drives the historicist towards reconstructing the *author's intention*, best recovered through fixed attention to the text's original *context*.

The drawbacks of such an approach are legion. From a non-theological perspective an uncritical attachment to history and origins can blind the scholar to the ideological and subjective forces at work in historical reconstruction. For H. G. Gadamer, historicism revealed itself in scholars who neglected their own historicity, and hence could not grasp that a truly historical understanding always involves our pre-understanding of the history of effects of the text we are seeking to understand. Ironically, therefore, the naïveté of historicism is precisely a misunderstanding of the inevitably historically shaped form of our interpretations.[5]

From the theological perspective of revelation to be defined below, historicism clouds the theological claim that the Christian life is ener-gised, defined and sustained by that of which the text speaks, *not* the origins and original context of the text. What ultimately matters is not the putative situation behind the text, but the divine–human encounter that both drove the text's original composition *and* continues to sustain the text's interpretation. The historicist affords little space to the church as an interpretative community. In the perspective which equates meaning with origins,

> Scripture is no longer understood as mutually constituted by the story it narrates and the community to whom it is narrated – a community already contained within the story, as the story within it.[6]

[4] P. Ricoeur, *Interpretation Theory: Discourse and the Surplus of Meaning* (Fort Worth: Texas Christian University Press, 1976), pp. 89–90.

[5] H.-G. Gadamer, *Truth and Method*, tr. W. Glen-Doepel (London: Sheed and Ward, 1975), pp. 299, 314.

[6] G. Loughlin, 'The Basis and Authority of Doctrine', in C. Gunton, ed., *The Cambridge Companion to Christian Doctrine* (Cambridge: Cambridge University Press, 1997), p. 47.

Historicist Biblical scholars have a tendency to work with erroneous models of authority. All authority is transferred to the (reconstructed) author's intention, a reconstruction that often enjoys the first and last word, and is deemed to be recoverable through attention to the text's original context. This is an incipient form of epistemological foundationalism, an assumption that in a text's original context we have the absolute and unsurpassable meaning of the text. For Karl Barth, the historicist mistakenly locates the revelation of the Biblical texts, the aspect of the text through which God communicates his will, in the events lying behind them.[7] Such an approach mistakenly bifurcates the form and content of the text, for it is the very form of the text communicating its content that acts as God's revelation pointing *beyond* the text. In line with this, and as will be insisted throughout this monograph, the ultimate authority within any theological understanding of Scripture is that to which its authors witness, *not* the context within which they articulated their witness.

At this slippery level of inquiry, attention to metaphors and prepositions is important. True attention to the text, unhindered by distraction with the events *behind* the text, draws us closer *to* the text, and yet in this drawing us closer to the text, the text itself comes to disappear, as we seek meaning either *within* the text of Scripture[8] or by looking *towards* that to which the text directs our attention. (This image of looking towards the text's witness was central to Barth's theology of reading Scripture, for whom Paul was like the pointing hand of John the Baptist in Grünewald's painting of the crucifixion, signalling something far greater than himself.[9]) In contrast to the historicist fascinated by the origins of the text, Barth implores us to keep together the form and ultimate content of Scripture, and so to avail ourselves of the opportunity to

> leave the curious question of what is perhaps behind the texts, and to turn with all the more attentiveness, accuracy and love to the texts as such.[10]

1.2   Revelation

In referring to revelation we are, as before, employing a term that has been the focus of considerable debate. Revelation is unmistakably to do

---

[7] *CD* I/2, p. 492.

[8] This image is important in Maximus the Confessor's interpretation of the transfiguration, in which Jesus' shining clothes become a symbol of illumination akin to spiritual reading of Scripture. As at the transfiguration, where Jesus' ultimate divine reality is revealed, so too does a reading of Scripture which seeks the meaning *within* understand the divinity witnessed to by the Bible's humanity. See Maximus the Confessor, 'Difficulty 10', in A. Louth, *Maximus the Confessor* (London: Routledge, 1996), p. 109.

[9] Barth, 'Biblical Questions', p. 65.   [10] *CD* I/2, p. 494.

with the communication of God's will to the world, but the mode through which we understand or conceptualise this communication is open to much interpretation. Some prefer a divine-speaking model,[11] a verbal model in accordance with a conception of revelation as demanding more than human inference of God's will. Basil Mitchell gives voice to such a proposal of revelation as God 'speaking' to us when he defines revelation as God communicating 'to his creatures fundamental truths about his nature and purposes which they otherwise could not discover'.[12] Others, like David Brown, posit a developmental model of revelation, a mode of divine communication that continues through the life of the church.[13] Still others, like Maurice Wiles, posit a non-interventionist model of revelation, stressing receptivity and apprehension more than divine (verbal) communication.[14] But Wiles' tendency to emphasise creation as revelation leaves him exposed to charges of deism.[15]

A Barthian understanding of revelation would articulate it as an 'event', puncturing linear time and proceeding from a point 'outside and above us'.[16] As such it interprets us; we do not interpret it.[17] Revelation as a process, developed by Anglo-Catholics like David Brown, would arouse suspicion with Barthians, who portray revelation as God's communication *to* the church's members, not as something generated internally from *within* the church's discourse.[18]

By positing the doctrine of revelation we have, indisputably, entered a realm of considerable complexity, a world containing a panoply of issues and unresolved debates. Since revelation is always the revelation *of God*, this only makes our language even more vertiginous. Despite the inevitable complexity of the issues, no theological project can afford to ignore discussion of how God reveals his will, 'the first and last question for faith'.[19] In the exposition that follows we shall turn to the work of a number of theologians, two of whose merit and usefulness to our

[11] E.g. W. J. Abraham, *Divine Revelation and the Limits of Historical Criticism* (Oxford: Oxford University Press, 1982).

[12] B. Mitchell and M. Wiles, 'Does Christianity need a Revelation? A Discussion', *Theology* 83 (1980), 103.

[13] E.g. D. Brown, 'Did Revelation Cease?', in A. G. Padgett, ed., *Reason and the Christian Religion: Essays in Honour of Richard Swinburne* (Oxford: Clarendon Press, 1994), pp. 121–41. D. Brown, *The Divine Trinity* (London: Duckworth, 1985), pp. 57–70, presents a critique of W. J. Abraham's 'divine-speech' model of revelation.

[14] Mitchell and Wiles, 'Does Christianity need a Revelation?', 109–14.

[15] E.g. E. L. Mascall, *Theology and the Gospel of Christ* (London: SPCK, 1977), p. 203.

[16] *CD* I/1, p. 142.

[17] K. Barth, 'Revelation', in *God in Action: Theological Addresses*, tr. E. G. Homrighausen and K. J. Ernst (Edinburgh: T. & T. Clark, 1936), pp. 3–4.

[18] *CD* I/2, p. 65.

[19] P. Ricoeur, 'Toward a Hermeneutic of the Idea of Revelation', in *Essays in Biblical Interpretation*, ed. L. S. Mudge (London: SPCK, 1981), p. 73.

project were set out in the book's introduction. Especially prominent will be the work and writings of a Reformed, an Anglican and an Orthodox theologian: Karl Barth, David Brown and Dumitru Stăniloae. This eclecticism, typical of this monograph, is not meant to reduce the very important theological differences between these theologians, but to investigate how they can be convened in an attempt to understand the ultimate unity lying at the heart of Christian theology.

When Christian theologians speak of revelation, it is the revelation revealed in Jesus Christ that they must prioritise. Keeping revelation and Jesus Christ together as synonyms reminds us that when we speak of revelation it must be God's revelation, or God's acts apprehended only by faith, of which we speak. The Christian revelation is, to put it starkly, God in Christ. This revelation is normative, because it is in this event that the gospel is disclosed: that God met humanity in Jesus of Nazareth and, in the risen Jesus Christ, shows himself to be radically able to meet humanity still. The revelation that is God's manifestation in Jesus Christ is *the* defining event of Christian faith and history, and no Christian theology that wants to talk of God (let alone God's revelation) can afford to ignore this doctrinal concept.[20] My thesis is that although God's revelation in Christ is complete and unsurpassable, it is a fullness whose pressure is released into an eschatologically directed future.

Orthodox and Anglican theologians, like David Brown and Dumitru Stăniloae, conceive of revelation as a progressive process through time, a growth in apprehension and understanding in different times, sustained by the complete and constant revelation of God in Christ and the church animated by the Spirit. This apprehension of revelation, founded in the person of Jesus Christ, has the capacity to expand ceaselessly, an expansion in line with God in Christ's infinite depth. And the more we understand, the more revelation both expands and evades our full perception. Revelation, then, is an infinite and ceaselessly progressive movement experienced through the church, an intrinsically eschatological experience, for it is 'a road leading towards the goal of our perfection in Christ'.[21]

---

[20] These forcefully programmatic statements are not evasive of the metaphysical issues surrounding the incarnation's importance. From our perspective, the incarnation is important for what it reveals to humanity of the nature of God *and* for establishing the means by which God wants to make himself known to humanity. To talk of the importance of an 'incarnational revelation' is to talk of a genuinely reciprocal relationship, where our conception of revelation is shaped exclusively by what is revealed in and through the incarnation, and our understanding of the incarnation's meaning and significance is properly shaped by a growing sense of *how* God reveals.

[21] D. Stăniloae, *The Experience of God. Orthodox Dogmatic Theology. Volume I: Revelation and Knowledge of the Triune God*, tr. and ed. I. Ionita and R. Barringer (Brookline: Holy Cross Orthodox Press, 1994), p. 50.

The sole revelation interpreted by the church is the complete fullness of God in Christ. The church is aided in this task of discerning amplification through the sustenance of the Holy Spirit, who comes so that we might know Christ's benefits more exactly. The church, gathered by God in response to his Word, is then the locus of revelation, but is not in any way to be confused with what it both proclaims and lives in. Theology must find the vocabulary with which it can articulate revelation being *experienced* as a continuing and deepening salvific reality without eliding the church within revelation itself. Revelation is something that the church is continually absorbed by and within, without ever feeling that it governs revelation more than it is itself governed by it.

Again, the primary commitment must be to the normative and foundational event of revelation that is Jesus Christ. It is in the person of Christ that the absolute and unsurpassable 'dynamic' character of revelation has been grounded.[22] All that Christ makes known is that his fullness is apprehended only 'in successive presents'.[23] To say this is to affirm that the revelation that is God in Christ can only be embraced in its complete richness insofar as it is understood that different elements of its revelatory potential will be revealed successively through time, rather than definitively in any one time. As the Lord of time, Christ will always spill out of our attempts to confine apprehension of him in any one time.

Scripture, as a textual witness to the revelation of God in Christ, is an agency within this eschatological dynamic, for in every context of reading Scripture, as it interacts with an interpretative community that holds it as authoritative, revelation's profundity is more deeply explored. In every context led by the Spirit, Christ as the centre of revelation 'seeks to be known and appropriated more and more deeply, and to be loved more and more intensely'.[24] The Biblical texts are themselves clearly the pioneers of this interpretative tradition, the four-fold diversity of the gospels a reminder, were reminder needed, of the diversity of interpretation which Jesus Christ, as the subject matter of the text, can bear. In this very important way, the text (insofar as it is read through Christocentric lenses) is constitutive and formative of the amplifying tradition with which it is partner.

---

[22] *Ibid.*, p. 37.

[23] R. Morgan, 'Expansion and Criticism in the Christian Tradition', in R. Morgan and M. Pye, eds., *The Cardinal Meaning: Essays in Comparative Hermeneutics, Buddhism and Christianity* (The Hague: Mouton Press, 1973), p. 65.

[24] Stăniloae, *The Experience of God*, p. 45.

To deploy Clodovis Boff's metaphor, revelation is a 'spring of mean-ing' more than it is a 'cistern',[25] which is to say that Scripture is not some stagnant reservoir of meaning, whose historically controlled meaning is static and stultified in one time. Scripture, being a witness to revela-tion, witnesses to the nature of revelation in the way it endlessly con-veys meaning and spiritual profundity through the time of the church.[26] Gathering in meaning throughout its rich and varied course, Scripture points to a revelation eschatological in scope and direction. The rev-elation of Scripture, what God makes known throughout the course of Scripture's interpretation, is that interpretation is directed towards a *telos*.[27]

This notion of revelation, with the principle of its end already in opera-tion, is exceedingly pertinent to a Biblical text like 1 Thessalonians, with its heavy eschatological tones. This notion of an eschatologically directed revelation, balancing out our place in time alongside the eschatological principle at work in the church, repudiates any notion of the church's understanding through time improving and perfecting itself sounding like a principle of idealism. Just as our understanding now is not down to our ingenuity, so full understanding will never come in the church's time of ever-growing amplification, but at the *eschaton*, which is proleptically at work in the church already. There is no sense of fulfilment within the time of the church. Rather this is what the church is continually advancing towards, for the life of the church is *not* in this time, as Sergius Bulgakov would assert, 'identical with itself'.[28] Keeping the end of revelation's time as an eschatological end, and not as an end in any way achievable by us, ensures that revelation is free from being seen as merely a player in the results of historical processes. What revelation makes known is not that God has somehow been enclosed by history, but that the *eschaton* is itself driving history and time. It is God in eternity who enters into time. It is not we, in time, who decide how and when we enter into eternity.

---

[25] C. Boff, 'Hermeneutics: Constitution of Theological Pertinency', in R. S. Sugirthara-jah, ed., *Voices from the Margin: Interpreting the Bible in the Third World* (London: SPCK, 1991), p. 19.

[26] An appeal to the authority of the church as the interpretative community of Scripture, the community in which the Spirit is active, need not be confused with the authority of any hierarchy or Magisterium. Barth, not perhaps immediately associated with appeals to ecclesial authority, appealed to the authority of the interpretation of the whole people of God, albeit an authority continually punctured and pierced by the Word. See K. Barth, *The Göttingen Dogmatics: Instruction in the Christian Religion*, vol. I, tr. G. W. Bromiley, ed. H. Reiffen (Grand Rapids: Eerdmans, 1991), pp. 227–49.

[27] Stăniloae, *The Experience of God*, p. 39.

[28] S. Bulgakov, 'The Church as Tradition', in *The Orthodox Church*, tr. E. S. Cram (London: The Centenary Press, 1935), p. 26.

Working with a model of revelation defined by its *telos*, the church's amplification of revelation remains properly governed by its end in God.

The boundaries and norms of this dynamic model of revelation are ones shaped, defined and justified by the ever-normative revelation: God in Christ. Keeping our conversation fixed on the revelation energising all Christian discourse reminds us of the need to distinguish carefully between the *referent* of our discourse and the *form* of our discourse. The dynamic form of this model of revelation is essentially eschatological and dialectic. It is eschatological because it understands itself as part of a movement directed towards a *telos*. Revelation also has a dialectical shape, for it operates by moving and growing in understanding *around* its constant axis and referent – Jesus Christ. This image of an expansion from the unifying centre and return to Christ as central referent (whose perception is continually being transformed) naturally points us to our third concept ripe for definition – 'conversation'.

1.3   Conversation

> Neither interpreter nor text but the common subject matter takes over in genuine conversation.[29]

In a conversation about the normative revelation of Jesus Christ, as sketched above, there will be one pivotal aim, which will be to direct the interlocutors in their task to create the spaces in which God's revelation might be heard. This is best achieved through a faithful attentiveness to the subject matter of which Scripture speaks, which shapes and determines our conversation – Jesus Christ. From the theologian David Tracy we learn much about the potential of conversation as a hermeneutical exercise. To be sure, Tracy's model of conversation (emerging from his reading of Gadamer and Plato) is developed independently of the concerns motivating our project, for Tracy has consistently attempted to relate Christian theology to pluralistic religious and cultural contexts. The charges provoked by Tracy's openly correlationist theology, based on notions of common human experience, need not detain us.

The model of conversation can only be accepted on the basis of two predicates. First, and here we start at the most elementary level, to converse, the interlocutors must be alive, and possess enough energy to be able to respond, question and provoke. There simply is no conversation

---

[29] D. Tracy, 'Is a Hermeneutics of Religion Possible?', in L. S. Rouner, ed., *Religious Pluralism* (Notre Dame: University of Notre Dame Press, 1984), p. 124.

when one of the interlocutors is dead or, less starkly, passive. Our interpretation of 1 Thessalonians will maintain the liveliness of the Word in
the words by a two-pronged activity that will pay attention to the interpretations provoked by the text *and* continues to open out the text's subject
matter to new interpretation. Reading the text as witness, as something
continually pointing away from itself and willing us to understand the
reality of which it speaks, keeps the text alive by allowing it to disclose
the Word *to us*. This connects us back, by contrast, to historicism, for
where historicists are distracted by what lies behind 1 Thessalonians,
there is the promise that opening out in front of the text, 'we recognise
nothing less than the disclosure of a reality we cannot but name truth'.[30]

But a text that has the capacity to be enlivened, rather than deadened
some 2,000 years after its original production, is no ordinary text. So
where first we called for the necessity of a live text, the second predicate
is part of the first, for only a classic can still provoke and question centuries after its first appearance. A conversation is in need of a live text,
and it is in need of a classic text, if the conversation is going to produce
any light. The problem which Tracy presents, and one where postliberal
theologians like Lindbeck would charge him with failing in his duty as
a *Christian* theologian, is that a 'classic' is more thought of as a literary
than a Christian theological term. By importing such a correlationalist
term Tracy is faced with the task of teasing out the difference represented
by the Christian classic – Scripture – from the literary classics of Shake-
speare, Milton or Keats.[31] After all, if for Tracy a classic bears 'a certain
permanence and excess of meaning that resists a definitive interpretation',[32] it is hard to see how the Bible holds more authority than a copy
of *King Lear*.

Nevertheless, the virtues of a conversational presence are exceedingly
attractive. Werner Jeanrond aptly articulates Tracy's vision:

> The other must not be swallowed, but affirmed as other, if I
> really want to accept the possibility of becoming to some extent
> an-other, that is, the possibility of learning and of changing, of
> transformation and conversation.[33]

[30] D. Tracy, *The Analogical Imagination: Christian Theology and the Culture of Pluralism* (London: SCM, 1981), p. 108.

[31] D. Tracy, 'Creativity in the Interpretation of Religion: The Question of Radical Pluralism', *NLH* 15 (1984), 303: a classic 'will provoke, vex, elicit a claim to serious attention'.
But a religious classic will *also* 'provoke some fundamental existential question for the
human spirit'.

[32] *Ibid.*, 296.

[33] W. Jeanrond, 'Theology in the Context of Pluralism and Postmodernity: David Tracy's
Theological Method', in D. Jasper, ed., *Postmodernism, Literature and the Future of
Theology* (Basingstoke: Macmillan, 1993), p. 158.

At one level, conversation may just be the name we give to the necessary form of the interchange between the interpreter and the phe-
nomenon to be interpreted.[34] But a conversational hermeneutic has a
lot more potential than this inauspicious description would indicate. A
hermeneutical conversation, one committed to understanding and interpreting, will be committed to listening to the claim of the other voice
as truly *other*, for it is in the different contributions of the interlocutors to the *same* subject matter that understanding is achieved. Correspondingly, a hermeneutical conversation is kept alive by the constancy
and liveliness of the to-ing and fro-ing that pertains to any genuine
dialogue.

As we shall see in our examination of Krister Stendahl's proposals, and
his own 'history of effects', a model of conversation realistically accom-
modates the necessarily two-way process between text and interpreter
that is interpretation. Moreover, a conversational model of hermeneutics
would seem well fitted to our understanding of revelation's dynamism.
For a conversation has a predisposed reluctance to foreclose findings, possesses an enduring openness to new disclosures, and hence is compatible
with our model of revelation as process, grounded in the revelation that
is God in Jesus Christ. At the centre of the conversation we are hoping to
conduct with 1 Thessalonians lies Jesus Christ as common to the interests
of both the text and the interpreter situated within the life and discourse
of the church.

To converse with, in and through the text is something worked out in
practice more than it is articulated and theorised. Consequently, the virtues
of a conversation – listening to all the interlocutors as other, without
swallowing them up into an interpretative mélange – will be something
aspired to in practice throughout this monograph.

These three terms – historicism, revelation and conversation – are set
out in exploratory fashion, as perspectives which will both guide the
course of the book and be worked out in greater detail through the various readings of 1 Thessalonians we undertake. Just as these terms display
a certain preliminary quality in our understanding, so too is it important
to pay attention to their mutual connections. Our model of revelation
informs our anxieties in relation to historicist tendencies within Biblical
studies. Likewise, the outworking of this model of revelation is only possible through the intrinsically *integrative* vision at the centre of Tracy's
model of 'conversation', a feature exhibited in this book's eclecticism
and inter-disciplinarity (incorporating Biblical studies, historical theology and systematic theology).

---

[34] D. Tracy, *Plurality and Ambiguity* (London: SCM, 1987), p. 10.

2   Case-study and critique of the work of two historical critics

Now that preliminary explanations of some guiding concepts have been set out, we can turn our attention to specific historical-critical work. Our case-studies of the work of two historical critics will begin with an examination and critique of a classic defence of the past as past by J. D. G. Dunn.[35] Moving on from this more general overview, we shall turn specifically to historical-critical work on 1 Thessalonians, examining K. P. Donfried's work on the theology of the Thessalonian correspondence.[36]

It seems apt to begin this critique of the work of specific historical critics with James Dunn's essay, in which he programmatically sets out the propriety and necessity of historical-critical work. It is no surprise that Dunn, as a scholar who has dedicated his academic career to meticulous and historically rigorous work, seeks to establish the case for historical criticism. My critique of his argument will provide a helpful introduction to the more sharply focused critiques I shall present of specific historical-critical work on 1 Thessalonians (section 3).

In his 1995 essay 'The Historical Text as Historical Text: Some Basic Hermeneutical Reflections', Dunn essentially has two arguments with which, in isolation, no reasonable scholar could disagree. First, Dunn argues for the necessity of 'Lower Criticism', the work concerned with the actual Greek of the New Testament requiring exegesis. In his argument that the church (and presumably the academy) 'will always need to be able to call on members or specialists who are familiar with the Greek text' nobody could disagree.[37] One need only read any exegetical excursus of Barth's *Church Dogmatics* to realise how serious systematic theologians have long been convinced of that part of Dunn's argument. It is indisputable that some degree of linguistic competence is important to the understanding of the New Testament.

Dunn's second argument is for the 'Higher Criticism', charged with the aim of 'reconstructing the historical circumstances out of which the New Testament writings emerged', for 'the meaning of a historical text is dependent in some degree on its historical context'.[38] Dunn is right to argue that 'The historical text is linked to its historical context as a plant is rooted in the soil which first nourished it', but runs up against a whole host of hermeneutical questions and issues when he insists that

---

[35] J. D. G. Dunn, 'Historical Text as Historical Text: Some Basic Hermeneutical Reflections in Relation to the New Testament', in J. Davies et al., eds., *Words Remembered, Texts Renewed: Essays in Honour of J. F. A. Sawyer* (JSOTSup 195; Sheffield: Sheffield Academic Press, 1995), pp. 340–59.

[36] Donfried, 'Theology of 1 Thessalonians'.   [37] Dunn, 'Historical Text', p. 343.

[38] *Ibid.*, p. 344.

'to attempt to transplant that plant by ripping it clear from its native soil and shaking it free from that soil may work, but it is likely to kill the plant'.[39] The logical jump that Dunn makes here leaves him vulnerable to hermeneutically driven critiques. It is certainly true that in a very important sense *one* meaning of the Biblical text is that which is germane to its historical context. It is at the point where Dunn jumps from the assertion that there is a historical meaning (which there undoubtedly is) to the assertion that 'the NT is nothing if it is not first *and foremost* a series of documents written in the Greek of the first-century Mediterranean world' that I diverge from Dunn.[40] What has been canonised, after all, is not the authorial intention or the text's original context, but *the text itself as a witness to revelation*.

The hermeneutical questions provoked by Dunn's arguments proliferate. In what sense do historical origins really provide the 'firm rule and norm' for the meaning we find in the text now?[41] Why does Dunn appear to limit the 'truth' of the New Testament text to its historical referentiality?[42] In Dunn's positivist hope that we must 'transplant' the soil and plant together (i.e. original context and text) into our context now, is it not possible to detect an inappropriate prioritising of Christian origins, a move that risks limiting and foreclosing God's continuing revelation?[43]

In a Barthian mode, the truth of the text inheres in the subject matter of the text itself, not the authorial intention or situation behind the text. This observation reminds us that much historical-critical work often operates with an unspoken theology. Despite its claims to represent the virtues of objective and ideologically disinterested study, historical-critical scholarship has very often been closely concerned with establishing and defending particular theological positions.[44] James Dunn stands in a long line of Biblical interpreters who, through their historical work, explicitly or implicitly advocate a theology that situates doctrinal purity uncritically close to historical inquiry. It is where this theology is unspoken that a hermeneutics of suspicion is required, for a conversation's integrity is marked by the honesty (and self-awareness) of the interlocutors.[45] One

---

[39] *Ibid.*   [40] *Ibid.*, p. 346 (my italics).   [41] *Ibid.*, p. 347.

[42] Dunn, *ibid.*, p. 346, says of historical-critical interpretation, 'the goal in all these cases has been to be "true" to these texts, and that "truth" can never be separated from their character as historical texts'.

[43] This is something about which Dunn is candid. Without its established historical meaning 'the text is ever in danger of functioning merely as a puppet or a plaything' (*ibid.*, p. 347).

[44] Morgan, 'Expansion', p. 89.

[45] R. Williams, 'Theological Integrity', in *On Christian Theology* (Oxford: Blackwell, 2000), p. 3.

of the things which a theological interpreter of the Bible is interested in is transcending its original context in the hope of engaging with the eternal subject matter of the text, namely the true 'relevancy' and authority within the text. Dunn's imperative may be to keep text and original context together, but my imperative is to keep text and the subject matter of the text bound together, for if I am to be charged with the prioritising of anything, I hope that it is with the subject matter of the text, that to which the text witnesses. One of the things we know through the text is that the subject matter of the text has the capacity not just to engage with a host of different contexts, but also to point us to meanings distinct from any reconstructed intention of Paul. In the face of Dunn's observations I have, therefore, two central criticisms to make.

(1) Those interested in the 'history of effects' would remind Dunn of the rich meanings which the Biblical text can bear in different communities over the centuries. Such a stance, which takes into account the range of meanings the text bears over time, shows a greater fidelity to the 'historical text as historical text'. The reminder of David Steinmetz that to focus on authorial intention to the exclusion of a text's rich history of reception is '*historically* naïve' is one worth recalling in this perspective.[46] Such meanings remind us that the eschatological direction of the text's reference is much richer than its original meaning in its context of production,[47] radically questioning and destabilising the normative role which 'authorial intention' has long enjoyed.

It is timely to clarify our thoughts here on 'authorial intention'. Historical critics like Dunn presume that the author's intention is not just retrievable but essential for understanding the text in question; but there are two problems with the quest for the author's intention. First of all, I suspect that an author's intention is irretrievable. This stands for any text. Secondly – and here I am arguing with Scripture in mind – even if we could ever retrieve an author's intention, this could only ever act as a misplaced source of authority.

In relation to the first problem, it seems almost beyond question that what an author intended when he or she wrote a text is inherently irretrievable. Whilst we can *certainly* accrue information about the writer's context, his or her circumstances of writing and the likely situations he or she wanted to address, there is no way we can hope to enter into his or her

---

[46] D. C. Steinmetz, 'The Superiority of Pre-Critical Exegesis', *Theology Today* 37 (1980), 37 (my italics).

[47] Stăniloae, *The Experience of God*, p. 82.

'intentions' in writing. Once we start questioning the quest for an author's intentions, the questions proliferate. What do we mean by 'intentions'? Do we mean the surely futile attempt to tap into the mental processes within the human author's mind as he or she wrote?[48] Similarly, how do we account for those parts of the text that could not be part of the author's 'intention', the use of phrases and images over which the author had no control? What room are we willing to give to the author's lack of control of the text? Equally, how do we account for those 'intentions' that the author simply failed to communicate, assuming that there is no such thing as a perfect congruence between articulation and 'intentions'? The drive for the 'authorial intention' pays scant attention to the reality that there may be intentions of the text independent of the author, *and* that there may be intentions of the author independent of the text. In this sense, much talk of 'authorial intention' treats too dismissively the inevitably complex relationship between 'intention' and the words of a given text.[49] To move from knowledge of an author's context to a suggested 'intention' in writing is highly tempting, but ultimately it must remain a chimera.

Secondly, even if we could retrieve the author's intention, it is highly questionable just how useful or desirable such an 'intention' would be in understanding Scripture. All texts are, to a certain measure, released by their authors. In the context of Paul's letters, these texts become part of a very specific 'social treasury',[50] namely the discourse of the interpreting church, whose task it is continually to unfold revelation's meaning. This should not be seen as some subversive 'dethroning' of Paul as author, but a corrective against those who deploy Paul as a 'passive exegete',[51] a tactic that confuses the meaning of the text within its interpretative community (the church) with a verifiable authorial intention. Understanding 1 Thessalonians is about more than understanding Paul as author, an author whose intentions are presumed to hold the authoritative key to the meaning of the text. Our role is not to police the meaning of Scripture by appealing to a probable authorial intention, but to recognise that the meaning of Scripture is historically generated within the life of the interpreting church, and it is only from within this interpretative community that authority is most properly exercised.

[48] T. Eagleton, *Literary Theory: An Introduction* (2nd edn; Oxford: Blackwell, 1996), p. 99.

[49] *Ibid.*, pp. 58–60.

[50] U. Eco, 'Between Author and Text', in U. Eco, ed. S. Collini, *Interpretation and Overinterpretation* (Cambridge: Cambridge University Press, 1992), p. 67.

[51] S. Burke, *The Death and Return of the Author: Criticism and Subjectivity in Barthes, Foucault and Derrida* (2nd edn; Edinburgh: Edinburgh University Press, 1998), p. 23.

Releasing ourselves from the quest for the authorial intention need not mean that the meaning of Scripture is able to roam uninhibited in the ludic imaginations of its interpreters.[52] Insofar as Scripture's profundity is amplified from within the community of the church, the proper constraints and limits will always be there for members (or hierarchies) to declare what is and is not faithful to the wider faith of the church. Plurality and richness of meaning do not, at least not in the discerning will of the church, mean that 'anything goes'. In the face of fear of countless subjective readings, the presence of the church is a reminder that there is a *specific* community and tradition, normed by the Word, with the authority to determine the limits to particular interpretations.[53]

(2) The timeless aspect in any Biblical text is its revelation, what God makes known *through* the text. It is this aspect of the text that is authoritative, for it is this, rather than any irretrievable authorial intention, that has sustained its life in the church. The text's authority is thus sustained by its participatory quality – its constancy in encouraging people to engage with the transformation it points towards. Coming to terms with the subject matter of the text, Barth correctly apprehended the revelatory aspect of the text which points beyond to the text's boundless potential to unravel in meaning:

> It is rather a question of our being gripped by the subject-matter . . . really gripped, so that it is only as those who are mastered by the subject-matter, who are subdued by it, that we can investigate the humanity of the word by which it is told us.[54]

Properly subdued by the subject matter of the text and comprehending its potential to change *our* historicity, we shall therefore stand in congruence with the 'intention' of Paul (or any other Biblical author). One of our presuppositions is that Paul's intention was not to be bedazzled by his context of production, but to articulate how God's revelation in Christ has dramatically changed that context, and presumably every context. When we read the text as a sign and pointer to this revelation, our presuppositions are somewhere in line with the apostle Paul's – to communicate 'the Word of God which is at work within you' (2:13).

Dunn's essay represents a misplaced enthusiasm for the past, as if it were in itself authoritative, and an outmoded presumption that the past (the 'soil' of the text's context of production) can be cleanly 'transplanted'

---

[52] Cf. M. C. Taylor, *Erring: A Postmodern A/theology* (Chicago: Chicago University Press, 1984), p. 179.

[53] J. Stout, 'What is the Meaning of a Text?', *NLH* 14 (1982), 8.

[54] *CD* I/2, p. 470.

into our time. Grammatical and lexical reading of the New Testament is patently defensible, and essential to responsible readings of the text.[55] But when historical critics start alluding to entering into the spirit of an age and author, and claiming a hermeneutical priority and authority for these reconstructions, then the ground onto which they have stumbled becomes immediately more treacherous.

This examination of Dunn's work clarifies my concerns about historical criticism. What is 'first and foremost' for us is the subject matter discerned by close attentiveness to the text and not the historical context of the text, for it is the text, as witness and pointer to revelation, which has through history always pointed beyond itself, to encourage readers to grapple with what it is *really* saying. To connect with the reality of what Paul was transfixed by is not to connect with the text's 'historical otherness',[56] as if it were this that fascinated Paul. What Paul is absorbed by is the revelation of God revealing his will for us. Dunn would no doubt claim that he is defending the integrity of the text. Ironically, however, what he is actually doing is defending the predilections of historical critics, and neglecting Scripture's own claim to be a witness to God's revelation.

Karl Donfried's contribution to *The Theology of the Shorter Pauline Letters* on the theology of 1 Thessalonians is not so much a dynamic work of interpretation as an example of historical theology. Barth's critique of historical criticism could just as well apply to Donfried's work. There is little in Donfried's work that demonstrates the integration of close textual reading with the reality indicated by the text.[57] Far from grappling with the subject matter of the text until the walls of the twentieth century and the first century become translucent,[58] possible only through a genuine engagement with the text's subject matter, Donfried works with the text at a level which stultifies the dynamic reality residing as the text's centre.

---

[55] Since, when it comes to our exegesis of 1 Thessalonians, we shall be paying attention to the original Greek, it would seem propitious to set out some hermeneutical parameters for this 'Lower Criticism'. Eco, 'Between Author and Text', p. 68, points out that responsible readers are aware of, and take into account, the state of language at a text's time of writing. When translating the phrase 'sons of light' in 1 Thess. 5:5 it is, for example, important to know that φωτός should be translated as 'of light' and not anything else like 'of God'. Careful rendering of Paul's words is a useful reminder that language is not something with which we are free to do whatever we like. There is, however, a very real difference between this *basic* responsibility towards language and the presumption to know what was in Paul's head as he used certain words.

[56] Dunn, 'Historical Text', p. 358.

[57] T. F. Torrance, *Karl Barth: Biblical and Evangelical Theologian* (Edinburgh: T. & T. Clark, 1990), p. 118.

[58] K. Barth, *The Epistle to the Romans*, tr. E. C. Hoskyns (2nd edn; Oxford: Oxford University Press, 1933), p. 7.

Donfried's interpretation of the theology of 1 Thessalonians moves from establishing the setting of the correspondence to expositing the theology itself, setting out the relationship between 1 Thessalonians and Acts, and then suggesting some ways in which 1 Thessalonians may hold some contemporary relevance. In other words, he moves in a way Dunn would approve. Assuming the text is a *product* of its context, what it says is judged in the light of its reconstructed context of production (and not in the light of its subject matter), and from this perspective Donfried moves to 'transplant' this reconstruction into our contemporary context to see what it might say. Donfried's candid opening assertion itself indicates this move: 'It is a major contention of this analysis that an awareness of the social situation in Thessalonica . . . will greatly assist the task of *understanding* the theology of 1 Thessalonians.'[59] For Donfried what 'will greatly assist' in understanding 1 Thessalonians in reality always sidelines the text's richness of meaning in contexts other than its origins.

It will be one of the criticisms below that historical critics tend to slip into a simplistic correspondence between text and context, seeing the text too often as a subsidiary or servant of its context. Historical criticism has the capacity to ossify the power of language, seeing it merely as a pale reflection of its original context rather than something with the potential to transform both its original context and all subsequent contexts. In Donfried's purported theological study of a Pauline text, there is little engagement with the text as a revelatory text. It is my contention that if we really want to understand the theology of 1 Thessalonians, we must commit ourselves to a conversation about the subject matter which unites both us as readers and the Thessalonians, a subject matter which historical critics will be ill-disposed to perceiving insofar as, by its eternity, it transcends any one particular moment of history. The meaning of what is said in 1 Thessalonians is neither captured nor exhausted in first-century Thessalonica. For the historicist temptation that Donfried cannot resist is that the meaning of the text is its historically recovered meaning, which is certainly one meaning, but not *the* meaning of the text. By seeking, behind the ever-present historicity of the New Testament, for an engagement with what Barth calls 'the message itself', namely 'a unique event, a truly singular occurrence, with a significance far beyond anything the New Testament writers themselves or their contemporaries ever dreamed of', we will have the chance to do more than just write historical theology.[60]

---

[59] Donfried, 'Theology of 1 Thessalonians', p. 3 (my italics).

[60] K. Barth, 'Rudolf Bultmann – An Attempt to Understand him', tr. R. H. Fuller, in H.-W. Bartsch, ed., *Kerygma and Myth: A Theological Debate*, vol. II (London: SPCK, 1962), p. 85.

Donfried assumes that to understand the theology of 1 Thessalonians is to reconstruct (as far as is possible) the reasons why Paul wrote what he did. Thus Donfried argues that the Thessalonian Christians are undergoing severe persecution, even to the point of death,[61] and suggests that 'Paul's intention in writing 1 Thessalonians is to console a Christian community suffering the effects of persecution and death, to encourage the discouraged.'[62] Throughout his exposition of the theology of 1 Thessalonians, Donfried understands the theology purely in functional terms: 'the references to the suffering of the Lord himself, of Paul, and of other Christian congregations *serve* as a fundamental encouragement for the Thessalonian Christians, who find themselves in a difficult situation'.[63] Whilst this passes as an acceptable historical understanding of the text, it can constitute only the very beginnings of a suitably gripped exploration of the text's theological meaning.

My argument is therefore this: that Donfried (and many other colleagues) think that once you have got at the history behind the letter, you have got at the theology in explaining its function. Get the history right, and you will get the theology right, or so the historical-critical argument would seem to be. I remain suspicious of such a simple correspondence between history and theology. Rather, I would argue that it is vital to read the text in the complete richness of its historicity, striving to go beyond and reach out 'far beyond ourselves',[64] to grasp the same subject matter that drove Paul to undertake his missionary journeys. To undertake this task may well prove to be in complete fidelity to Paul himself, for Paul too was driven to seek that which was always above and beyond him; he too was 'totally absorbed by something (Someone!) other than himself'.[65]

Since the history which Donfried wants to reconstruct is largely inaccessible, and there can be no possible chance of re-creating the experiential circumstances of 1 Thessalonians, if we do want to get at the *theology* of 1 Thessalonians it may be wise not to invest everything in the historical project. The only thing that the text makes as accessible now as then is the subject matter to which Paul, as apostle, witnesses.

Donfried's work falls short of what I would term a 'theology of 1 Thessalonians' not because of his historical-critical approach (which stands to show his considerable learning), but simply because the text's historical

---

[61] Donfried, 'Theology of 1 Thessalonians', pp. 22–3.

[62] *Ibid.*, p. 5.   [63] *Ibid.*, p. 44 (my italics).

[64] K. Barth, 'The Strange New World within the Bible', in *The Word of God*, p. 33.

[65] B. L. McCormack, 'Historical Criticism and Dogmatic Interest in Karl Barth's Theological Exegesis of the New Testament', in M. S. Burrows and P. Rorem, eds., *Biblical Hermeneutics in Historical Perspective: Studies in Honor of Karlfried Froehlich on his Sixtieth Birthday* (Grand Rapids: Eerdmans, 1991), p. 326.

origins are Donfried's *only* conversation partner. There is no engagement with the history of effects, or with the subject matter of the text. In this sense there is no attempt to confront the subject matter that generates the text's revelatory potential through time. Since it has been consistently argued above that the theology of 1 Thessalonians is only accessible via a multi-layered conversation, it should be clear where the points of divergence from this book will lie.

The poverty of Donfried's project becomes all the clearer when we move to a consideration of his final chapter, where he evaluates the contemporary relevance of the theology he has just outlined. For Donfried, the theology of the Thessalonian correspondence is of 'remarkable relevance' for the contemporary church.[66] Donfried locates this relevance in the fact that the Thessalonian church was 'surrounded by pagan religions and a threatening political environment', and similarly the modern church is not only in 'a minority position' but surrounded by 'atheistic ideologies and deconstructed versions of "Christianity"'.[67] Whilst I am sympathetic to the analogical relationship Donfried is trying to construct here, I am not convinced that his project possesses sufficient hermeneutical sophistication to construct and sustain such a move. It is not so clear that one can cut off the past from present conceptions (for that is the project of historical criticism), and then immediately cast that into the present as an authority. In order to project the past into the present as an authority, there needs to be an appropriate means of getting between the two, and an agreement concerning what precisely is authoritative. In short, Donfried may know where he wants to go, but he may not know how to get there. As Brevard Childs shrewdly points out, to assume that historical insights can be neatly transposed into theological statements is 'simply a presumption of historicism'.[68]

It is not immediately clear that the necessarily contingent and unstable meanings of the past can *automatically* play a normative role within the life of the church without some kind of hermeneutical framework. Accepting the text as authoritative only works within a framework which allows for a conversation between the past and present, respecting the two as different spheres, and yet convinced that the two can be brought to a point of unity insofar as they converse about the subject matter of the text, a subject matter which rules and determines the interpretation. Viewed from this perspective, Donfried's highlighting of Paul's understanding of

---

[66] Donfried, 'Theology of 1 Thessalonians', p. 73.   [67] *Ibid.*
[68] B. S. Childs, 'Interpretation in Faith: The Theological Responsibility of an Old Testament Commentary', *Interpretation* 18 (1964), 438.

faith as a dynamic event[69] or Donfried's emphasis on the abiding validity of the sexual ethics[70] are valuable conversation pieces, purely as examples of historical theology. My point is that much more work, time and patience are required to justify the claim that such (historically mined) information is of 'remarkable relevance for the contemporary church'.[71]

This consideration of Donfried's theological project has outlined some of the reservations that I have in the face of the claims he makes. It must be stressed again that my criticism is not of the work of historical criticism *per se*, but rather of the claims its practitioners make for it. Donfried's work may be historically illuminating, but theologically it shows how much more work there is to be done.

3   Three critiques of the historical-critical project

Our examination of the work of two respected historical-critical scholars has encouraged us to engage with historical criticism as it actually operates within the guild of Biblical studies. Our continuing engagement with historical criticism moves us along the way to launch three criticisms of the historical-critical project:

> First, historical-critical studies operate with a limited notion of meaning and truth.
> Secondly, historical criticism is disabled by a historicism that fixes the language into a restrictively reflective relationship between text and original context.
> Thirdly, the latent historicism within historical criticism distracts historical critics from the actual subject matter of the Biblical texts.

3.1   Meaning and truth

Our first critique is that historical criticism works with a restricted notion of truth and meaning, prioritising the original meaning of the text over the neglect of the wealth of meaning generated by Scripture's life in the interpretative community of the church. We shall explore this critique by initially focusing on a general example of Biblical scholarship, after which we shall examine work directly pertaining to 1 Thessalonians.

The exemplar of descriptive New Testament study – distinguished by its attempts to bifurcate the meaning of the Bible into a meaning 'then' and

---

[69] Donfried, 'Theology of 1 Thessalonians', p. 74.
[70] *Ibid.*, p. 76.   [71] *Ibid.*, p. 73.

a meaning 'now' – is Krister Stendahl, lately of Harvard Divinity School. Stendahl himself should properly be located within a broad trajectory stretching back to J. P. Gabler in the eighteenth century and W. Wrede in the nineteenth century and continuing to find expression now in scholars such as Heikki Räisänen.

The root of Stendahl's influence lies in his 1962 article in *The Interpreter's Dictionary of the Bible* entitled 'Biblical Theology, Contemporary', in which he pressed for the distinction between descriptive theology and normative theology. For Stendahl these are two distinct labours. It is the job of the Biblical scholar to establish 'what the text meant', and the job of the systematic theologian to move towards an explanation of 'what the text means'. Stendahl credits the *religionsgeschichtliche Schule* with pushing for a distinction between what the text means and what the text meant, a distinction easier to appreciate when you are as acquainted with the religious and cultural diversity of first-century Mediterranean life as the proponents of the *religionsgeschichtliche Schule* attempted to be. The *religionsgeschichtliche Schule* is applauded for fostering an attitude that saw 'the experience of the distance and strangeness of biblical thought as a creative asset, rather than as a destructive and burdensome liability'.[72] The *religionsgeschichtliche Schule* led to two different responses, what Stendahl terms 'liberal' and 'orthodox' stances. The liberal interpreters of the nineteenth century allowed their predilections concerning what was of continuing meaning to feed into their historical reconstructions, so that the two realms of past and present meanings became suspiciously correlated, and the reconstructed words 'happened to square well with the ideals of the modern age'.[73] Likewise the orthodox interpreters were also poor historians, systematising the Bible and thereby silencing more awkward texts.[74]

Stendahl proceeds to examine the work of three scholars who were acutely aware of the time difference between the time of the text's production and now: Barth, Bultmann and Cullmann. Not surprisingly, Barth fails to impress, promising in his *Der Römerbrief* a commentary but delivering what 'turns out to be a theological tractate'.[75] Bultmann is out of favour, for his primary interest is in establishing what texts can say of kerygmatic and existential significance, an interest that clearly militates against the import of establishing what the text *meant*.[76] Cullmann, finally, is recognised as 'the most productive contemporary writer in the

---

[72] K. Stendahl, 'Biblical Theology, Contemporary', in H. Räisänen et al., eds., *Reading the Bible in the Global Village* (Atlanta: SBL, 2000), pp. 72–3. This is a reprint of the 1962 original.
[73] *Ibid.*, p. 71.   [74] *Ibid.*   [75] *Ibid.*, p. 74.   [76] *Ibid.*, pp. 75–6.

field of NT theology',[77] but nevertheless he too lacks the hermeneutical agility to translate his findings into contemporary meaning and relevance, and so unwittingly allows the descriptive method to 'transcend its own limitations'.[78] For Stendahl, the work of these three scholars reveals that the relationship between what the text means and what it meant is primarily 'competitive' in nature,[79] with now one side losing out, now the other. Stendahl's clarity as to the distinct natures of the descriptive and the normative tasks of theology is designed to eliminate any such confusion.

In subsequent articles Stendahl has elaborated on this two-stage hermeneutical process. In a paper presented to the SBL in 1964 and published in 1965, Stendahl attempts to divest Biblical theology's historical descriptive task of any authority, allotting authority to the work of normative thinkers who establish 'what it means'. The descriptive role of Biblical scholars must be applied without distinction, 'This limitation of descriptive biblical theology must be imposed rigorously. We remember that everything called "biblical" easily becomes adorned by the authority of the Scriptures.'[80] The Biblical scholar is thus the historian in the midst of theologians, *describing* the thoughts of the first Christian theologians whilst keeping a safe distance from the normative tasks of systematic theologians. The overriding objective is the urgent attempt 'to rescue the church from the arrogant imperialism of biblical theology', and so to harness the 'freedom and creativity of systematic theology'.[81] Stendahl's atomising tendencies do not end there, for although he adopts the language of 'dialogue',[82] in reality he wants to close off Biblical studies 'from the heavy layers of interpretations accumulated over the centuries' in pursuit of the original meaning.[83]

A number of criticisms have been ranged against Stendahl,[84] some more theological than others. At this preliminary stage it is apt to echo James Barr and express concern about the use of the words 'means' and 'meant'.[85] It is very clear that establishing what the text 'meant' is largely determined by the questions we ask about it – rhetorical, sociological, theological, historical. In short, it is not clear that there is any

---

[77] *Ibid.*, p. 76. [78] *Ibid.*, p. 78. [79] *Ibid.*

[80] K. Stendahl, 'Method in the Study of Biblical Theology', in J. P. Hyatt, ed., *The Bible in Modern Scholarship* (London: Carey Kingsgate Press, 1965), p. 203.

[81] *Ibid.*, p. 204. [82] *Ibid.*, p. 208. [83] *Ibid.*, p. 207.

[84] E.g. F. Watson, *Text, Church and World: Biblical Interpretation in Theological Perspective* (Edinburgh: T. & T. Clark, 1994), p. 33, who problematises Stendahl's presumption that he can arrive at some clean, neutral meaning which he can present to the academy.

[85] J. Barr, *The Concept of Biblical Theology: An Old Testament Perspective* (London: SCM, 1999), pp. 189–208.

one 'meaning' of the text that can be articulated univocally and used, in Stendahl's metaphor, as a 'baseline' for subsequent interpretations.[86]

If what the text 'meant' is a polysemous field, then so too is the field of the text's present meaning crowded with possibilities. Apart from the consideration that it is obvious that the church holds no monopoly over the contemporary meaning of the texts, the church itself witnesses (wittingly or unwittingly) to a pluriform interpretative tradition. To say this is a variant upon the adage that church history is the history of the interpretation of Scripture. For literary theorists, quite apart from theologians who stress the excess of meaning pertaining uniquely to the Scriptures, it is evident that all texts can be interpreted as many times as there are interpreters. It is precisely this open-ended nature of the interpretative activity that makes texts so engaging.[87] And besides the rich potential of what the text is to 'mean' now, there is the subsidiary but no less important consideration that we construct contemporary meaning from previous forms of meaning, and so too conceptions of what the text meant are partly shaped by what we think it means now. The very business of interpretation is not hospitable to any notion that 'description' and 'normativity' are mutually exclusive. In short, the attempt to force a division between what the text meant and what it means is illusory, for what meaning means itself is far from clear![88]

It is not hard to see the wider influence of Stendahl's hermeneutical drive. Those following Stendahl's programme explicitly, such as Heikki Räisänen, call for a strict division of labour between the work of the Biblical scholar and the theologian, and there are many others implicitly influenced who try to do 'New Testament Theology'. Having already dealt with Donfried's analysis of the theology of 1 Thessalonians, we shall now examine a theological interpretation emanating from a recent SBL consultation. We shall examine to what extent such theological treatments are testament to the 'history of effects' of Stendahl's strikingly modern programme,[89] a manifesto that talks of New Testament *theology* but delivers a history of early Christian thought.

---

[86] K. Stendahl, 'The Bible as Classic and the Bible as Holy Scripture', *JBL* 103 (1984), 10. This metaphor reveals a historicist prejudice – that there is one recoverable historical meaning to texts and that this should in some sense *limit* all other meanings.

[87] Stout, 'What is the Meaning of a Text?', 8.

[88] Frequently, however, Stendahl displays a robust hope that somehow, he as a Biblical public health officer can get at the original meaning, free of all the meanings which have contaminated the text. For such optimism see Stendahl, 'Bible as Classic', 9.

[89] For the modernism latent within Stendahl's project see A. K. A. Adam, *Making Sense of New Testament Theology: 'Modern' Problems and Prospects* (Macon: Mercer University Press, 1995), pp. 82–6.

The Pauline Theology Consultation of the Society of Biblical Literature, which ran from 1985 for ten years, commenced with the earnest concern that the theologies of Paul which were being produced in the 1970s and 1980s 'tended to reflect the theological perspectives of Paul's interpreters more clearly than the theological emphases of the apostle himself'.[90] The Pauline Theology Consultation group desired to get at Paul's theology as 'it came to expression in each letter',[91] and so contribute to the task of understanding the mind and thought of Paul. Their work has been published in four volumes.

Earl Richard's contribution to the consultation, entitled 'Early Pauline Thought: An Analysis of 1 Thessalonians', follows (as the title suggests) a rigorously descriptive pattern. As a feature of this interest, questions of background fascinate Richard, and certainly students of Paul interested in the background of his thought have a large field in which to play, with Hellenistic Jewish, Greco-Roman and Jewish Christian sources of thought all being important.[92] From the commencement of his analysis Richard reveals his preoccupation with preparatory historical questions – debates about chronology, the relevance of Acts 17, the textual integrity of 1 Thessalonians itself (a tendency which breaks apart the final form of the text), and Hellenistic epistolary parallels.[93]

Despite the project's aim of getting closer to understanding Paul, there is little evidence in Richard's work that he has found himself absorbed and gripped by the reality Paul makes known in 1 Thessalonians. It might be unfair to charge Richard with not reading 1 Thessalonians as Scripture, for he makes no claims that this is one of his presuppositions. For Richard the background against which 'one must read the letter' is the community to which it was sent.[94] Where we are on *terra firma* is in criticising Richard's hermeneutical decisions. For there is in Richard's analysis a historicist tendency to silence any chance of conversation by refusing to participate in the patient struggle and discovery that is the hermeneutical conversation. Richard sees the meaning *behind* the text rather than the world in *front* of it, and as one absorbed in historicist questions he remains deaf to the provocations and questions of the text. Richard thus silences the text, eliminating any chance of its questioning, provoking or propositioning. Neglecting to read the text in line either with its

[90] J. M. Bassler, ed., *Pauline Theology, Volume I: Thessalonians, Philippians, Galatians and Philemon* (Minneapolis: Fortress Press, 1991), p. ix (preface).
[91] *Ibid.*
[92] E. J. Richard, 'Early Pauline Thought: An Analysis of 1 Thessalonians', *ibid.*, p. 39.
[93] *Ibid.*, p. 42.   [94] *Ibid.*, p. 48.

(or Paul's) verifiable intention – as a witness to God's revelation – Richard fundamentally misreads the text's full potential.

A purely historical-critical understanding of the text represents what David Tracy would term a methodology of control,[95] a means by which Richard ensures that *he* remains impervious to the provocations of the text which would pull him into *its* understanding. In Richard's analysis the historian remains in control, breaking up the text into two letters – the so-called 'Early Letter' and 'The Later Missive'[96] – and interpreting the ethical exhortations against their Hellenistic and Judaeo-Christian background.[97] Splitting up the letter might not have been so damaging if Richard had proposed a whole or a unity to which these parts could be related, but for Richard there is no overarching whole to Paul's witness that is 1 Thessalonians.

In many ways, then, Richard, is a faithful disciple of Stendahl, committed to a 'descriptive approach',[98] free from the ecclesial confusions resulting from immersion within the text's form and reference. By setting himself the task of description from the beginning of his study, Richard remains in control, never really letting himself be governed by the flow and form of the text, breaking it up as an extra measure, lest it exercise any such authority over his interpretation. In the historicist mindset of Richard, the text's meaning is exhausted by its historical significations. By imposing the Stendahl grid, a distinction which encapsulates the motivations behind our first critique, based on the premise that the primary task is to establish historical meanings in detachment from contemporary meanings, Richard both contains and limits the text's full potential.

This examination, and preliminary critique, of Stendahl's and Richard's work leads to my first critique: historical-critical studies operate with a limited notion of meaning and truth. Allies from both non-theological and theological perspectives will consolidate this thesis.

Considering that the texts which the historical critics expose to historical scrutiny are themselves part of a rich history of meanings within (and outwith) the church, it is profoundly ironic that historical-critical scholars have given so little attention to their own rootedness in space and time, to the fact that they too are part of the texts' common history of interpretation. Historical critics have applied insufficient critical attention to their own interpretative location, as the intellectual historian Dominick LaCapra highlights: 'the past is not simply a finished story to be narrated but a *process* linked to each historian's own time of narration'.[99] The

---

[95] Tracy, 'Creativity', 297.   [96] Richard, 'Early Pauline Thought', pp. 49–50.
[97] *Ibid.*, p. 50.   [98] *Ibid.*, p. 39, n. 1.
[99] D. LaCapra, 'Rethinking Intellectual History and Reading Texts', in *Rethinking Intellectual History: Texts, Contexts, Language* (Ithaca: Cornell University Press, 1983), p. 18.

irony of historical-critical scholars being insufficiently attuned to their own historicity, and participation within history, is palpable.

The reluctance of many Biblical scholars to discern how meaning in a text is linked to our present situation is widespread. Examples of this malaise abound in historical reconstructions of the New Testament, not least in 'Historical Jesus' research. Critics often point out that the Jesus established by the historians' toil frequently turns out to be a pale reflection of the historian's social and political outlook: a politically involved and radical Cynic divested of any eschatological or apocalyptic teaching is common to many contemporary North American constructions. George Tyrrell's comments about Harnack's nineteenth-century Liberal Protestant reconstruction of the historical Jesus are still strikingly apposite to our situation: 'The Christ that Harnack sees, looking back through nineteen centuries of Catholic darkness, is only the reflection of a Liberal Protestant face, seen at the bottom of a deep well.'[100]

'Historical Jesus' research is a good example to highlight for another reason, for it brings to light many of the complex issues surrounding faith and history. Much Historical Jesus research works with the assumption that historically established facts can be translated straight into Christological truths. Indeed, the crusading ethos of the much-maligned Jesus Seminar would appear to be that the 'truth' of Jesus is established only via historical purity. The reality is that behind reconstructions of the 'real' Jesus have often been lurking subtle, or not so subtle, Christologies. L. T. Johnson, writing of the recent attempts to locate the historical Jesus (with the Jesus Seminar a particular target), aptly comments that such attempts are grounded in the theological assumptions, first that 'origins define essence' and secondly that subsequent developments are bound to be inferior to the original copy.[101]

Much historical criticism operates with a remarkable dissonance between the critical energy applied to the texts and the critical energy applied to the current context of interpretation. However, this is to assume that the texts are part of a rich world of meanings, that in our moments of location, our interpretation must give proper weight to the 'excess of meaning' of which the text is constitutive, and that matter I now seek to demonstrate.

We have seen that many theologians and non-theologians read the Bible as a 'classic', a book whose meanings unravel over time, and a text whose power and potential are not exhausted by its original provenance.

---

[100] G. Tyrrell, *Christianity at the Cross-Roads* (London: Longmans, 1913), p. 44.
[101] L. T. Johnson, *The Real Jesus: The Misguided Quest for the Historical Jesus and the Truth of the Traditional Gospels* (New York: HarperCollins, 1996), p. 55.

Historical criticism, with its propensity to examine 'behind the text', is quite unequipped to examine the worlds of meaning that unravel out of and 'in front of' a classic text. It was the German philosopher H.-G. Gadamer in his *Truth and Method* who most famously elucidated this aspect of the text, the *Wirkungsgeschichte*, or 'history of effects'.[102] The corollary of examining the history of effects of a text may well be a more rigorously attuned sense of the text's history, for the question of the history of the text as a classic text incorporates questions of the text's historical effects as much as it does questions surrounding the text's context of production. To read a classic text like 1 Thessalonians without giving space to the worlds of meaning provoked by a reading *within* marks a failure to engage with what is most profoundly enduring within the text.

An exemplar of a Biblical scholar who is interested in precisely these questions is Yvonne Sherwood, author of *A Biblical Text and its Afterlives: The Survival of Jonah in Western Culture*.[103] Sherwood, whose interests are in literary theory and cultural studies, is self-consciously writing against the grain of a guild still largely enthralled by historical-critical questions. For Sherwood, however, Biblical texts are always 'sustained' by interpretation, for so potent a force is interpretation that it 'overwhelms, eclipses, *and always precedes* the biblical "original"'.[104] The study of Jonah and its afterlives reveals that knowledge and meaning in relation to Jonah as a text are '*agglutinative*'.[105]

Sherwood's book is a fascinating catalogue of the various interpretative contortions (as she regards them) which the book of Jonah has experienced in the hands of both Jewish and Christian interpreters. In the interpretative hands of the Fathers, Jonah is interpreted typologically, as a sign pointing towards Jesus and, subsequently, a living representation of 'carnal' Israel.[106] If, in the interpretations of Augustine and others a creeping anti-Judaism can be detected, so too, in the hands of the Reformers was the text used and deployed with political and strategic ends in mind.[107] And, in the nineteenth century, the text was subject to all sorts of fantastic and ingenious interpretative strategies with those anxious to read the narrative as God's scientific textbook.[108]

For Sherwood, the interest lies in the sheer weight of interpretative positions and strategies which the text of Jonah can bear. For her, the stimulation does not lie in the historical origins of the text, but in the rotation

---

[102] Gadamer, *Truth and Method*, esp. pp. 267–74, 305–41.
[103] Y. Sherwood, *A Biblical Text and its Afterlives: The Survival of Jonah in Western Culture* (Cambridge: Cambridge University Press, 2000).
[104] *Ibid.*, p. 2 (italics in the original).   [105] *Ibid.*, p. 5.
[106] *Ibid.*, pp. 11–21.   [107] *Ibid.*, pp. 32–42.   [108] *Ibid.*, pp. 42–8.

of the various interpretations, which reveal the text to be 'a gigantic echo chamber'.[109] The history of effects, of which the text is constitutive, is an alienating process, requiring the deconstructive skills of an archaeologist of interpretation. For Sherwood, such an examination of the history of effects reveals the text in a less than flattering light: 'I am left holding a heavily encrusted, rusted, text, covered in barnacles and ideas that hold on, like limpets.'[110]

Sherwood is clearly a non-theological partner who does not talk of revelation, but of deconstruction. Nevertheless, in her implicit criticism of historicist tendencies, and her commitment to establish how the text gathers and grows in meaning over time, she is an ally for whose company I am grateful.

Theologically, what I am calling for in this argument is a close attentiveness to the ultimate witness and reality of the Biblical text – something requiring scrupulous clarification – that is constantly generative of new readings. The revelation of the text, its subject matter, is that to which the text is witness. Historical criticism confuses the text's revelation with its original moment of delivery, as if somehow the factuality of the text's origins represented its revelation. If we read the revelation of the text's witness as God's revelation, this revelation will always transcend our attempts to freeze it into any one historical context. The difference here, with a non-theological ally like Sherwood, is worth pointing out. For where we too may be interested by the kind of questions raised by such theories as reader-response, theologically we will want to speak of the generative revelation that is God in Christ.

Historical criticism is therefore not criticised because it isn't necessary, for the Biblical texts are indisputably historically constituted texts. We can and must say that in 1 Thessalonians the text acted as witness to revelation, and this cannot have happened in anything other than a historical moment, for revelation properly makes itself known in the particularity of human history.[111] But reading 1 Thessalonians as a text witnessing to revelation asks us to read a text witnessing to the 'Lord of time', the one in whom all time finds (or will find) its unity. The text points to a God whose capacity to reveal himself in different times is boundless. My critique of historical criticism revolves around the limits of its vision, limitations which hinder the historical critic's attempts to get at the *enduring truth* of the text, a truth outwith the historicist's horizon.

Those who perceive a mutually constructive relationship between *ekklēsia* and text *cannot* read the Bible as they would 'any other book'.

---

[109] *Ibid.*, p. 78.   [110] *Ibid.*, p. 87.   [111] *CD* I/2, p. 50.

It is because historical criticism is chronically ill suited to reading the Bible with such sympathy that it will be limited to a marginal role in any explicitly theological interpretation of the Biblical texts.

Working towards an understanding of the text's meanings is possible only through a hermeneutical dialogue between the text's revelatory subject matter (disclosed from *within* the text) and each new context in which the text finds itself part of new meanings, and is performed and interpreted. Such an approach undoubtedly signals a departure from any putative 'authorial intention'. The assertion that the original context and authorial intention are not normative in the quest for meaning is as alien to Stendahl as it is heresy to most historical-critical scholars.[112] In reality, all we are calling for is a realisation that in writing 1 Thessalonians the apostle Paul witnessed to realities which it was not his role to control or contain, but merely to make known. If these realities of revelation are allowed their proper freedom, what 1 Thessalonians points to acts as host for an abundant field of meaning.

Historical-critical scholars not only suppose that they can, but also demand, that the text is divorced from the situation of its interpreters. The text is read as alien, divorced and separate from our context – it is put at a distance. What I have been arguing is that such a project is unrealistic and limited. The truth of revelatory texts like those of Scripture is to be discerned not by merely casting them into their original situation but by repositioning their eternally valid revelatory power – to which they witness – in the living stream of the community that holds them as authoritative. The truth and meaning of 1 Thessalonians reside within the relationship of creative tension between the text, the world of meanings opened up by the text, and its faithful location within the worship, life and tradition of the church.[113] Within this setting, Paul's authorship of 1 Thessalonians is only a *preliminary* concern to the *secondary* role that the texts can and do play in hermeneutical conversations. Far from the meaning of the texts being frozen in one time, and in one context, the texts of the Bible find themselves in the canon because they have found themselves consistently able to speak from *their* particular context to *our* context.

---

[112] See K. Stendahl, *Paul among Jews and Gentiles and Other Essays* (Minneapolis: Fortress Press), p. 96, where he posits the possibility of the Biblical original functioning 'as a critique of inherited presuppositions and incentive to new thought'. The seemingly normative nature of Stendahl's descriptions is typical of the confusion of his project.

[113] The term 'tradition' is another term heavy with possible meanings. Here I am deploying it *not* to refer to official pronouncements from the Magisterium, but in the widest sense, to point to the church's continuing reading of Scripture.

This first critique therefore calls for an end to the bifurcatory tendencies dominant within Biblical studies, classically given shape by Stendahl's (in)famous distinction between 'what it means' and 'what it meant', and found most recently in Heikki Räisänen's work.[114] Far more fruitful would be to construct a model of interpretation with an indisputable centre, whilst we remained committed to a process of continual refinement and infinite progression. In such a hermeneutical conversation now one voice will be heard to speak, and now another, but all the participants will enjoy an organic relationship, where previously an unrealistic 'relay-race model' reigned.[115] Nicholas Lash, in response to Stendahl, embodies much of what we aspire to when he wrote,

> we do not *first* understand the past and *then* proceed to seek to understand the present. The relationship between these two dimensions of our quest for meaning and truth is dialectical: they mutually inform, enable, correct and enlighten each other.[116]

What is called for, therefore, is an integrative conversation driven by an imaginative fidelity to the witness of the texts. Within this conversation guided by the witness of the text it is quite proper to read 1 Thessalonians in the light of later Christian tradition. Indeed, it will prove to be disclosive of new meanings within the text, for the real fallacy lies in supposing that historical truth is attained by divorcing ourselves from our present context, which, in truth, is like trying to flee from our own shadow.

Liberation theologians, distinguished by their critique of Western scholars for failing to realise entrenched ideological biases, further consolidate our argument against atomised ways of thinking. For liberation theologians the truth of Biblical texts is not to be garnered by the kind of unattainable disengagement with the ultimate reality of the texts which historical criticism preaches, but by a consistently *engaged* reading of the subject matter of the texts that manifests itself in praxis and performance.[117] Moreover, many liberation theologians remain suspicious of what one distinguished practitioner terms 'semantic positivism', an attitude which freezes the meaning of the texts into controlled etymological understandings, so they can be deployed at will. For Clodovis Boff, such

---

[114] E.g. H. Räisänen, 'Comparative Religion, Theology and New Testament Exegesis', *Studia Theologica* 52 (1998), 124: 'The goal of a history of early Christian religion is not to proclaim a message. It tries to analyse and to understand.'

[115] As set out by N. Lash, 'What Might Martyrdom Mean?', *Ex Auditu* 1 (1985), 16–17.

[116] N. Lash, 'Interpretation and Imagination', in M. Goulder, ed., *Incarnation and Myth: The Debate Continued* (London: SCM, 1979), p. 25.

[117] E.g. J. Miguez Bonino, 'Hermeneutics, Truth, and Praxis', in *Doing Theology in a Revolutionary Situation* (Philadelphia: Fortress Press, 1975), p. 99.

a technique heralds all the living relevance of a 'museum', all the fertility of a 'cemetery'.[118]

Miguez Bonino equally criticises the Western atomisation of truth as theory and, separately, truth as application. For Miguez Bonino, the Western mindset is hindered by a belief that first the theoretical conceptions of truth have to be worked out, and then this truth is to be applied in concrete historical situations. The brunt of Miguez Bonino's criticism is that in the Western mindset there is no belief that the applicatory role can be a corrective to theoretical conceptions, theoretical truth representing 'a universe complete in itself'.[119] And, of course, in his highlighting of the importance of the community which performs and interprets Scripture Miguez Bonino is not alone amongst liberation theologians. For Boff, likewise, priority must be given to the actual practice of the church over theoretical contributions.[120]

Whilst liberation theologians are primarily reacting against the intellectual obscurantism of the Western academy, it is not hard to see the parallels with our critique of historical criticism. Liberation theologians provide us with two central insights. First, just as historical critics have divorced themselves from the story of Biblical performance that is the theological and spiritual tradition of the church, they must stand with the Western theologians critiqued by Miguez Bonino who attempt to construct a world of truth 'complete in itself'.[121] Where Miguez Bonino and his associates talk of exegesis marrying with praxis, it is equally imperative to construct a similar relationship between the text and those contributions which might *serve* to illuminate the witness of that text.

And so secondly, liberation theologians helpfully talk of understanding the meaning of Scripture within the life of what Clodovis Boff terms 'the living spirit of the living community',[122] from within the mystery-laden and mutually dynamic relationship between Scripture and the *sensus fidelium*.

Theologically, therefore, I am keen to assert that the truth of the text is not located here *or* there, but is worked out over time. The reader is thus called to a dialogue with the text, reading the text itself in the richness which the time of the church offers. As we read the text we inevitably read in our time, with our contextual concerns and questions, and hope to be encountered by a text that reminds us that there is more at work than just our time. Theologically, the revealing truth is not the text

---

[118] Boff, 'Hermeneutics', p. 15.
[119] Miguez Bonino, 'Hermeneutics', p. 88.   [120] Boff, 'Hermeneutics', p. 32.
[121] Miguez Bonino, 'Hermeneutics', p. 88.   [122] Boff, 'Hermeneutics', p. 14.

itself (as per historical critics and Biblical literalists), or in the original context of textual production, but in the act of reading the text in the time of the faithful community produced, sustained and nourished by the Word. Truth thus lies in the discernment of how the God who through the incarnation has interwoven himself amidst our time can bring that which the text speaks of to new meanings and understandings over time, through time and history itself. Correspondingly, the process of discernment takes place in time and through the unfolding history of theological tradition. Meaning and truth, in short, are produced over time, and therefore cannot be fixed to any one point.

Such a reading of 1 Thessalonians is possible only by accepting two presuppositions.

First, as was emphasised in our preliminary definition of revelation, the excess of meaning is possible precisely because we are dealing with a text faithfully witnessing to revelation. As was argued above (section 1), it is in the very nature of revelation to be always spilling out, over and beyond its context of production. To acquire what Biblical scholars and theologians alike call a 'Scriptural imagination' is to read the text with eyes open to realities continually indicated by the text. So, we shall find that this theological assertion is unmistakably related to our understanding of inspiration within the co-constitutive relationship that inheres between church and Scripture. Attesting that we too can be participants within the living stream of Scriptural interpretation is to attest that we too can be part of a community where God ceaselessly discloses his purposes for the church and for the world, where God's revelation is experienced and can be (deficiently) articulated as a dynamic flow of grace.

Secondly, to recognise a continuity between the specific time of 1 Thessalonians and our time is to recognise and affirm that the contemporary church is united to the same grace to which 1 Thessalonians points. Where the historicist examines the text with the presupposition that it is necessarily alienated and different from our interests, the ecclesially situated reader must assert in reaction the essential continuity that inheres between the interpretative location of the church now and the church we read of in the texts. God is perceived as working through time, not just in one time, for the benefit of increased and sustained communion. The Biblical texts, therefore, will be understood as creative of meaning *then* as much as they are *now* continually re-creative of meaning. Such a perspective is likely to transcend the concerns of historical critics in locating the meaning of the text in its original context.

In summary, historical criticism is predisposed to militate against the polyvalent meanings of the text, preferring single meanings, where the text is host to a wealth of diverse meanings over time. Where historical criticism treats the text as productive of a single historical meaning, in a particular context, we replace this model of *stasis* with a model sensitive to the rich production of meaning through the interpretative traditions that emerge over time.

The approach outlined here, rooted in an affirmation of the mutually corrective and supportive relationship between Scripture and church – insofar as the church generates new levels of understanding of Scripture's essential subject matter – has two closely related though subtly distinct implications.

First, as was stressed above, insofar as we are committed to historical understandings of the text, we will want to sustain a lively interest in the church's tradition, which has amplified the text's profundity. From this perspective our readings of Thomas' and Calvin's commentaries on 1 Thessalonians emanates.

There is, however, a second corollary. In many ways this implication is quite distinct from the previous implication, for a conversation with the text, a conversation shaped by the text's inherent subject matter, must be genuinely dialogical, now allowing one voice to speak, and then letting another voice be heard. Both the text and the subject matter will be absolutely regnant. Theologically, our conversation will be given its integrity by ceaseless fidelity to the text's subject matter, that which is disclosed purely and only by the text. We shall be looking for something more than the *Rezeptionsgeschichte* of the Biblical texts, because we shall be seeking roadways into explorations of the text's profundity, a profundity that is of necessity present because this is a text attested to be witnessing to revelation.

Relating this model to 1 Thessalonians compels us to think imaginatively, confident that we are inheritors of the same dynamic of grace communicated to the Thessalonian Christians. Such a mindset calls us to grapple with the same issues they were grappling with, being absolutely gripped by the same subject matter Paul was gripped by. This kind of faithful imagination therefore works towards a theology that discloses how the *same* subject matter that generated 1 Thessalonians can be explored in its endless profundity in the context in which we are now located.

3.2   Historicism freezes the eschatological language of Scripture into a reflective relationship between text and original context

Our second complaint against historical criticism is closely related to the first. There is a dangerous and unspoken bias prevalent within historical criticism to which we need to be alert. The assumption of much historical-critical methodology is that the text is a mirror of the world in which it was written, an assumption in line with reading the Scriptural text as *sources*. Not only does this have a tendency to freeze the text's meaning into one particular context (a point which we have noted above), but it also assumes an unsophisticated correspondence between experience and language, seeing language merely as a translator or filter through which we feed our experiences. In this perspective the language of Scripture becomes a purely passive player.

Reading the documents of the early church as mimetic aids to seeing into the lives of the communities (putatively) behind them divorces the texts from the participatory and reciprocal roles they have the capacity to play in the communities in which they took shape. Our allies here are not just theological. Jean Howard, writing of the new historicism in Renaissance studies, warns of the danger of ignoring the extent to which texts can *constitute* history as well as *reflect* it.[123]

The assumption of historical criticism is that the language of the New Testament is a reflection of the experience of the early Christian communities, language being a mirror into which inquisitive historians can peer. Historical critics are thus predisposed to reading texts as reactive to situations within their communities, rather than as a medium through which God himself works his continually creative will. This predilection is not surprising given that history is a subject generated and sustained by questions of causality, questions that ask how, why and when certain events happened. In pursuing these questions of causality the text is constrained within an *assumed* continuum of cause and effect. In the historicist mind-set of analogy, there is little or nothing in the text lacking the potential to be explained in terms of prior circumstances or contexts. For the historicist it is the constructs of historical inquiry rather than the church's unfolding of revelation which makes sense of the Bible's language.

The argument here pivots around the concern that historical critics read the language of Scripture as pointing back to putative thought-processes and worldviews, where theologically it is imperative to press the text forwards into the world which the language of Scripture simultaneously proposes and expands. There is, in this sense, an eschatological fullness and ripeness to the language of Scripture, the full meaning of which is only brought about through the church's ever-expansive time of reading. Just as the revelation of Christ is complete and unsurpassable, but nonetheless is progressively amplified through time, so too is the fullness

---

[123] J. E. Howard, 'The New Historicism in Renaissance Studies', *ELR* 16 (1986), 25.

of Scripture present from its genesis, but it too is progressively under-stood and comprehended through its inexhaustible reading. Metaphors of Scripture being the 'seed' and tradition being the 'harvest' of meaning have their place here.[124]

Given the claim in this book that there is at work in the language of Scripture the promise of eschatological fullness, it seems highly pertinent to examine historical-critical readings of Paul's directly eschatological discourses. The exemplar I have chosen is Ernest Best's commentary on the Thessalonian correspondence.[125] Best does not claim that his work is theological exegesis – his interests are purely textual, grammatical and historical. I shall, therefore, base my critique not so much on what Best writes (for exemplary scholarship should not be carped at), but on what he doesn't write, and on how his omissions are dictated by his presupposition that 1 Thessalonians is a historical source to be mined for background information.

The most eschatological section of Paul's text is 1 Thess. 4:13–18, a section Best refers to as 'The Dead and the Parousia'.[126] In this section, establishing the historical context is clearly not unconnected to under-standing the passage, but it is far from the whole task facing us. Whilst it is important to recall that Paul wrote these verses with the Thessalonians in mind, as indicated above, what is more interesting for a theological exegesis is examining the new worlds of understanding which the text itself has opened up, quite independent of its original context. It is clear, however, which position Best is predisposed towards: the text is a *reaction* to events in Thessalonica, and the text can be read as a mirror through which Paul's purpose is faithfully reflected. Thus, for Best, 'Paul's pri-mary purpose in writing is not to enunciate doctrine but to reassure' the Thessalonian Christians.[127] Paul is read as a historically grounded pur-veyor of well-chosen advice, a reading which misses the excitement of reading Paul as an apostle with a timeless message.

A symptom of historical critics' reluctance to interpret the eschatolog-ical potential of Scripture's language is a fervent interest in the world behind the text (the etymology of specific words, the background of con-cepts, the context of utterances) which clouds out any possible interest in the world proposed by the text. Whilst this is certainly not reading the Bible in line with its classic status, in line with its inexhaustible inter-pretation, it is equally not reading it in line with its role as revelatory

[124] E.g. Bulgakov, 'The Church as Tradition', p. 29.
[125] E. Best, *A Commentary on the First and Second Epistles to the Thessalonians* (BNTC; London: A. & C. Black, 1972).
[126] *Ibid.*, p. 179.   [127] *Ibid.*, p. 180.

Scripture, texts which the church attests to as holding an abiding revelatory significance.

In reliable historicist fashion, Best understands the texts solely by means of the words' background and etymology. He shows understandable interest in the background to 'sleeping' (4:13), tracing its meaning back to the Old Testament, but there is little evidence that pushing the word's meaning further and further back into history is necessarily the best, let alone the only way, to perceive that to which the text witnesses. In Best's approach the only semantic depth words enjoy is by being pushed back into their pre-history, and into the likely meanings which Paul intended, but not into the lives they come to enjoy in successive interpretative communities. This curator-like drive to 'reconstruct the original form' of words contrasts with the reading proposed in Part III, where we explore the meaning that Christian tradition has discerned in the reference to the sleeping (κοιμώμενος) Thessalonians.[128] In Best's commentary, however, no space is given to the text's performance within the reading community of the church.[129]

Best's over-riding interest in the historical origins of the words of the text is taken to extremes in some cases, for in eschatological material there is much to occupy the industrious historical critic. Biblical eschatology brings with it its own jargon, words which tease the historical critic and sap all his or her energies. But if Best satisfactorily exposits the background of such words as 'archangel', 'trumpet' and 'clouds',[130] there is no interest in extending the words' meaning forwards into their eschatological fullness. Even in his concluding postscript on eschatology, where most historical critics would try (perhaps ineptly) to translate their historical findings into some form of theology, Best keeps firmly to his own 'patch', giving yet more information on the background to Paul's eschatological teaching.[131]

It needs to be stressed that I am not criticising the actual findings of Best's commentary. His close reading of the Greek speaks of a serious responsibility to the text. Ultimately, however, my presuppositions and Best's are divergent. For Best, the texts are sources to be dug into for their meaning, and correspondingly he provides the reader with a pre-history of Paul's eschatological images. Theologically it is necessary to insist that any eschatological assertions we want to make on the basis of 1 Thessalonians must rest not on scholarly hypotheses surrounding Paul's

---

[128] *Ibid.*, p. 189.

[129] Indeed, where ancient commentators are cited they are treated dismissively, and are said to have avoided the 'plain meaning' of the text: Best, *A Commentary*, p. 195.

[130] *Ibid.*, pp. 197–9.   [131] *Ibid.*, pp. 349–54.

influences, but rather on studied and loyal attention to what is indicated in the actual text. Such presuppositions are somewhat different from Best's, for in particular, I am aroused by the witness of the text, not in the manner of a historicist seeking past meanings, but in the search for continually expansive meanings. With this perspective, the limited value of Best's commentary in relation to my interests becomes evident.

The limitations of Best's project will be brought into sharper focus by comparing his findings with Karl Barth's reading of Rom. 8:18–25, in the second edition of his Romans commentary.

Barth locates the meaning of the passage in his grappling with the subject matter as it arises from the final form of the text. Thus, the background to the words Paul uses does not distract him, and he constantly refers to Paul as 'the writer' as if in an effort to help the reader focus on the text in hand. Part of Barth's task is to demolish any hints of religion, any suggestion that we can conceptualise or contain God in our image or desires. There is no direct knowledge of God.[132] Such a God is truly a 'No-God', a false step from 'the true and Unknown God'.[133] Given this absolute and utter distinction between humanity and God, Barth is uneasy with Paul's use of 'I reckon' (Rom. 8:18). Where Paul can say this as an apostle, we must invert this statement, 'God reckoned with me.'[134]

Provoked by the content of the text, Barth is seeking an answer to the question, 'What place does suffering, that vast and immeasurable factor of human life, occupy in the context of our Sonship?'[135] Any answer to this question must base itself on the radical distinction between God in heaven and humanity on earth. All knowledge we have is inherently dialectical:

> it is precisely our not-knowing what God knows that is our temporal knowledge about God, our comfort, light, power, and knowledge of eternity.[136]

It is suffering, and its eschatological resolution, which fires and provokes Barth throughout most of his commentary on this section, and he seeks to find the answer in God, in whom truth resides. Not surprisingly, Barth finds part of the answer in Christology, 'the secret and the revelation of

---

[132] Barth, *The Epistle to the Romans*, p. 314: 'Direct communication from God is no divine communication.'

[133] *Ibid.*, p. 303. Cf. B. L. McCormack, *Karl Barth's Critically Realistic Dialectical Theology: Its Genesis and Development 1909–36* (Oxford: Clarendon Press, 1995), pp. 246–9.

[134] Barth, *The Epistle to the Romans*, p. 303.   [135] *Ibid.*, p. 304.

[136] *Ibid.*, p. 310.

suffering', through which it is revealed that in our sharing of Christ's suffering we are promised the hope of his deliverance.[137] Our present sufferings are representative of nothing less than 'the frontier where this life is dissolved by life eternal'.[138]

Barth relates the modern drive to explore and discover the extremes of the world to his commentary on 8:19, a verse which talks of creation waiting for the manifestation of the sons of God. Barth relates our modern angst to the resolution that will be offered by God, urging his readers to see, through the text, the need to come to terms with the optimism by which we refuse 'to see the vanity of the creature'.[139] Eschatology, for Barth, is thus a matter of perception, of knowing and seeing rightly where the world is heading, that the world is in God's hands. As Barth puts it, 'We must recover that clarity of sight by which there is discovered in the COSMOS the invisibility of God.'[140] And the same God, precisely as God, who subjects us to vanity is the same God of hope, insofar as we apprehend that 'All those things which are so manifestly observed by men are hidden in God.'[141] Barth's eschatology is based on a radical time–eternity dialectic, an assumption that eternity is a state free from the constraints of time. Consequently, whilst eternity can never become time (for it would then cease to be what it is), it can encounter or graze any and all moments of time in equal measure.[142] This is what Barth means with his persistent juxtaposing of Now, time, and eternity, 'the "Now" which is time's secret'.[143] So also Barth writes of this 'Now' 'that it bears in its womb the eternal, living, unborn Future'.[144] This grazing of time with eternity (the 'Now') is a perpendicular irruption of time, the meeting of eternity with time which is *both* radically distant and near.[145]

Hope, for Barth, is 'to dare to think what God thinks',[146] and we wait in expectation because we see what 'to us is invisible'.[147] But, above all, we know that the world of sorrow in which we wait is linked to the sorrow of the cross, the locus where God was revealed as God.

The distinctiveness of Barth's treatment of this eschatological pericope from Romans is clear. True to his stated intention in his 1920 lecture 'Biblical Questions, Insights and Vistas', he has put the findings of historical critics 'behind' him.[148] The findings of historical critics are unstated, though clearly in the background of Barth's commentary. In contrast to

---

[137] *Ibid.*, p. 305.   [138] *Ibid.*   [139] *Ibid.*, p. 308.   [140] *Ibid.*, p. 309.   [141] *Ibid.*
[142] McCormack, *Karl Barth's Critically Realistic*, pp. 263–5.
[143] Barth, *The Epistle to the Romans*, p. 313.   [144] *Ibid.*, p. 306.
[145] McCormack, *Karl Barth's Critically Realistic*, pp. 144, 164.
[146] Barth, *The Epistle to the Romans*, p. 314.   [147] *Ibid.*, p. 315.
[148] See Barth, 'Biblical Questions', p. 61.

Best, however, what Barth reads in and through the text is not Paul's context, or the background of the words which he employed. Barth reads Paul not as a historical source, but as a witness to an eternal 'truth',[149] that all Christian theology must be based on a consistently eschatological outlook:

> If Christianity be not altogether restless eschatology, there remains in it no relationship whatever with Christ.[150]

Reading the text as a witness to something totally other and beyond our range of perception radically upsets the assumption that there is a neat correspondence between the text and its original context. There is more at play and at work within the text than can be adjudged by the historicist endeavour for origins. Thus where historical-critical scholars are predisposed to detecting putative experiences of early Christian communities lurking behind the text,[151] I would post a reminder of the continually creative role which the language of Scripture bears through time. Where our first criticism centred on how historical criticism militates against the polysemous nature of the Biblical texts, this, our second criticism, focuses on the tendency of historical criticism to ignore the creative roles of the text within both its original context and each new context within which it strives for revelatory value. For it is clear that texts merely understood as reflections of historical happenings are servile to, or in partnership with, a particular moment of history. In its transcendence, revelation is always puncturing and interrupting history, *continually* speaking through history to communicate God's will and action. The Biblical texts are always much more than mere reflectors of their immediate social reality. Rather – in witnessing to God's revelatory will – they are always active participants in creating new realities. Both within their original locus of production and within the communities reading them as authoritative, the texts of Scripture are continually creative of new meanings, much more than they are mirrors which can be peered into by historicist scholars.

The argument here *is* primarily theological, for I am talking about the very nature of revelatory language, language with an infinite capacity to open out into successive 'presents'. My assertion is that when we want to talk of Scripture we must talk of a text whose potential has transcended its original context, whose horizons are always wider than its original context of production. This is to say that whatever Paul's historical intentions might or might not have been, theologically our interest lies with

---

[149] Barth, *The Epistle to the Romans*, p. 308.   [150] *Ibid.*, p. 314.

[151] E.g. U. Luz, 'The Disciples in the Gospel According to Matthew', tr. R. Morgan, in G. Stanton, ed., *The Interpretation of Matthew* (Edinburgh: T. & T. Clark, 1995), p. 124.

the abiding revelatory potential of the text in manifesting a 'proposed world'.[152] In this sense the language of 1 Thessalonians, as *Scripture*, eludes its context of production and constantly seeks to speak in new contexts; thus the revelatory significance of the Scripture is only to be grasped through the church's time of reading. In this perspective, Scripture is the Word of God that creates the church and is also itself formed in and by the church. The texts, far from being murky mirrors of their original context, are discourses striving for participatory, if not contestatory, roles, setting in motion an endless field of meanings. The focus here being largely the language of revelation, our criticism is that historical criticism has a tendency to pass over the complex and revelatory roles which language did and *does* play in the life of communities where the text is taken up in performance. Reading 1 Thessalonians as a source, rather than as Scripture, historical criticism unwittingly reveals itself as a profoundly limited exercise, because it neglects to read 1 Thessalonians in line with what it is *really* attempting to communicate, 'the Word of God which is at work in you' (2:13).

The revelatory language of 1 Thessalonians can therefore be cast in a mode of event and process. The event, whose voice is still to be heard, is that of the significance of God in Christ, as it impacts (in our instance) upon the Thessalonian church and beyond. Our argument here profitably draws upon Ricoeur's formulation of the importance of the historical forms of revelation in the Bible, events whose historical significance is attested to by their 'transcendent character',[153] events whose meaning stands apart from the normal course of history. Moreover, Ricoeur does not shy away from the conclusion that the task of understanding the texts may lie in divorcing ourselves from the author's intentions.[154]

Modifying Ricouer's seminal essay on the hermeneutics of revelation, I would assert that it is the language of Scripture witnessing to the perfection of God in Christ's revelation, more than the events of which it speaks, which is truly transcendent. It is not that there is anything special or revelatory about first-century Thessalonica, only that Christ's significance as an event was set out in its first, primordial form in this place. But far from holding its meaning in any one fixed time, the language of Scripture transcends even its original context of production. This is how Scripture is constantly experienced in the life of the church. One example might be Paul's statement in 1 Thess. 5:10 that the Lord Jesus Christ died 'for us'. We cannot say that it was any part of Paul's historical intention to communicate this creed to early twenty-first-century Christians.

---

[152] Ricoeur, 'Toward a Hermeneutic', p. 102.   [153] *Ibid.*, p. 78.   [154] *Ibid.*, p. 108.

He might have been sharing this creed with the Thessalonians, but his language has been and is released, taken on and experienced by countless others. Paul's words, released into the life of a community endlessly tracing their own experience of a graced reality through the text, witness to a revelation radically free from any 'original context' or tentatively reconstructed 'authorial intention'.

Christian language, even Scriptural language, can only ever be an imperfect shadow of the real experience of graced transformation. Correspondingly, the language of 1 Thessalonians can only be inadequately understood from within an understanding of its original context. The least imperfect way to understand Scripture, as Scripture, is to wrestle with the process that is its unfolding over time. As we have seen, historical criticism, marked by an objectivity predisposed against reading language as revelatory, that is in generating and sustaining new ways of perception and living, is bound to neglect this complex role played out by Scriptural language. Theologically, therefore, what we see in the text is less a mirror of an original context, and far more an expression of linguistic dissatisfaction with the inability of language to correspond to the 'power' (1:5) of God. For theologians, it is necessary to grapple with the Biblical text's charge of speaking of that which cannot be adequately spoken of in our limited language, namely God. In this way the words used by Paul reveal *to the reader* a hope of 'communication surviving the perils of words',[155] and an awareness that we understand the language only in part against its original context, and far more fully within every interpretative context within which the language encounters, interprets and is brought to fresh expression.

The expansion of Scriptural understanding is thus experienced as a process, a process that enjoys a dialectical relationship with the event on which it is founded. To state this programmatically: *the process of revelation is a continual unfolding of Christ's complete revelatory significance.* God in Christ has committed himself to time, and so enabled all time to be seen eschatologically, as constant expansion and progress towards the promise of eternity. The significance of God in Christ's revelation is something deepened and amplified through time, and never in any one time we prioritise – original context or otherwise. Where historical criticism is interested in questions of text and original context, there is a greater theological need to relocate this energy in a drive to understand the revelatory language through the church, which is continually prolonging, extending and deepening its understanding of Scripture's referent.

---

[155] R. Williams, 'Poetic and Religious Imagination', *Theology* 80 (1977), 182.

It is through the text that we understand this imperative, for it is only through reading the text with attention and love that we come to see the limitations of understanding the language wholly against its original context. Reading the text as a text through which God is continually willing to communicate, we shall be seeking ways which help us engage with the revelation of the text in an ever-expanding way, which connects us with the story of the text's performance and interpretation in the church.[156]

Lest the argument seems suddenly to have become opaque, it is important to clarify my meaning here. The revelatory capacity of the Bible can only be grasped through time, rather than in just one moment, because the Bible speaks of revelation transcending the *particular* and communicating to all time. This is presumably what Barth was trying to articulate when he opened his first Romans commentary with the words,

> Paul, as a child of his age, addressed his contemporaries. It is, however, far more important that, as Prophet and Apostle of the Kingdom of God, he veritably speaks to all men of every age.[157]

The meaning and significance of Scripture's texts cannot be wholly contained within any one time, for their revelatory capacity can only be unfolded through the church's ruminative reading. To be sure, this very process is only made possible because of the complete and unsurpassable *event* that is God's revelation in Christ. In Christ, God has entered into time and endorsed our time as capable of the text's creative reading and expansion. The inexhaustible richness of Scripture's language is now to be read in the context of 'the catholicity of the whole of time'.[158] In this way, revelation as event and revelation as process, far from being mutually exclusive, are intrinsically bound together. Only because of the event do we become participants in the process. As we shall see in our own theological reading of 1 Thessalonians (Part III), it is close reading of the text itself that engages us with the complex unravelling of revelation contained within the form of the words. The meaning that God has for any given Scriptural text is not exhausted within the reflective relationship that historicists construct between text and original context. The Scriptural text has more work to do in the church besides this, for we have in Scripture 'a seed capable of progressive and continual growth'.[159]

---

[156] See M. Blondel, 'History and Dogma', in *The Letter on Apologetics, and History and Dogma*, tr. A. Dru and I. Trethowan (London: Harvill Press, 1964), p. 244.

[157] Barth, *The Epistle to the Romans*, p. 1.

[158] G. Florovsky, 'The Catholicity of the Church', in *Bible, Church, Tradition: An Eastern Orthodox View* (Belmont: Nordland, 1972), p. 49.

[159] Blondel, 'History and Dogma', p. 275.

3.3   Historicism blinds historical critics to the text's apostolic witness

Our third complaint in relation to historical criticism is exclusively theological. To claim that historical critics are hampered by their historicism and so fail to engage with the ultimate witness of the apostles is likely to attract support only from theologians. Nevertheless, despite the potential loneliness of our quest, it is worth attempting to counter the presumption that the historical-critical mode of interpretation is really the most faithful and attentive reading of Scripture.

The assumption of much historical criticism is that the most truthful understanding of the text will be achieved by an interpretation that puts the most distance between the modern reader and the world of the first-century church. This is the thesis evident in Stendahl and Räisänen: the church will only hear a new and possibly offensive voice from the church of the past if it commits itself to a maximal distance between the current context of interpretation and the text. However, in the desire to avoid the excesses of eisegesis, historical critics may well be working with a defective model of exegesis. Exegesis, in attempting to bring *out* the meaning of a passage, requires the kind of open and frank discussion which commences with the presupposition that, at root, the texts we are working with are texts whose meaning lies within their subject matter witnessed to as true and valid in all times. In this key, Christ as the Lord of time, the one in whom all time mysteriously finds its purpose and unity, radically destabilises the distancing preached by historical critics.

Prior to dealing with historical criticism as it is actually practised, I shall first discuss a programmatic article of Brevard Childs which assists in the clarification of the criticisms I shall direct towards 1 Thessalonians scholarship. Developing the argument, I shall examine Jeffrey Weima's work on the events 'behind' 1 Thess. 2:1–12, and how he completely misses that which is most striking about these verses: Paul's role as apostle and witness to God's revelation.

In his 1964 article 'Interpretation in Faith: The Theological Responsibility of an Old Testament Commentary', Brevard Childs outlined many of his concerns about 'the serious lack of good Old Testament commentaries' at the time he was writing.[160] Childs is aware that it would be grossly unfair to judge commentaries by norms foreign to their guiding interests, to questions to which they are not seeking answers. Nevertheless, Childs *is* unashamedly interested in the scope of theological commentaries, and

---

[160] Childs, 'Interpretation in Faith', 432.

seeks the normative as well as the descriptive categories which will sustain such a project. The questions which Childs asks are exactly the same questions which I want to pose to 1 Thessalonians scholarship, questions generated by my dissatisfaction with the historical-critical project: 'can the theological task of a commentator be exhausted when he remains on the level of the witness? Is there not a responsibility to penetrate to the substance towards which the text points?'[161]

For Childs, theological exegesis of the Old Testament would have three distinguishing features. First, it would be committed to reading a single Old Testament text in the light of the whole Old Testament, or as Childs articulates it, 'from the single text to the whole witness'.[162] At this stage all the traditional textual and philological apparatus of the historical-critical method is brought to the fore – the difference is that it is circumscribed within a theological matrix. Secondly, the commentator will be committed to examining the inter-relationships between the Old and New Testaments, for although they form a dual witness, they witness to the univocal purposes of God.[163] Thirdly, there will be a dialectic movement from 'substance to witness' and back again from the witness to the substance,[164] a task which seeks to hear the Word of God anew. So, the task is here to 'penetrate to that reality which called forth the witness',[165] a task which surely lies at the heart of all theological exegesis.

Where do these observations take us? Childs suggests that the mark of historicism is getting stuck in the rut of history, when there is no real clarity on how one 'goes beyond this [the descriptive task] to enter into the full theological dimension'.[166] And yet, as happens with many ideological fallacies, we are blinded by our assumption that the difficulty lies in translating 'what it meant' into 'what it means', whereas in truth the problem lies less in this point of crossover and far more in the presumed objectivity of the descriptive task. For, as Childs and others point out, *how* we decide to read the Bible determines in a large measure what we get out of it.[167] The protestations of New Testament scholars that reading the New Testament texts as historical texts is consensual and neutral will not drown out the nagging question: why not read the New Testament texts as canonically shaped literature or as religious literature which attests to revelation, or texts which witness to the Word of God lying beyond them, a summons which requires our attention? Historical critics may think that by reading the New Testament texts as sources they are standing on cool, objective, neutral ground on which everybody can stand, but there

[161] *Ibid.*, 436.   [162] *Ibid.*, 440.   [163] *Ibid.*, 440–2.   [164] *Ibid.*, 443.
[165] *Ibid.*, 444.   [166] *Ibid.*   [167] *Ibid.*

is much truth in Childs' comment 'that the fundamental error lies in the starting point'.[168]

For any theological exegesis *the* starting point must be that in reading 1 Thessalonians we are reading the words of an apostle and witness, one urging us to look towards that to which he is gesturing. Paul's words are those of a witness willing us to look towards the reality indicated by his words. As an apostle and witness Paul is constantly pointing beyond and away from himself. His words are best read not as bound within their historical context of production, but as constantly extending beyond it, because Paul's words are the words of an apostle aware that God in Christ's revelation is the ultimate authority. It is this apostolic sensitivity, the awareness that his authority is transcendent in origin,[169] which is precisely at work in 1 Thess. 2:1–12, and throughout the letter.

As part of this emerging apostolic self-understanding, Paul's courage in the face of great opposition is courage 'in our God' (2:2). Entrusted by God with the gospel, Paul directs his words not towards the pleasing of humanity, but God (2:4). Paul's very behaviour and delivery of the gospel are witnessed to by God himself (2:5, 10). In short, what Paul is recounting in 1 Thess. 2:1–13 is the conduct of an 'apostle of Christ' (2:7), as one set aside by God to witness to God's revelation. As an apostle, Paul is always acutely aware of the need to point away from himself and direct attention to the real salvific force at work, '*God's word which is also at work in you believers*' (2:13, my italics).

It is perhaps typical that much of the debate surrounding 1 Thess. 2:1–12 has been concerned with its origins and purpose rather than its actual content. Such readings are remarkably unfaithful to Paul as witness and apostle, paying more attention to why Paul says what he does rather than to what he is actually saying. Looking for the historically conditioned purpose of texts, historical critics miss the witness of the Scriptural text, the ultimate reality or substance towards which the text's author, as witness, is pointing and which he is willing us to encounter. The historical-critical debate instead chases around those who see the original purpose of these verses as paraenetic and those who see them as apologetic in purpose.[170]

Jeffrey A. D. Weima's article 'An Apology for the Apologetic Function of 1 Thessalonians 2:1–12' is a recent reassertion of this tendency.

---

[168] *Ibid.*

[169] See S. Kierkegaard, 'Of the Difference between a Genius and an Apostle', in *The Present Age and Two Minor Ethico-Religious Treatises*, tr. A. Dru and W. Lowrie (London: Oxford University Press, 1940), pp. 137–63.

[170] For a helpful summary of the various arguments see Still, *Conflict* , pp. 137–49.

For those who argue that in 1 Thess. 2:1–12 Paul was defending himself against opponents the possible list seems endless: Judaisers, Gnostics, Spiritual Enthusiasts, or Millenarianists from within the church, or indeed non-believing Jews from outwith the church in Thessalonica.[171] Weima interprets every word and phrase of Paul's not as pointing beyond itself to a world unfolding in front of the text, but rather as pointing to some situation that may or may not lie behind the text. Weima's argument thus distorts the full (and most obvious) narrative effect of the peri-cope, dividing the text from its ultimate reference, which allows him to posit what he confesses are only 'probable' backgrounds.[172] There is no hint of reading the text just as it stands. Weima assumes that there is an inherent transparency to the text, allowing him to advance his real interest – the text's background. For Weima it is identifiable historical events which the text ultimately conveys, not the witness of Paul the apostle.

Now that it has been argued that Paul's intention in 1 Thess. 2:1–12 is apologetic, and thus reactive, the cast is set for how Weima reads the verses. For Weima's argument to sustain itself, he can *only* mir-ror read the text, for his argument will look the stronger the more enthusiastically he mirror reads the text. We have here, then, a good example of a closed methodology, where Weima, by his argument that freezes the language into its original context of production, is predis-posed to reading the language as a mirror reflective of 'a historical reality'.[173] Correspondingly, Weima argues that antithetical statements can be mirror read to conclude 'that the attacks against Paul focused on his integrity'.[174] Paul's opponents are the compatriots mentioned in 2:14, aggrieved at the Thesssalonians' anti-social conversion from idolatry to Christianity.

The deficiency in Weima's reading of 1 Thessalonians lies in his read-ing of it as a *source*, and not as *witness*. This results in the irony that the very verses in which Paul is most keen to articulate his apostolic witness, that there is Something else at work in him, are mined by Weima for possible historical contexts. Weima's reading is purely illustrative of a wider malaise that reads the referent of the text as its historical back-ground, and so consistently misreads that to which the text is ultimately witnessing.

Weima's assumption is that the meaning of 1 Thessalonians is what lies 'behind' it. Theologically this is deficient because the text's revelatory

[171] J. A. D. Weima, 'An Apology for the Apologetic Function of 1 Thessalonians 2:1–12', *JSNT* 68 (1997), 73–4.
[172] *Ibid.*, 84.   [173] *Ibid.*, 85.   [174] *Ibid.*, 96.

quality is found not *behind*, but *in* the witness of the text itself, and thus a close attentiveness to the text is required at all times. Theologically shaped exegesis insists, therefore, that each Biblical text is read as a witness, and not as a source. Only in this way can we be faithful to Scripture's capacity to make known the reorganising power of the Word of God.

Weima misreads the text of 1 Thessalonians, and spectacularly misses its apostolic witness, because for him the *res*, that which the text is really speaking about, is its historical situation. In Barth's language, Weima leaps out of the circularity between the texts and their quality of witness, and so finds something quite alien from what Paul is *really* communicating.[175] If Weima had displayed as much preoccupation with the text and the subject matter which Paul is witnessing to through the form of the text as he had done with the text's background, he would have discerned the communicative will of 1 Thess. 2:1–12, the sheer miracle of the 'Word within the words'.[176]

4   Conclusion

The assumption that the most faithful reading of Scripture will be the one most disengaged from the Bible's central message needs itself to be exposed for what it is – an unrecognised bias, the lingering embers of positivist modernity. Theologically, it is quite justified to decide against siding with the assumptions of the modern reader in favour of the Biblical author.[177] Just as Paul was not transfixed by his context of deliverance but by the subject matter of which he is apostolic witness, so too we must resolve to be gripped by that which Paul was gripped by, if we want to interpret Paul's words with a sense of rigour and attention. In contrast to all the historical critics we have been reading, our movement throughout this book will not be from the text *back* to its historical context, but from the text *forward* into its history of reading in the church, and *forward* into a sympathetic reading alongside its subject matter. It is this *forward expansion* into the text's fecundity, an eagerness to grapple with the text's ultimate significance, that will be as much present in our reading as it was in Barth's (in)famous declaration that

[175] Barth, *The Göttingen Dogmatics*, pp. 215–16.
[176] Barth, *The Epistle to the Romans*, p. 9.
[177] A similar point is made by Barth in Preface Draft 1A to the First Edition of his *Der Römerbrief*, translated in R. E. Burnett, *Karl's Barth's Theological Exegesis* (Tübingen: J. C. B. Mohr, 2001), p. 281.

As one who would understand, *I must press forward* to the point where insofar as possible I confront the riddle of the subject matter and no longer merely the riddle of the document as such, until I can almost forget that I am not the author, until I have almost understood him so well that I let him speak in my name, and can myself speak in his name.[178]

This declaration, read correctly, is not a call for attention to 'authorial intention'. Paying attention to the apostle Paul as an authority means paying attention to that to which his words witness. It is this subject matter – the Word in the words, God's will in the feebleness of human words – which bears the ultimate authority, and not our reconstructed authorial intention. The challenge here is to release *our* models of authority – in reconstructions of Paul's 'intention' – and dare to confront the ultimate authority within the text, the subject matter. Confronting the subject matter, accompanying this struggle with a ceaseless attention to the text itself, we shall discipline ourselves to pass from any interest in Paul as author to that which he was transfixed by. Only from this perspective, as the subject matter takes over, will any hankerings after authorial intention dissolve.

From our critiques of historical criticism, which have been interwoven with our positive proposals about where the meaning of the text *is* to be found, the rest of the argument flows successively.

Initially, it is worth reminding ourselves of the emphasis consistently put earlier in the book on the text itself. Consequently the rest of the book will demonstrate a relentless fidelity and reference to the text of I Thessalonians.

In Part II, true to my stated interest in the voices of tradition through which this text has been interpreted, I shall examine the readings of I Thessalonians in the hands of Thomas Aquinas and John Calvin. Chapters 2 and 3 will endeavour to be examinations of the readings of the text. We shall look closely at both Thomas' and Calvin's *reading*, namely how they do the business of interpretation, and whether there is anything we can learn from their hermeneutics in the light of our criticisms of prevailing historical-critical tendencies. Secondly, we shall look closely at their reading of *the text*, examining what both Thomas and Calvin state the text is saying and establishing what we have learned from their commentaries. Reading these neglected commentaries, we shall thus be pointed afresh to the witness of I Thessalonians.

[178] Barth, *The Epistle to the Romans*, p. 8 (my italics).

Allowing the witness of the text to emerge slowly through our study of Thomas' and Calvin's commentaries on the text and methodologically adopting some of their pre-modern methods of exegesis, we shall turn in Part III to our own exploration of the text's depth. Exploring the text in conversation with an eclectic range of voices, I shall endeavour to show in exegetical practice the infinite depth of 1 Thessalonians' ultimate content.

PART II

**An exploration of some pre-modern readings
of 1 Thessalonians**

2

THOMAS AQUINAS AND 1 THESSALONIANS

Introduction

Thomas Aquinas is too rarely revered as a Scriptural theologian. The theologian for whom sacred revelation was directly equivalent to Scripture ('sacra Scriptura seu doctrina'[1]) would doubtless have approved of the symbolism implicit in the Council of Trent's decision to place his *Summa Theologiae* aside the altar Bible throughout their deliberations. For Thomas, knowledge and understanding of Scripture were co-dependent on the *scientia* that is *sacra doctrina*. Examination of Thomas' exegesis therefore demands an awareness of the reciprocity between his expositional studies and his more 'systematic' works.[2] Thomas would not understand, or probably appreciate, our study of 'systematic theology' as distinct from 'Biblical studies'. Study of Thomas' exegetical method and contribution must respect his conviction: that theology, as the supreme science, is the most unified of studies working from indemonstrable first principles to a deeper knowledge of itself.[3]

Thomas' teaching career began at the University of Paris in 1251/2 as a *baccalaureus biblicus* where, as a *cursor biblicus*, he lectured on the entirety of Scripture.[4] In 1254 Aquinas was elevated to the post of *baccalaureus Sententiarum*, obliging him to comment on the *Sentences* of Peter Lombard (c. 1095–1160). By 1256 Aquinas had graduated to the position of Master in theology (*magister in sacra*

---

[1] *ST* 1a q. 1 a. 2 ad 2. A cursory glance at the frequent citation of Biblical references in the *sed contra* sections of the *Summa Theologiae* articles impresses upon the reader the authority which Thomas invests in Scripture. Note, however, that he is not shy of drawing in the interpretation of the church (*ST* 2a2ae q. 1 a. 8 s.c.), or of Fathers like Augustine (*ST* 1a q. 1 a. 2 s.c.) as an authority.

[2] J.-P. Torrell, *Saint Thomas Aquinas, Volume I: The Person and his Work*, tr. R. Royal (Washington: Catholic University of America Press, 1996), p. 55.

[3] *ST* 1a q. 1 a. 7 re; 1a2ae q. 66 a. 5 ad 4; 2a2ae q. 171 a. 4 re.

[4] J. A. Weisheipl, *Friar Thomas d'Aquino: His Life, Thought and Work* (New York: Doubleday, 1974), p. 72, holds that Thomas was never a *cursor biblicus* at Paris. Instead he argues that Thomas lectured on Lombard's *Sentences* between 1252 and 1256.

pagina), which for the next three years obliged him to lecture on the Bible daily, to conduct public classroom discussions (*quaestiones disputatae*), and to preach sermons to clergy and laity. Thus, the three functions of the *magister* were *legere*, *disputare* and *praedicare*. Between 1259 and 1268 Thomas was heavily involved in teaching Scripture and preaching in Italy, before returning to Paris University in 1269 for another three years. While he is most famous for his two great works, the *Summa Contra Gentiles* and the *Summa Theologiae*, and for his commentaries on Aristotle, his formative teaching was actually composed of commenting and lecturing on Scripture. It is worth bearing in mind the implications of the academic hierarchy Thomas ascended so quickly: the highest task for any medieval university teacher was teaching Scripture.

Given Thomas' context this emphasis should come as no real surprise. Despite our propensity to view scholasticism as indicative of a period of abstraction and philosophical indulgence, Thomas' context was a time of evangelical revival, a time when the basic text for the masters' classes could have been nothing *but* the Bible.[5] This revival was embodied by Thomas' own controversial decision to join the newly established Dominican Order (1216), an order that practised evangelical mendicancy and preaching.[6]

Aquinas was a prolific Scriptural commentator. There are extant commentaries on Psalms 1–54, Job, Isaiah, Jeremiah and Lamentations in the Old Testament; and in the New Testament on Matthew, John, Romans, 1 and 2 Corinthians, Galatians, Ephesians, Philippians, Colossians, 1 and 2 Thessalonians, 1 and 2 Timothy, Titus, Philemon and Hebrews. Traditional assignations to Aquinas of a commentary on the Song of Songs lack documentary evidence and are deemed spurious. As well as these commentaries there is the impressive *Catena Aurea* (*Golden Chain*), written between 1262/3 and 1267. This is a commentary on all four gospels by

---

[5] For this evangelical revival see N. Healy, *Thomas Aquinas – Theologian of the Christian Life* (Aldershot: Ashgate, 2003), pp. 24–33.

[6] Hence their epithet, 'Order of Preachers'. Thomas brings up the theme of preaching frequently in his Thessalonians *Lectura*. See *Lectio Thessalonicenses* V.II.134; *Commentary on Saint Paul's First Letter to the Thessalonians*, tr. M. Duffy (Aquinas Scripture Series; Albany: Magi Books, 1969), p. 52, where preachers are described as 'prophets'. This is especially interesting given that for Thomas prophecy is a 'gift of grace (which) raises man to something which is above human nature' (*ST* 2a2ae q. 173 a. 2 ad 3). See also *Lectio* I.I.19; II.I.28; II.II.40, 53. Thomas' decision to join the controversial Dominican Order was very far from the religious life his family had planned for him, and they imprisoned him for a year to test his resolve.

means of a skilfully woven sequence of writings taken from the Fathers of the East and West.

Thomas' commentaries fall into two groups: *reportationes* and *ordinationes* (also known as *expositiones*). A *reportatio* represents the notes taken down of a lecture on Scripture as it was actually delivered by Thomas. An *ordinatio*, on the other hand, represents something much more polished, and was always written or, at the very least, dictated by the author himself.

The commentary on 1 Thessalonians lies within the group of commentaries formed by Reginald of Piperno's *reportationes* on the lectures of Thomas. Mandonnet (who has been enormously influential) sought to tie down Thomas' commentaries to specific academic years,[7] and divided Thomas' teaching on Paul into two distinct periods: Italy between 1259 and 1265 and Naples between October 1272 and December 1273,[8] the second round of teaching motivated by a desire to improve upon the first attempt. The extant commentaries on Job, Isaiah, Jeremiah, Lamentations, Romans and as far as 1 Cor. 7:9 represent these improved *ordinationes*. It would appear that the section from 1 Cor. 7:10 through to chapter 10 represents an insertion from the *postilla* of Peter of Tarentaise.[9] Thomas' death interrupted any further progress on the remaining commentaries, and so our immediate concern is that Thomas' commentary on 1 Thessalonians remains as a *reportatio*.

Perhaps the wisest course is to echo Jean-Pierre Torrell's tentativeness and opt for Thomas' teaching in Orvieto and Rome between 1265 and 1268 as the context for his 1 Thessalonians lectures.[10] If Thomas followed the order of the Vulgate, we can assume that his lectures on 1 Thessalonians would be a little over half way through his course. Thomas' lectures on 1 Thessalonians are therefore posterior to his *Summa Contra Gentiles* (1259–64), yet very close in time to (if not concurrent with) the composition of the *Summa Theologiae* (1266–73), both theological resources we shall draw upon.

---

[7] P. Mandonnet, 'Chronologie des écrits scripturaires de s. Thomas d'Aquin', *Revue Thomiste* 33 (1928), 222–45. For criticisms of Mandonnet's thesis see Torrell, *Saint Thomas*, pp. 251–2.

[8] See C. T. Baglow, *'Modus et Forma': A New Approach to the Exegesis of Saint Thomas with an Application to the* Lectura super Epistolam ad Ephesios (Rome: Editrice Pontificio Istituto Biblico, 2002), p. 115.

[9] I. T. Eschmann, 'A Catalogue of St Thomas' Work', tr. L. K. Shook, in E. Gilson, *The Christian Philosophy of St Thomas Aquinas* (London: Victor Gollancz, 1957), p. 399.

[10] Torrell, *Saint Thomas*, p. 255.

One final matter needs to be discussed prior to launching into detailed study of Thomas' commentary. The reliability of the text we are working from could be legitimately queried, given that it is not from the hand of Thomas himself, but that of a secretary (for the Pauline commentaries, Reginald of Piperno). Just how safe is it to build up an argument upon the foundations of a text written by a scribe and not the author himself? There are, fortunately, good grounds to retain confidence in the reliability of the text. Mandonnet's comparison of Thomas' *reportationes* and *expositiones* uncovered little difference in style between the two, indicating the care with which Thomas' lectures were transcribed. As Christopher Baglow further notes, were we to make only documents written by Thomas' own hand admissible for scholarly scrutiny, we would have to set aside most of Thomas' *œuvre*.[11] Certainly many other medieval texts which scholars work from are the fruits of lecture transcriptions, and there is evidence from Bernard Gui that Thomas had time to check the transcriptions of his lectures.[12] Indeed, stories of Thomas dictating to three secretaries simultaneously are indicative of a famed energy that could only have been realised with the aid of secretarial assistance. Faced with a text which bears all the hallmarks of Thomistic exegesis, and unwilling to relinquish much of Thomas' other work, we are probably best advised to affirm the authenticity of our commentary, despite its being written by a secretary.

Taking our cue from the concluding remarks in Part I, we shall be concerned in our study of Thomas' commentary first of all with Thomas' *reading*, with how he does the business of interpretation. We shall examine his use of *auctoritates* in commenting on the text (section 1.1). We shall pay especially close attention to the way in which, throughout his exegesis, Thomas nests his comments within Biblical citations. We shall also see how he reads and deploys the Patristic inheritance, engaging with one instance of Thomas' use of the interpretative tradition. In section 1.2 we shall examine Thomas' disciplined, Aristotelian reading of the text. These two sections – examining the influence of the canon, the Fathers and Aristotle – will equip us in examining Thomas' profoundly theological exegesis of 1 Thess. 4:13–18 (section 2). We shall conclude (section 3) with some reflections on Thomas' theological and exegetical contribution to our reading of 1 Thessalonians in Part III.

[11] Baglow, '*Modus et Forma*', p. 120.

[12] M. Lamb, 'Introduction', in Thomas Aquinas, *Commentary on Saint Paul's Epistle to the Ephesians*, tr. M. L. Lamb (Albany: Magi Books, 1966), p. 23.

**1 The hermeneutical principles of Thomas'
1 Thessalonians *Lectura***

1.1 Thomas and *auctoritates*

(a) Thomas and the canon

The misconception that Thomas was steeped in a dry and introspective scholasticism has long given way to the realisation that, for somebody who at one time was lecturing on Scripture up to four times a week, he is rightly recalled as a Biblical theologian.

The manner in which Thomas reads Scripture throughout his Thessalonians *Lectura* is foreshadowed in the prologue. Thomas begins by citing Gen. 7:17, 'The waters increased and bore up the ark and it rose above the earth', as words 'appropriate' ('competent') to the subject matter of 1 Thessalonians.[13] Thomas clearly gives the 'ark' a spiritual interpretation, a meaning guided by the providence of God, who 'has the power, not only of adapting words to convey meanings (which men can also do), but also of adapting things (res) themselves'.[14] For where the literal sense of this Genesis passage could not refer to the church, a spiritual interpretation allowing God's direction of events permits the ark to symbolise the church (presaged by 1 Peter 3:20), since in both, 'only the elect will be saved' ('soli electi salvabuntur').[15] In this spiritual interpretation, the 'waters' of Gen. 7:17 'signify' ('significantur') the tribulations afflicting the church. This is so first, because (Mt. 7:25) waters have a tendency to 'strike like tribulations'; secondly, because (Ecclus. 3:30) water extinguishes fire, and tribulations can quell the fiery 'force of desires' which threaten the church's good order; and thirdly, because (Lam. 3:54 and Jonah 2:6) water threatens to inundate the church, but the church is not yet overcome by flooding. The Thessalonian church is signified by the ark because just as the ark rose up on the deadly waters of the flood, so too the Thessalonian church in its tribulations is assured not of its destruction, but its uplifting. Much of this assurance lies in God's providential direction of events.[16]

Thomas' prologue is interesting for the way it weaves the *literal* referents of diverse Scriptural passages into a coherent *spiritual* truth (that in times of suffering 'the Church is not destroyed but uplifted').[17] Moreover,

---

[13] *Prologus*; Duffy, *Commentary*, p. 3.   [14] *ST* 1a q. 1 a. 10 re.
[15] *Prologus*; Duffy, *Commentary*, p. 3.
[16] Cf. the same spiritual interpretation of the ark in *ST* 2a2ae q. 173, a. 3 re, where the ark is 'ordained to be prophetically significant'.
[17] *Prologus*; Duffy, *Commentary*, p. 3.

not being restricted to literal meanings of texts, Aquinas reads Gen. 7:17 more expansively than the human authors could have intended. This is because God, as principal author of Scripture, has the capacity of 'adapting things [in our case, the ark] themselves', and so 'the things meant by the words also themselves mean something'.[18]

That Thomas should rely so heavily on such an intratextual reading of the Bible is not surprising. If, for Thomas, God is the primary author and mover of Scripture, then it will be a text constantly explaining itself *through* itself. What is vague or obscure in one part will be explained by another part.[19] Thomas' keenness for extracting the meaning of 'the Bible by the Bible' is evident throughout his lectures.[20]

There are some 340 Scriptural citations in the 1 Thessalonians *Lectura*. The vast majority of these citations are from the New Testament (211, or 62 per cent of the total), with 129 (38 per cent) from the Old Testament.[21] The majority of the New Testament citations are from Paul's epistles (including the Pastorals and Hebrews) – 115 out of 211 total New Testament citations. When we add to this figure citations from the other non-narrative texts (the Catholic epistles), the figure rises to 134. The gospels, Revelation and Acts (what we may call here 'narrative' texts) account only for 77 (36 per cent) of the total New Testament citations.

That 34 per cent of the total Scriptural citations are drawn from the Pauline literature is not surprising given Thomas' stated high regard for Paul's theological contribution.[22] Neither is it surprising that Romans is the most cited of the Scriptural texts – the epistle of grace is for Thomas an interpretative and explicative key.[23] Moreover, that 39 per cent of the Scriptural citations (and 64 per cent of the New Testament citations) come from the non-narrative sections of the New Testament supports those who claim that Thomas prefers to work with non-narrative texts that convey their theme in the most direct manner.[24]

When it comes to the citation of the Old Testament, Thomas' reliance upon the Psalms is often noted, and his *Lectura* on 1 Thessalonians is no exception. Psalms account for 18 per cent of the total Old Testament citations. Thomas' knowledge of and passion for the Psalms is undoubtedly

---

[18] *ST* 1a q. 1 a. 10 re.   [19] *ST* 1a q. 1 a. 9 ad 2.

[20] T. McGuckin, 'Saint Thomas Aquinas and Theological Exegesis of Sacred Scripture', *New Blackfriars* 73 (1993), 205.

[21] It has been surmised that when quoting Scripture, Thomas was doing so from memory, a skill mastered during his imprisonment at the hands of his family. See Torrell, *Saint Thomas*, p. 11.

[22] See Thomas' prologue to the Pauline commentaries, translated *ibid.*, pp. 255–6.

[23] In the Prologue to his Pauline commentaries, Thomas spoke of Romans as the epistle that dealt with Christ's grace most fully. See *ibid.*, p. 256.

[24] Baglow, *'Modus et Forma'*, p. 132.

related to his daily liturgical use of them in worship.[25] Certainly, Thomas reserved a consistently high regard for them, reading their subject matter as Christ and the church. So high was Thomas' regard for the Psalms that he thought they read more like a gospel than a prophet.[26] Isaiah and the Wisdom literature also emerge as heavily cited books.[27]

Aside from this quantitive analysis of Thomas' use of Scripture it is necessary to pay attention to *how* he actually worked with Scripture to generate understanding of 1 Thessalonians.

Scripture for Thomas is its own interpreter, and thus the meaning of a phrase employed by Paul in 1 Thessalonians can be clarified by reference to further texts within Scripture. But, unlike modern exegesis (and, as we shall see, Calvin), which prefers to explain what Paul says in one text with reference to what he says in another Pauline text, Paul is explained by reference to *any* part of Scripture. This is perhaps not surprising given that, for Thomas, God was the author of Scripture, and so in inspiring the writers to write understood everything he was doing.[28] There is, for Thomas, 'a radical unity of scriptural truth',[29] a conviction born from the belief that God was Scripture's principal cause.[30]

There are two obvious ways in which Thomas deploys Scripture in his Thessalonians *Lectura*.

(1) Thomas uses Scripture as an authority to illuminate the reference of 1 Thessalonians. A good example of this deployment is Thomas' exposition on 5:5, which talks of the Thessalonians being 'sons of light and sons of the day'. Thomas delves deeper into the meaning of Paul's description of them as 'sons' by turning to Isa. 5:1, in corroboration of his point that what 'Scripture says'[31] is that 'someone is said to be the son of something because he abounds in that thing'.[32] The Vulgate refers here to 'filio olei', that is 'the son of oil'. Modern translations render this as 'very fertile', but Thomas would appear to read this reference to 'son' as a warrant for demonstrating his main point: that sons are those who share and abound

[25] Torrell, *Saint Thomas*, p. 34.

[26] Psalms, *Prooemium*. See Torrell, *Saint Thomas*, p. 34, for a translation.

[27] Torrell, *Saint Thomas*, p. 34, suggests that Wisdom literature was popular at the time because it lent itself easily to moral instruction.

[28] *ST* 1a q. 1 a. 10 re, 'auctor autem sacrae Scripturae Deus est qui omnia simul suo intellectu comprehendit'.

[29] C. C. Black, 'St Thomas' Commentary on the Johannine Prologue: Some Reflections on its Character and Implications', *CBQ* 48 (1986), 688.

[30] H. Pope, *St Thomas Aquinas as an Interpreter of Holy Scripture* (Oxford: Basil Blackwell, 1924), pp. 24–7.

[31] *Lectio* V.I.115; Duffy, *Commentary*, p. 44.

[32] *Lectio* V.I.115; Duffy, *Commentary*, p. 44.

in the same thing as the father, in this case the fertility of the land. Turning to Isaiah in order to understand Paul's reference to 'sons', Thomas deploys Jn. 8:12 and 12:36 to exposit the reference to 'light' as a reference to the 'faith of Christ' ('fides Christi').[33] This extrapolation enables him to draw an elegant parallel which exposits Paul's reference to 'the day'. Just as out of light comes day, so out of the light that is the faith of Christ (note that for Thomas it is Christ's faith rather than our faith in Christ which would appear to be operative here) comes the day of 'good works' ('bonorum operum').[34] Appropriately, Thomas inserts Rom. 13:12, 'The night is far gone, the day is at hand.' More than being a decorative proof text, Scripture is itself part of the interpretative sequence.

In Thomas' reflections on 5:5, and other verses, we also get some clues as to how he worked. It has been suggested by Jean-Pierre Torrell that Thomas worked with an early form of a concordance,[35] and indeed many citations seem to be selected on account of their word association.[36] Certainly, in expounding the meaning of the word *lux* in 5:5 it is not unreasonable to contend that Thomas turned to some form of concordance which directed him to Jn. 8:12, 'Ego sum lux mundi', and Jn. 12:36, 'Credite in lucem.' So too do we see this spiral of word associations in other places of the commentary. In the first *Lectio* on chapter 1, Thomas turns to 1 Cor. 15:10, 'Gratia Dei sum id quod sum', when talking about the *gratia* which Paul asks as a blessing upon the church. It seems quite possible then to agree with Torrell that Thomas worked with some form of concordance.

Another example of Scripture acting as a primary explanatory source in Thomas' exegesis is in his comments on 1 Thess. 2:18, 'we wanted to come to you – I, Paul, again and again – but Satan hindered us'. Thomas turns to Rev. 7:1 ('four angels standing at the four corners of the earth so that no wind could blow on earth or sea or against any tree') in an attempt to understand the nature of the obstacles put in Paul's way.

(2) As a canonical and scholastic theologian, Thomas uses Scripture in a secondary mode to prompt its own *quaestiones*, the *responsiones* to which prompt new understanding. Just as Scripture is self-explanatory, so too for Thomas can it act as a source of *quaestiones* and means for

---

[33] *Lectio* V.I.115; Duffy, *Commentary*, p. 44.   [34] *Lectio* V.I.115; my translation.

[35] Torrell, *Saint Thomas*, pp. 33–4.

[36] *Lectio* V.II.139; Duffy, *Commentary*, p. 54, where Thomas, commenting on Paul's direction to 'greet each other with a holy kiss' (5:26), contrasts it unfavourably to the 'passionate' ('libidinoso') kiss of the woman in Prov. 7:13, and the 'treacherous' ('proditorio') kiss of Judas in Mt. 26:49. Of course, it might just be that Thomas knew his Scriptures so well that he could cite these texts from memory.

combating error, a profoundly scholastic drive.[37] The nature of Thomas' canonical tendencies is emphasised by an extended reflection in *Lectio* I.I.12–13. Thomas considers how Paul's report of his successful preaching is at risk of contradicting what is said elsewhere in Scripture (a frequent concern to medieval exegetes), in this case Ezek. 3:26, 'And I will make your tongue cleave to the roof of your mouth, so that you shall be dumb.' Extraordinarily (to our modern sensitivities) Thomas suggests that Paul was aware of this contradiction, stating that it was 'For that purpose' Paul first called to mind with what power he preached to them, and also how they were witness to these events.[38]

This same concern, that Scripture cannot contradict itself and so be shown to be untrue in any way,[39] is evident in Thomas' comments on the ethical advice in 4:11, where Paul urges the Thessalonians to 'mind your own affairs'. Here, in *Lectio* IV.I.90 Thomas sets up his own mini-scholastic disputation, asking if Paul's advice contradicts what he says in Rom. 16:2, to 'Help her in whatever she may require from you.' Confirmation that Thomas is constructing his own little disputation comes in the next line, where he signposts his *Respondeo*.[40] Thomas' resolution of this apparent tension is somewhat enigmatic:

> I elaborate by pointing out that things occur in a disorderly manner if they are not governed within the limits of reason, for example, when somebody drives himself excessively; they occur in an orderly manner if the dictates of reason are observed in regulating them.[41]

In these instances Scripture, prompting its own questions of inquiry, is used to delve deeper into the meaning of the text.

There is another conclusion to be drawn from Thomas' use of Scripture in his Thessalonians *Lectura*. His apparent naïveté in the ways of historical awareness and text-critical issues is often remarked upon,[42] though there is evidence that he was not as unsure in the ways of Biblical (or at least

[37] O. M. Pesch, 'Paul as Professor of Theology: The Image of the Apostle in St Thomas' Theology', *The Thomist* 38 (1974), 588.

[38] *Lectio* I.I.13. My translation slightly differs from that of Duffy, who finds the infinitive 'to counter' in the text.

[39] *ST* 1a2ae q. 103 a. 4 ad 2.

[40] Similar 'mini-disputations' are in *Lectio* IV.II.98, 101, 102; V.I.108, 111; V.II.128.

[41] *Lectio* IV.I.90; Duffy, *Commentary*, p. 33.

[42] E.g. E. Stump, 'Revelation and Biblical Exegesis: Augustine, Aquinas and Swinburne', in A. Padgett, ed., *Reason and the Christian Religion: Essays in Honour of Richard Swinburne* (Oxford: Clarendon Press, 1994), pp. 186–7.

textual) criticism as many have thought. One such representative, Henry Pope, argues for Thomas' probable knowledge of Hebrew, and warns us against associating knowledge of the Biblical languages exclusively with the Reformation era.[43]

Thomas was certainly no historical critic (not, of course, that this was something he was consciously opposing). His fervent espousal of gaining meaning from Scripture by citing other parts of Scripture reveals that it was the canonically narrated history, and the canon's organic history within the tradition of the church, which held the interpretative authority.[44] Thomas' understanding and tolerance of history were not unusual for a medieval theologian: the history worth considering is the history of God's saving relationship with his created people. Even a cursory reading of the Thessalonians *Lectura* quickly assaults the reader with a very alien concept of time and history, with Thomas frequently opining that Paul is giving advice about how to behave in relation to priests.[45] In Thomas' conception of time, wholly informed by the divine–human relationship, history had been definitively defined by the transition from the age of Israel to the age of the church.[46] This is not the endeavour of historicism, the misguided attempt to attempt to find meaning and truth in the reconstruction of what lies 'behind the text'. Instead, Thomas' love of the different texts of Scripture and the different texts of interpretation reveals a deep fidelity to a conviction that truth is something discerned through the history of God's saving ways with his people, principally made known through the textuality of Scripture itself.[47]

A short section of Thomas' exegesis may help corroborate what I am saying here about him viewing history through the lenses of Scripture. Towards the end of his *Lectura* Thomas engages in what, at first reading, looks like speculative mirror reading of the text. Commenting on 1 Thess. 5:27, Thomas says that 'Paul feared that those in charge of the assembly might suppress it because of some of the things contained in it.'[48] But this is clearly a conjecture drawn from the deep well of Thomas' Scriptural knowledge, the authority behind the claim being Scripture. For Thomas

---

[43] Pope, *St Thomas*, p. 17.

[44] For the authority of the church see *Lectio* V.II.137; *ST* 2a2ae q. 1 a. 7 re; 2a2ae q. 5 a. 3 ad 2.

[45] E.g. *Lectio* V.II.125.

[46] J. Moltmann, 'Christian Hope: Messianic or Transcendent? A Theological Discussion with Joachim of Fiore and Thomas Aquinas', tr. M. D. Meeks, *Horizons* 12 (1985), 332.

[47] A. Maurer, *St Thomas and Historicity* (Milwaukee: Marquette University Press, 1979), p. 33.

[48] *Lectio* V.II.139; Duffy, *Commentary*, p. 54.

Scripture always explains Scripture, and in this case 1 Thess. 5:27 is explained by Prov. 11:26.

(b)   Thomas and the Fathers

One of the surprising features about Thomas' *Lectura* is the freedom he evidences from citing copious Patristic references. References to the Fathers, or Peter Lombard's *Gloss*,[49] are more notable for their scarcity than their preponderance. In total there are a mere eight direct references to the Fathers.[50]

Part of the reason for Thomas' apparent reticence on this is his relatively eirenic context. To be sure, Thomas was sometimes drawn into defending the newly established Dominican Order, of which he was a member. But Thomas' situation was much less polemical than that of later interpreters, in particular the Reformers, and he certainly did not need to establish his continuity with the early church tradition. Whilst he was of the opinion that those 'who were closer in time to Christ . . . had a fuller knowledge of the mysteries of faith',[51] Thomas' credentials and his church's apostolic continuity were unquestionable, and so this may be one reason why he has the confidence to appeal so rarely to the Fathers as an authority. Nobody aware of his other works could be in any doubt that for Thomas the authority of the church was coinherent with the authority of Scripture and that Scripture lived within the discourse of the interpreting church.[52]

Thomas' reference to Augustine in *Lectura* V.I.3 affords an opportunity to examine how Thomas deploys the Patristic inheritance. Thomas is vexed by the apparent contradiction between 1 Thess. 5:3 and Lk. 21:26. The problem is that one text says that the persecutors of the church will think they have 'peace and security' (1 Thess. 5:3), whilst another says that in the end times people will faint 'with fear and foreboding' (Lk. 21:26). To resolve this problem Thomas appears to draw upon the

---

[49] As B. S. Smalley, *The Study of the Bible in the Middle Ages* (Oxford: Blackwell, 1952), p. 334, notes, medieval exegetes understood Scripture and the *Gloss* to be virtually coinherent.

[50] Thomas refers to Gregory the Great in the *Prologus* to Lombard's Gloss, *Collectanea in Epistolis S. Pauli* (Folio CXCIV), in *Lectio* III.I.62; to Augustine in III.I.64; IV.II.98; V.I.3; to unattributed tradition in IV.II.102; to Jerome in IV.I.85; IV.II.101; to a Gloss which I have not yet been able to identify in V.II.130; and to *The Lives of the Fathers* in V.II.130. There is an indirect (and uncited) reference to John Damascene's Christology in *Lectio* IV.II.95, discussed below in section 2.

[51] *ST* 2a2ae q. 1 a. 7 ad 4. See also *ST* 2a2ae q. 174 a. 6 re.

[52] *ST* 2a2ae q. 5 a. 3 ad 2.

thirty-sixth chapter of Augustine's letter to Heschyius.[53] Equally vexed by this seeming inconsistency in Scripture's witness, Augustine proposes that the 'peace and security' of 1 Thess. 5:3 refer to the evil people, whilst the 'fainting' and 'foreboding' of Luke refer to the plight of the good people (at the hands of the evil in the end times).[54] In this citation Augustine thus serves to maintain Scripture's unified witness to God's saving will.[55]

In his attention to the voice of Paul the apostle, the Fathers are guardians of Paul's revelation and are enlisted when they serve to free his voice from confusion or contradiction. Consequently Thomas turns to the Patristic inheritance to clarify what might seem obscure in 1 Thessalonians or even contradictory in relation to the rest of the canon. There is no questioning of Scripture's pre-eminence, for it is the 'superior science',[56] and faith rests on the revelation made to the apostles and prophets, not on any doubtful revelation to 'any other teacher'.[57] The combination of the revelation directly mediated to the apostles and the words of Sacred Scripture makes our faith certain.[58] Nevertheless, the authoritative words of Augustine can be enlisted, insofar as he himself turns us to hear with clarity the *teaching and insight* of those who were closest to the brilliance of Christ:

> Apostles are put first because they had a privileged share in all of Christ's gifts. They possessed a plenitude of grace and wisdom regarding the revelation of divine mysteries . . . They also possessed an ample ability to speak convincingly in order to proclaim the gospel . . . Moreover, they also had an exceptional authority and power for looking after the Lord's flock.[59]

1.2   Thomas, Aristotle and the text of 1 Thessalonians

Steeped in Aristotle's thought, Thomas consistently emphasised acquisition of knowledge through sensible forms.[60] This assertion of knowledge

---

[53] Augustine, Letter 199, in *Saint Augustine. Letters: Volume IV (165–203)*, tr. W. Parsons (FOC 30; Washington: Catholic University of America Press, 1977), pp. 356–401.

[54] Thomas touches upon this possible contradiction again in *ST* (*Supplementum*) 3a q. 73 a. 1 ad 1.

[55] W. H. Principe, 'Thomas Aquinas' Principles for Interpretation of Patristic Texts', *Studies in Medieval Culture* 8 (1978), 115.

[56] *ST* 1a q. 1 a. 8 re.   [57] *ST* 1a q. 1 a. 8 ad 2.

[58] *ST* 1a q. 117 a. 2 ad 2; 1a2ae q. 103 a. 4 ad 2; 2a2ae q. 110 a. 3 ad 1; 2a2ae q. 174 a. 6 re.

[59] *Lectio Ephesios* IV.IV.211; *Commentary on Saint Paul's Epistle to the Ephesians*, p. 163. See also *ST* 1a2ae q. 106 a. 4 ad 2; 2a2ae q. 1 a. 7 ad 1 and ad 4; *Lectio Ioannis* I.VIII.183; II.II.383; IV.IV.651.

[60] *ST* 1a q. 1 a. 9 re; 1a q. 84 a. 3 re; 2a2ae q. 175 a. 5 re; 2a2ae q. 178 a. 1 re; 3a q. 30 a. 3 ad 2.

through sensible matter is marked by, at one level, a repudiation of Plato's notion of 'Ideal Forms', and at another level a reassertion of the composite role of the soul *and* the body in understanding. One does not have to look hard to see this polemic jutting through the surface of Thomas' 1 Thessalonians commentary.[61]

The exegetical implications of Thomas' enthusiasm for Aristotle are well documented, particularly in the studies of Thomas Torrance and Beryl Smalley. For Thomas, just as any spiritual meanings in the Biblical text are to be firmly supported by the literal sense of the text,[62] so too do we only know spiritual realities through sensible matter. Philosophically, Thomas pays close attention to the external, assuming that our knowledge must conform to *things themselves*. Thomas' concentration on the external corresponds to a close attentiveness to the text itself, and its plain, literal sense. It is then quite logical that for Thomas the literal sense of the text acquired a new foundational significance, as that upon which any further meanings should be grounded.[63]

Two aspects of Thomas' exegesis of 1 Thessalonians speak loudly of Aristotle's influence. The first aspect of Thomas' hermeneutics which affords an examination of Aristotle's influence is his relentless division and subdivision of the text. The second aspect – the deployment of Aristotelian causality – is directly related to Thomas' theological exegesis of 1 Thess. 4:13–18, and will be left to closer examination in section 2.

Beginning with Thomas' division of the text is apt, for his lectures would themselves have begun with a reading aloud of the text, partly a matter of pragmatics given the expense and shortage of printed bibles. Following this the text would have been broken up into appropriate rhetorical structures. Thomas divides and subdivides the text of 1 Thessalonians throughout his *Lectura*. At this stage let us therefore focus on how he divides up, and so understands, the order of 1 Thess. 4:13–18, an analysis that we shall utilise in section 2. Table 1, under the rubric of Thomas' own stated theme for the verses, sets out how he divides Paul's text (with the canonical references Thomas appeals to underneath). Uncovering the shape of the text in this manner should not be read as Thomas' attempt to recover the mind 'behind' the text. Rather, it is expressive of a deep fidelity to the text and its movements, confident that an Aristotelian understanding of its shape and contours is an understanding of the *sacra doctrina* revealed by the text. Thomas *is* fascinated for the 'reasons' the apostle

---

[61] *Lectio* I.I.21; IV.II.93; V.II.137. Cf. *ST* 1a q. 1 a. 6 ad 2. [62] *ST* 1a q. 1 a. 10 ad 1.
[63] *ST* 1a q. 1 a. 10 ad 2; 3a q. 5 a. 3 re. See R. G. Kennedy, 'Thomas Aquinas and the Literal Sense of Sacred Scripture', unpublished Ph.D. thesis, University of Notre Dame (1985).

Table 1. *Thomas' structuring of 1 Thess. 4:13–18*

Paul's argument: 'he urges them to lessen their inordinate sorrow'

---

1 4:13: 'he provides a warning'
   Sir. 41:1; 1 Sam. 15:32; Rom. 6:23; Eccles. 7:2; Sir. 22:11; Phil. 3:20;
   Jn. 11:11; Psalm 40:9; S. of S. 5:2; 1 Cor. 15:52
2 4:14f.: 'he provides a reason for the warning'
   (2.1) 4:14: 'he establishes the resurrection'
          1 Cor. 15:12; Zech. 14:5; Isa. 3:14
   (2.2) 4:15: 'he rules out the faint suspicion of a delay'
          2 Thess. 2:2; 1 Cor. 15:52
   (2.3) 4:16: 'he outlines the order of resurrection'
          (2.3.1) 4:16a: 'he discusses the cause(s) of the resurrection'
                   (1) '*the trumpet of God*' = 'the divine power'
                        Wisdom 5:20
                   (2) '*the Lord himself*' = 'the power of the humanity of Christ'
                        Acts 1:11; Phil. 2:8; Lk. 21:27; Jn. 5:28
                   (3) '*with the archangel's call*' = 'a ministering cause'
                        Rev. 12; Isa. 9:6
          (2.3.2) 4:16b–17: 'he presents its order and manner'
                   (1) 4:16b: 'he treats the resurrection of the dead'
                   (2) 4:17a: 'he considers the meeting of the living with Christ'
                        1 Cor. 15:51; 1 Cor. 15:22; Rom. 5:12; 1 Cor. 15:52;
                        Mt. 24:28; Phil. 3; Acts 1:9; 1:11; 1 Kgs. 8:12; Mt. 25:6
                   (3) 4:17b: 'he refers to the happiness of the saints with Christ'
                        Jn. 14:3; Phil. 1:23
          (2.3.3) 4:18: 'he ends with a consideration of their mutual consolation'
                   Isa. 40:1

---

says what he says,[64] but these 'reasons' are found by sticking closely
to the argument of the text itself.[65] It is of note, as close reading of the
Lectura reveals, that the text divisions are formed quite independently
from the canonical conversation that follows the divisions. Thomas'
chief conviction, of which the divisions speak, is that the text is to be
revered as a carefully crafted web with the God of order as its primary
author.[66]

Thomas' incessant desire to break up 1 Thessalonians in the task
of understanding its meaning in relation to the whole of the letter and
the whole of Scripture can be more exactly traced to his Aristotelian

---

[64] *Lectio* IV.I.91; Duffy, *Commentary*, p. 33.
[65] E.g. *Lectio* III.I.72; Duffy, *Commentary*, p. 27.
[66] Pesch, 'Paul as Professor', 589–90, 597–8.

background in two ways.[67] The first is relatively undisputed, but the second, while linked to the first, is more complex.

First, Thomas aims to *understand* the text as Aristotle said an artisan should understand his creation. Working from the text of Scripture as his 'first principle', Thomas hopes to understand the contours of the text by a process of composing and dividing, an intellectual mode of understanding promoted by Aristotle.[68]

Secondly, the rigour with which Thomas endeavours to understand the text is testimony to the seriousness with which he wants to *understand through the sensible form of the text*. This Aristotelian insight that we know universal ideas through the objects of the sensible world represented a departure from those who saw endless allegories spinning off from the language of the text, these allegories themselves akin to the Platonic world of order above the form of this world.[69] Thomas Torrance, who is otherwise critical of Thomas' hermeneutics, pronounces approvingly upon this restrained aspect of Thomas' exegesis.[70]

Reading Aristotle encouraged Thomas to see how letter and spirit, language and thought, history and spiritual meaning could be fruitfully read together. For Thomas, via Aristotle, the intellect, in its unavoidable involvement with the soul–body composite, understood the 'quiddity' of things in their material existence. Hence the importance of words, and extracting the meaning of words by a forensic (*not* genetic) examination of their co-text. Thomas' reading of (and commentary on) Aristotle's *On Interpretation* had convinced him that words were the outward expression of interior thoughts.[71] In contrast to Platonic understandings of the text, the text was no mere copy, for there is a truth in the 'whatness' or 'materiality' of the text itself:

> with us men, a perfect judgement of the mind obtains through turning to sense-objects which are the first principles of our knowledge.[72]

---

[67] H. Meyer, *The Philosophy of St Thomas Aquinas*, tr. F. Eckhoff (St Louis: Herder, 1946), p. 22, also points to the influence of Boethius (c. 480–525) in Thomas' zeal for the division of the text.

[68] E.g. Aristotle, *On the Soul*, tr. W. S. Hett (London: Heinemann, 1935), III.vi.430a26ff.

[69] Cf. *ST* 1a q. 84 a. 5 re. See T. F. Torrance, *Divine Meaning: Studies in Patristic Hermeneutics* (Edinburgh: T. & T. Clark, 1995), p. 19.

[70] T. F. Torrance, 'Scientific Hermeneutics according to St Thomas Aquinas', *JTS* N.S. 13 (1962), 262.

[71] E.g. *ST* 1a q. 34 a. 1 re.

[72] *ST* 2a2ae q. 173 a. 3 re. So Smalley, *The Study of the Bible*, p. 292, notes the correspondence between the Aristotelian perspective on the relationship between the body and the soul and that between the letter and the spirit of the Biblical text. Just as the body cannot

Since it is from knowledge of material things that human beings acquire an intellectual knowledge of everything else,[73] we should expect nothing from Thomas *other than* a close attention to the understanding of the words in the text. The division of the text may, at first blush, seem alienating and scholastic, but it is rooted in a conviction that exegesis must be disciplined by painstakingly following each word of the text so that everything which follows can be seen to rest upon the letter of the text and the structure in which the text is located.

It is important, however, to end with a corrective. Thomas' attention to the text ultimately derives from the conviction that the Scriptural text itself is the very 'foundation of faith'.[74] The text is the access point to the revelation distilled into the prophet's or apostle's intellect and hence calls for serious reading.[75] What the Holy Ghost has revealed is the absolute norm for what we can and cannot say about God.[76] For Thomas, Scripture's prophetic-apostolic momentum is essential for humanity's salvation:

> The ministers of God are those who preach, namely, Christ, the prophets and apostles. Preaching is performed by Christ as the one from whom the doctrine originates, by the prophets who prefigured this doctrine, and by the apostles who carry out the injunction to preach.[77]

2   Thomas' theological exegesis of 1 Thess. 4:13–18

Equipped with some awareness of *how* Thomas reads Scripture, we are now ready to undertake a study of his reading of 1 Thess. 4:13–18. Throughout this study we shall refer to the divisions of the text set out in table 1. As we shall soon see, this is a section that discloses Thomas' exegetical triad in operation: the canon, the Fathers and Aristotle.

For Thomas, Paul's central message is an admonition: the Thessalonians should 'lessen their inordinate sorrow'.[78] Thomas is aware of the benign dispositions of those who grieve, for the grieving person is mourning the 'dissolution of the frail body', a body which should be taken care of 'for the sake of the soul'.[79]

---

be understood in distinction from the soul (and vice versa), so too the Bible's spiritual sense cannot be studied in distinction from its literal sense. In this vein Aristotelians could be expected to understand the 'spirit' of Scripture as something vitally linked to the text itself.

[73] *ST* 1a q. 87 a. 3 ad 1.   [74] *ST* 3a q. 55 a. 5 re.
[75] *ST* 2a2ae q. 171 a. 6 re.   [76] *ST* 1a q. 36 a. 2 ad 1; 2a2ae q. 11 a. 2 ad 2.
[77] *Lectio* II.II.44; Duffy, *Commentary*, p. 19.
[78] *Lectio* IV.II.92; Duffy, *Commentary*, p. 34.
[79] *Lectio* IV.II.93; Duffy, *Commentary*, p. 34.

Thomas' understanding of death was distinct from the Platonic ideal of the eternal soul's separation from the mortal body. Thomas hovered neatly between the Platonists, who held that the human person is the soul imprisoned within a perishable body, and contemporary 'physicalists', who saw the human person as body alone. He consistently stressed the importance of the psychosomatic unity.[80] The most perfect form of the human person is the soul–body unity. Death, far from freeing the soul and allowing it to enter into the eternal realm of truth as in Plato's account of the death of Socrates in *Phaedo*, is a sign that things are not how they should be. Death is a 'metaphysical horror',[81] signifying the 'frail' nature of our bodies:[82]

> life and health of body depend on its being possessed by soul . . . And so, to the contrary, death, disease and all bodily defects imply the lack of control of body by soul.[83]

The divorce between body and soul at death is unnatural, for our 'form' is provided by the soul,[84] the immortal soul animating the body.[85] Death's rude interruption is a rupture of what is a God-endowed unity, a horror well elucidated by Thomas' citation from Sir. 41:1, 'how bitter is the reminder of you to one who lives at peace among his possessions'.[86]

Despite the importance of the soul to Thomas' anthropology, as we have seen Thomas emphasised the acquisition of knowledge through sensible forms,[87] a role performed through the soul's union with the body. Thus there is a 'natural' relationship in the soul's union with the body, for it is through the body–soul composite that we are rational beings who understand through sensible forms. Death, marking the divorce of the body from the soul, is a perilously unnatural state of being, a state only God's resurrection of our bodies can rectify.

But there is more to say on death. Death is a constant reminder of what Rom. 6:23 teaches, 'the wages of sin is death', a wage which robbed man of what was originally his by virtue of justice – his natural desire for immortality. Since the Fall of man, we can be assured of one thing, that, in the words of Eccles. 7:2, death is 'the end of all men'.[88] This post-Fall implication is also obliquely suggested later in the lecture, when Thomas

---

[80] M. Potts, 'Aquinas, Hell and the Resurrection of the Damned', *Faith and Philosophy* 15 (1998), 341–51.

[81] M. F. Rousseau, 'Elements of a Thomistic Philosophy of Death', *The Thomist* 43 (1979), 600.

[82] *Lectio* IV.II.93; Duffy, *Commentary*, p. 34.   [83] *ST* 2a2ae q. 164 a. 1 re.

[84] *ST* 2a2ae q. 175 a. 5 re; 3a q. 8 a. 1 re; 3a q. 54 a. 1 re.

[85] *Lectio* V.II.137.   [86] *Lectio* IV.II.93.

[87] *ST* 1a q. 84 a. 3 re; 1a q. 84 a. 6; 3a q. 8 a. 2 re; 3a q. 30 a. 3 ad 2.

[88] *Lectio* IV.II.93.

refers to angels collecting the dust (*pulveres*) of the dead,[89] quite likely a reference to the punishment of Gen. 3:19.

Thus, to follow the divisions of the text set out above (table 1), in section 1 death is the rupture of the natural soul–body composite; it marks a painful separation from loved ones; it is a reminder both of original sin and of our own inevitable death, and for these reasons some sorrow is permitted.[90] But Paul's warning is that, aware that the dead are merely in a state of 'rest' (Sir. 22:11), we must not grieve like those who believe that the wounds of death are eternal in effect. We need to be reminded that those in Christ are not dead but asleep, that our ultimate destiny is not death but heaven (Phil. 3:20). Like the twelve in John's story of Lazarus, we need to hear that the dead are merely asleep (Jn. 11:11), and at the call of Jesus will come to new life.

As people of faith who do not die, but fall asleep in Christ, we believe that we shall 'rise again' from where we lie (Psalm 40:9). But more, just as when we sleep our soul remains awake, so when we die our soul will remain 'vigilant' ('vigilat').[91] Interestingly, drawing on S. of S. 5:2, Thomas likens our soul to the heart – that which gives the body its life and energy.[92] Therefore, although the physical body is corruptible, the soul is incorruptible,[93] extending beyond death. Whilst the body sleeps at death, the soul remains alert and awake. Finally, the restoration we feel after a good night's sleep is a foretaste of things to come, the time when our bodies will be 'raised imperishable' (1 Cor. 15:52), and in so becoming incorruptible will enjoy an eternal, deathless union with the soul.[94]

In section 2 of the text's division we turn in 4:14f. to the reason for the warning that we must not grieve 'as others'. There are three stages to Paul's warning: first, 'he establishes the resurrection' (2.1); secondly, 'he rules out the faint suspicion of a delay' (2.2), and thirdly, 'he outlines the order of resurrection' (2.3).

Thomas understands Paul's words in 4:14 by turning first to 1 Cor. 15:12, 'if Christ is proclaimed as raised from the dead, how can some of you say there is no resurrection of the dead?'. It is this very same verse which Thomas cites in the first question of the *Summa Theologiae*, where he discusses theology's status as a *scientia*. For Thomas *sacra doctrina* advances from what it takes on in faith to demonstrate what is caused by this first principle. Taking the resurrection of Christ as a first principle, a principle known only by faith, Thomas seeks to articulate (via Aristotle's

---

[89] *Lectio* IV.II.98.   [90] *Lectio* IV.II.93.   [91] *Ibid.*; Duffy, *Commentary*, p. 35.
[92] *Lectio* V.I.120; Duffy, *Commentary*, p. 46, the heart 'is the source of life'.
[93] *ST* Ia q. 75 a. 6 re.   [94] *Lectio* IV.II.93.

insight that 'whatever is first in a given genus is the cause of all that comes after it'[95]) how our resurrection is captured within a continuum of cause and effect.[96] At this early stage we are therefore introduced to how reference to Aristotelian 'causal analysis'[97] aids Thomas in understanding Paul's dramatic claim of 1 Thess. 4:14: that the resurrection of *Jesus* is the assurance of *our* resurrection.

Expanding his exegesis, Thomas claims that Christ is more than just the 'cause' of our resurrection: he is also its 'exemplar' ('sed etiam exemplar').[98] In assuming flesh and rising in bodily form,[99] Christ is thus an exemplar for our resurrection. Christ embodies, models and prefigures what our resurrection promises to be if, through the sacraments, our lives participate in and replicate his life.[100] The issue here is one essentially of conformity to the reparation of our sinful human nature brought about by Christ, an expectation Thomas raises earlier in his commentary:

> We, however, are waiting for two things: first, for the resurrection, in order that we may clearly conform to Christ.[101]

At the centre of this exemplary causality, and our complete conformity to Christ, lies the hypostatic union between humanity and divinity represented by the incarnation of Christ, the event at which 'Christ assumed (accepit) flesh'.[102] But, more intricately, for Thomas the Word in human form and risen in human form communicates what is 'truly' ('vero') and 'simply' ('simpliciter') the function of the Word, 'to revive our souls'.[103]

---

[95] Aristotle, *Metaphysics* II.I.993b24. Cited in *ST* 3a q. 56 a. 1 re.

[96] *ST* Ia q. 1 a. 8 re.

[97] *Lectio* IV.II.95; Duffy, *Commentary*, p. 35. This is not the only place where Thomas says that Paul is arguing by the means of Aristotelian 'causal analysis'. See also his comments on 1 Thess. 2:5 in *Lectio* II.I.32 and on 1 Thess. 2:20 in *Lectio* II.II.53, where a correspondence is assumed between the goodness of the effect and the goodness of the cause.

[98] *Lectio* IV.II.95. Thomas is more suggestive as to the content of this conformity in *ST* 3a q. 56 a. 1 ad 1, where our moral conformity to Jesus' exemplary suffering and death sets us on a path to conformity with his resurrection.

[99] *Lectio* IV.II.95, 'Etenim eo quod Christus accepit carnem, et in ea resurrexit, est exemplar nostrae resurrectionis.'

[100] Or, as Duffy, *Commentary*, p. 35, translates it, Christ is the 'pattern' of our resurrection. See also *ST* 3a q. 56 a. 1 ad 3; *Comp. Theol.* §231. As N. Crotty, 'The Redemptive Role of Christ's Resurrection', *The Thomist* 25 (1962), 61, notes, Thomas' thinking on the exemplary causality of the resurrection undergoes some development. It is in the third part of the *Summa Theologiae* that Thomas articulates the principle that that which is perfected in the exemplar is imitated by the less than perfect.

[101] *Lectio* I.I.22; Duffy, *Commentary*, p. 11. Also *Lectio* IV.II.103.

[102] *Lectio* IV.II.95; Duffy, *Commentary*, p. 35. Cf. *ST* 3a q. 2 a. 2 ad 1, a. 3 ad 2; 3a q. 33 a. 3 re.

[103] *Lectio* IV.II.95; Duffy, *Commentary*, p. 35.

Thomas here alludes to the two-fold resurrection, spelt out with most clarity in his *Compendium of Theology*.[104] It is the job of the Word of God alone to give new life to the souls and restore them to life with God, and it is the job of the Word 'made flesh' to revive our bodies,[105] and so in the fullness of time to reunite our risen bodies with our revived souls. Christ, in reviving both our souls and bodies, has thus destroyed the two-fold death that is our soul's separation from God and the body's separation from the soul.

Lest this understanding of Christ as 'exemplar cause' obscure the real mover behind the resurrection Thomas hastily adds that Christ's resurrection is also the 'efficient cause' ('causa efficiens') of our own resurrection.[106] Christ's resurrection as 'efficient cause' thus points back to the first cause that is, for Thomas, always God, who is the ultimate cause of the resurrection. Thus Christ is the efficient cause of our resurrection, 'by the power of the divinity united in him' ('virtute divinitatis sibi unitae').[107]

The reason why *our* resurrection is guaranteed is that Christ's humanity was united to God. Christ's body which rose from the dead was no mere body, but 'a body united to the Word of life' ('corporis uniti verbo vitae').[108] Jesus' body operates as 'an instrument of divinity' ('instrumentum divinitatis').[109] This notion of Christ's instrumental humanity is found throughout Thomas' writing, and represents an idea which he openly adopted from John Damascene's *Exposition of the Orthodox Faith*.[110]

For Thomas, an instrument always enjoys a two-fold distinction: it is always moved by a superior cause, and it always acts in accordance with its own form.[111] Carefully distinguishing the various guises an instrument can take,[112] Thomas shows that Christ's humanity is not a passive player

---

[104] Whatever exact period this opuscule is dated to, it is undoubtedly a work written towards the end of Thomas' writing career. See M. D. Chenu, *Toward Understanding St Thomas*, tr. A.-M. Landry and D. Hughes (Chicago: Henry Regnery Press, 1964), p. 332.

[105] *Lectio* IV.II.95; Duffy, *Commentary*, p. 35. Cf. *Comp. Theol.* §231.

[106] *Lectio* IV.II.95; my translation. Cf. *ST* 3a q. 56 a. 1 ad 3. Thomas never saw the exemplary and efficient causalities of the resurrection as mutually exclusive: *Comp. Theol.* §239.

[107] *Lectio* IV.II.95; my translation. For the sovereignty of God in his role of 'first cause' (*causa prima*) see *ST* 1a q. 65 a. 3; 3a q. 56 a. 1 ad 2 and 4. For the notion of Christ's union with divinity see *ST* 3a q. 56 a. 2 ad 2, 'The efficacy of Christ's resurrection extends to the soul not through any power inherent in the body of the risen Christ but only through the divine power which he has from personal union with the divinity.'

[108] *Lectio* IV.II.95; my translation.   [109] *Ibid.*; my translation.

[110] John Damascene, 'Exposition of the Orthodox Faith', III.xv, in *NPNF*² tr. S. D. F. Salmond (Edinburgh: T. & T. Clark, 1898).

[111] *ST* 3a q. 19 a. 1 ad 2; q. 62 a. 1 ad 2.   [112] *ST* 3a q. 18 a. 1 ad 2.

in the act of resurrection.[113] At every stage, Christ's humanity contributes what is proper for it to contribute in this work of salvation. However, in his resurrection's capacity to raise the dead, Christ's humanity witnesses to a higher principle working through it effectually,[114] empowering it to produce an effect quite beyond its own nature.[115] The relationship between the 'verbo vitae' and Christ's humanity is not competitive,[116] for in communion they are working towards the same cause, the resurrection of the dead:

> the whole effect proceeds from each, yet in different ways, just as the whole of the one same effect is ascribed to the instrument, and again the whole is ascribed to the principal agent.[117]

In a fascinating parallel Thomas connects our future bodily resurrection with Jesus' miraculous healing of the leper, his favoured illustration of Christ's instrumental humanity. Just as through Jesus' touch of the leper the principal agency of God's power was at work, so too through Christ's resurrection is our resurrection being worked out. The parallel here is one of causality. Jesus' human touch had the effect of healing because of the divine power working through and with his ability to touch. So too Christ's resurrection has the effect of raising our bodies because through the resurrection 'the activity of the divine power is working'.[118] Just as through the human touch of Jesus, God's efficacious power was working to achieve an effect beyond the capacity of the instrument alone,[119] so too through the resurrection of Jesus' body is there working the 'verbum vitae' to which his risen body is united.[120] If we follow this intriguing parallel, it is not going too far to suggest that, just as Jesus' touch cured the leper by virtue of the divinity working through his capacity to touch, so too God's working through Christ's resurrection combines to effect something which neither God's power nor Christ's resurrection could achieve alone, namely 'our resurrection'.[121]

In positing Christ's humanity as an 'instrument of his divinity', Thomas is thus pointing to the transformation of Christ's humanity in being able to rise again, for 'the very definition of an instrument is that it effects change by being changed itself'.[122] Christ's humanity thus now promises

---

[113] *ST* 3a q. 7 a. 1 ad 3.   [114] *ST* 3a q. 13 a. 1 ad 2.
[115] *ST* 3a q. 62 a. 1 ad 2.   [116] *Lectio* IV.II.95.
[117] *SCG* III.lxx. See also *ST* 1a2ae q. 14 a. 3 ad 4.
[118] *Lectio* IV.II.98; Duffy, *Commentary*, p. 37.
[119] *ST* 3a q. 19 a. 1 ad 5. See J. S. Albertson, 'Instrumental Causality in St Thomas', *New Scholasticism* 28 (1954), 414.
[120] *Lectio* IV.II.95.   [121] *Ibid.*; my translation.   [122] *ST* 1a q. 110 a. 2 arg 3.

change in us – our resurrection – because Christ's divinity and humanity (and all that was achieved within this economy), the principal and the instrumental, are working towards a single cause, which none of them could do without the other.[123]

It is this interpretation, Thomas implicitly declares, which gets at what Paul was supposing when he wrote 1 Thess. 4:14 (Et ideo Apostolus, hoc firmiter supponens).[124]

Thomas' exegesis of 4:14 corroborates recent opinion that Aquinas fruitfully works with a triumvirate of *sacra doctrina seu sacra scriptura*, God revealed in Christ, and Aristotelian insights. For just as Aristotle had established that the first in any genus was the cause of all that followed it, so too is Christ's resurrection 'the cause of our resurrection'.[125] Through the instrumentality of Christ's humanity God occupies the role of 'first cause'.[126] That we know this is accessible only through the *sacra doctrina* that is 1 Thess. 4:14. Thomas' exegesis thus climaxes at the very point where Aristotelian insights, a Christocentric vision and a commitment to *sacra scriptura* intersect and cross-fertilise.

It would be wrong therefore to read Thomas as an exegete stupefied by Aristotle and blind to the ways of eisegesis. Thomas' exegesis is firmly Christocentric, though situated in an Aristotelian framework. In the narrative of the general resurrection, generated and propelled by the 'divine power' ('virtus divinitatis'),[127] Christ is the cause of our resurrection in his own incarnate right.[128] The very resurrection of our bodies is attributed to the power of the incarnate One, 'the Word made flesh' itself.[129] It is through this instrumental power that on the day of judgement (hence his citation of Isa. 3:14 and his persistent talk of the universal resurrection[130]) our bodies will be 'renewed' ('reintegratio'),[131] and our souls and bodies triumphantly reunited as one.

Having established the resurrection, with help from Aristotle, in 4:15 Paul turns to rule out any delay 'in regard to the resurrection' (2.2).[132] His concern is not to say something specific about the timing of Christ's coming – it was this misapprehension that led to 2 Thessalonians. Rather, he speaks with the Lord's words, words which 'do not fail', and he is speaking not to his contemporaries, but to all those who survive the persecution of the Antichrist. Such people can be reassured that the living will not receive their 'consolation' before the dead. Instead, to turn to 1 Cor. 15:52,

---

[123] *ST* 3a q. 19 a. 1 ad 5.   [124] *Lectio* IV.II.95.
[125] *Ibid.*; Duffy, *Commentary*, p. 35.   [126] *ST* 1a q. 84 a. 4 ad 1.
[127] *Lectio* IV.II.98; my translation.   [128] *Lectio* IV.II.98.
[129] *Lectio* IV.II.95; Duffy, *Commentary*, p. 35.   [130] *Lectio* IV.II.98 etc.
[131] *Lectio* IV.II.98; my translation.   [132] *Lectio* IV.II.96; Duffy, *Commentary*, p. 36.

both those who are asleep and those who are alive will receive the glory of the resurrection, 'in a moment, in a twinkling of an eye'.[133]

In the third and most complex stage of Paul's reason for the warning of 4:13, Paul outlines 'the order and manner of the resurrection' (2.3). This itself breaks down into three further subdivisions: the cause of the resurrection (2.3.1); the resurrection's order and manner (2.3.2); and finally, a consideration of their 'mutual consolation' (2.3.3).[134] It is in 1 Thess. 4:16a that these three causes of the resurrection are outlined.

The primary actor in the universal resurrection will be God himself, acting through his 'divine power' ('virtute divina').[135] Paul's reference to the 'trumpet of God' points to the principal mover behind the resurrection: the power of God, who 'arouses the dead'.[136] The resonance of this trumpet is appropriate to the God who calls his people together for war (Wisd. 5:20). Thomas suggests that the 'trumpet' can be understood as a metaphorical reference to 'the divine power of Christ (virtus divina Christi) present and manifest to the whole world'.[137] (Note here how God's power and Christ's power, as distinct from Christ's instrumental humanity, are interchangeable.)

Focusing on the primary cause of our resurrection as God's divine power, we are close to Thomas' thoughts as he outlined them in his *Summa Contra Gentiles*:

> Resurrection is natural if one considers its purpose, for it is natural that the soul be united to the body. But the principle of resurrection is not natural. It is caused by the divine power alone.[138]

Supplementing this divine power is the instrumental 'power of the humanity of Christ'.[139] As we have seen, *only* through this instrumental capacity is the resurrection made possible. In speaking of 'the Lord himself' descending, Paul is referring to the 'glorious humanity of Christ' as the cause of our resurrection.[140] He will 'come in the same way as you saw him go into heaven' (Acts 1:11), the way not of humility and obedience as in his first coming, but the way of risen, triumphant glory (Lk. 21:27). Indeed, it is with his return that the dead will not just be risen,

[133] *Lectio* IV.II.96; Duffy, *Commentary*, p. 36.
[134] *Lectio* IV.II.97; Duffy, *Commentary*, p. 37.
[135] *Lectio* IV.II.98; Duffy, *Commentary*, p. 37.
[136] *Lectio* IV.II.99; my translation.
[137] *Lectio* IV.II.99; Duffy, *Commentary*, p. 38.　　[138] *SCG* IV.lxxxi.
[139] *Lectio* IV.II.98; Duffy, *Commentary*, p. 37.
[140] *Lectio* IV.II.99; Duffy, *Commentary*, p. 37.

but reunited with their souls, which have remained vigilant throughout the body's slumber.[141] It is through Christ that the body will be
reunited to its 'form',[142] and so this coming will quite aptly be one of
glory.

In referring to the time when all 'who are in their graves will hear his
voice' (Jn. 5:28), Thomas points to that time when at Christ's call all
shall obey his voice. In Christ's presence, '*all* the dead' ('omnes mortui')
shall be raised.[143] This is a universal resurrection of the blessed and
damned (*communis resurrectio*),[144] of which Christ's resurrection is the
efficient cause. This resurrection of all, as a result of the power of Christ's
resurrection, stands distinct from the exemplary outworking of the resurrection which speaks more specifically of those 'who were conformed to
his death through baptism'.[145] Although all will rise, Christ's resurrection
is only of exemplary effect for those who have sought to be conformed
to his will, for there is in Thomas' perspective 'a difference between the
good and the evil'.[146]

Descending the hierarchy, Thomas refers somewhat ambivalently to
the third cause of the general resurrection, the archangel's ministry. With
God as 'principal cause' and Christ's humanity as 'instrumental cause',
Thomas coins the term 'ministering cause' to refer to the work of the
angels.[147] Their work will include such tasks as the collection of dust,
perhaps an implicit indicator of the role played by angels in the reversal
of the curse of Gen. 3:19.[148] Thomas is keen to limit the role played
by the archangel in the general resurrection. It cannot be the call that
raises the dead, for Jn. 5:28 would seem to indicate that this is a role
reserved for Christ. In an attempt to maximise the role played by Christ
in the resurrection, the effect is to consign the archangel's role to a rather
general-sounding 'ministry'.[149]

Having discussed the cause of the resurrection (2.3.1), Thomas then
turns to 4:16b–17, where Paul presents the resurrection's 'order and

---

[141] *Lectio* IV.II.98.   [142] *ST* 3a q. 25 a. 6 ad 3.

[143] *Lectio* IV.II.98; Duffy, *Commentary*, p. 37 (my italics).

[144] *Lectio* IV.II.98; Duffy, *Commentary*, p. 37.

[145] *Lectio* IV.II.95; Duffy, *Commentary*, p. 36. So too *ST* 3a q. 39 a. 5 ad 2, q. 63 a. 1
ad 3.

[146] *Lectio* IV.II.103; Duffy, *Commentary*, p. 40.

[147] *Lectio* IV.II.98; Duffy, *Commentary*, p. 37.

[148] Or, following C. Leget, *Living with God: Thomas Aquinas on the Relation between
Life on Earth and 'Life' after Death* (Leuven: Peeters, 1997), p. 78, Aquinas views the soul
as much stronger than the body. Held together by the soul, at death the body dissolves at
the soul's departure. Cf. *Lectio* IV.II.93; *ST* 3a q. 53 a. 1 ad 1.

[149] *Lectio* IV.II.99; Duffy, *Commentary*, p. 37. See *ST* 1a q. 112 a. 1 re; 2a2ae q. 172
a. 2 ad 3.

manner' (2.3.2).[150] Thomas subdivides these verses yet further into
three points. First, in 4:16b, 'he treats the resurrection of the dead';
secondly, in 4:17a, 'he considers the meeting of the living with
Christ'; thirdly, in 4:17b, 'he refers to the happiness of the saints with
Christ'.[151]

Thomas skips over his first point, not least because of the detail he has
just gone into above, and rushes to the exegetical problem presented by
4:17a, a problem which Aquinas treats as a mini-disputation.

Thomas refers to Jerome's letter 119, written to two monks (Minervius
and Alexander) from Toulouse. In this letter Jerome reports that some in
his time believed that they would never die, before going on himself to read
1 Thess. 4:17 metaphorically, to mean that believers will be 'assumed'
into the company of apostles and prophets. For Thomas, of course, such
a thought would be inconceivable: as he quoted from Rom. 6:23 at the
beginning of his lecture,[152] death represents 'the wages of sin'. Paul's
possible implication in 4:16b–17 that those found alive at the time of
the judgement would escape death must be avoided at all costs. In a
question on original sin in the *Summa Theologiae*, Thomas reveals just
exactly what is at stake in implying that some will evade the punishment
of death:

> That all men descended from Adam, Christ alone excepted, con-
> tract original sin must be firmly held according to Catholic Faith.
> The denial of this truth implies the error that not all would be in
> need of redemption through Christ.[153]

Correspondingly, in this *sed contra* section of this disputation in his lecture, Thomas turns to a catena of citations from Paul in 1 Corinthians
and Romans, authoritatively confirming that Christ's return will mark
a reversal of the death universally experienced by all those 'in Adam'
(1 Cor. 15:22).

Thomas proposes to improve upon Paul's reticence. When Christ comes
for judgement, those who are found alive will in that moment die and
'immediately' ('statim') be resurrected. So minimal will this time be that
such people will be 'regarded as living' throughout the process.[154] It
is interesting to compare Thomas' confident terseness with the notable
circumspection of the *Prima Pars* of his *Summa Theologiae* on this very
same subject:

---

[150] *Lectio* IV.II.97; Duffy, *Commentary*, p. 37.
[151] *Lectio* IV.II.100; Duffy, *Commentary*, p. 38.   [152] *Lectio* IV.II.93.
[153] *ST* 1a2ae q. 81 a. 3 re.   [154] *Lectio* IV.II.101; Duffy, *Commentary*, p. 39.

The more probable and generally accepted opinion maintains that all those living at the time of the second coming will indeed die, then rise again after a little while: more will be said about this in the *Tertia Pars*. If, however, it be true, as others hold, that these [the living] will never die, we should reply thus: even if these survivors were not actually to die, the obligation to undergo death as a penalty would remain in them, though the penalty itself would be remitted by God who has the power to pardon the punishment for even actual sins.[155]

No sooner has Thomas apparently dealt with this little local conflict than he bumps into the next exegetical quandary. Reading 4:16b and 4:17a together would seem to imply that at the general resurrection the dead will rise ahead of the living, who themselves go through their momentary death when they meet Christ. What this endangers is the notion of a simultaneous (*simul*) general resurrection,[156] as Paul taught in 1 Cor. 15:52, and as was no less important for Thomas' worldview.

Thomas turns to two (unattributed) sources of tradition. The first response, as Thomas reports it, resembles Augustine's views in the twentieth chapter of *City of God*. Here Augustine, commenting on these same verses, implies that those found alive at Christ's return will experience a short 'sleep' and resurrection as they are being caught up in the clouds. Thus, for Augustine, it is as the dead are 'being borne aloft through the air' that those found alive will undergo a sudden death and resurrection.[157] This is close to the school of thought which, as Thomas recounts, reads the 'moment' of 1 Cor. 15:52 as a 'brief amount of time' ('modico tempore').[158] Such a position endangers the universal resurrection which Thomas is eager to retain.

The other interpretative position reads Paul's statement that the dead 'will rise first' as a pronouncement of dignity, not of temporal order. Thomas, however, is unhappy with this response: it is not necessarily clear that those who suffer under the Antichrist will be less dignified than those who have had the fortune to die before such throes.

Thomas resolves the question in a different way, and so interestingly stands against the interpretative traditions he has cited. *All* will die and

---

[155] *ST* 1a2ae q. 81 a. 3 ad 1 (written, as noted on p. 71 above, roughly concurrently with his Thessalonians *Lectura*).

[156] *Lectio* IV.II.102.

[157] Augustine, *The City of God against the Pagans*, tr. R. W. Dyson (Cambridge: Cambridge University Press, 1998), XX/20.

[158] *Lectio* IV.II.102; Duffy, *Commentary*, p. 39.

rise simultaneously (*simul*). Reverting to the authority of the 'apostle', Thomas clarifies that Paul is not saying that there will be a temporal order of resurrection, that the dead will rise first and *then* the living. Before the living meet Christ, 'first' ('prius') the dead must rise from their slumber.[159] The text does not therefore endanger the necessity of the universal resurrection – for at the coming of the Lord, those alive will experience death and then 'immediately' ('simul') experience resurrection along with those who have died before them.[160] All will rise at the same time. The text thus clarifies the order of rapture – that before the living are taken up to meet Christ, first they must die, so that together with the already dead they can rise simultaneously and be taken up in the clouds.

In the clouds the bodies of the saints will be conformed to the glory of Christ's body.[161] Only the good will be conformed to Christ's glory.[162] The Marietti critical edition of the lectures makes clear that Thomas asks why this conforming of the saints to Christ should happen in clouds.[163] The reason for this gathering together around the body (Mt. 24:28) in the space of the clouds is that here the saints are 'to take on the appearance of God' ('deiformitatem'),[164] for God's glory is broadcast through clouds (1 Kgs. 8:12). Thus, through the same 'divine power' which is the principal cause of the general resurrection, the glory of the saints will be manifest. To those who remain in the world below – the realm which 'they loved' ('dilexerunt') – such 'transfigured' ('fulgentia') bodies will appear as clouds above.[165]

In his final subdivision (2.3.2) Thomas indicates the future beatific state of the saints. 'Taking delight in' ('fruentes') his company, they shall be with the Lord for ever, in the realm where death reigns no more.[166] And so as saints they will have realised their holy desire, 'to depart and be with Christ' (Phil. 1:23).

In his final division (2.3.3), Thomas ends with the consideration that Paul wanted his words to be words of comfort to those who grieve. The Thessalonians, and presumably we ourselves, can be assured that the saints will rise 'without suffering any loss'.[167]

---

[159] *Lectio* IV.II.103.   [160] *Ibid.*
[161] cf. *ST* 2a2ae q. 175 a. 3 arg. 2; 3a q. 45 a. 4 ad 2.
[162] cf. *ST* (*Supplementum*) 3a q. 75 a. 2 ad 3.   [163] *Lectio* IV.II.103.
[164] *Ibid.*; my translation. Cf. *ST* 1a q. 12 a. 5–6. For direct references to 'deiformity' in the *Summa Theologiae* see A. N. Williams, *The Ground of Union: Deification in Aquinas and Palamas* (New York: Oxford University Press, 1999), pp. 35–9.
[165] *Lectio* IV.II.103; my translation.   [166] *Lectio* IV.II.104; my translation.
[167] *Lectio* IV.II.105; Duffy, *Commentary*, p. 40.

3   Conclusions

Thomas' exegesis witnesses to a theologian who reads with total earnest-ness Paul's miraculous claim, in 1 Thess. 4:14, that the resurrection of Jesus is the pledge of our future resurrection. The use of Aristotelian-inspired causality and of Christ's instrumental humanity serves to make Paul's extraordinary teaching clearer. Thomas' exegesis is born from a deep and prayerful meditation on God's truth, as revealed in the mys-terious words of 1 Thessalonians. Contrary to Protestant critics, like T. F. Torrance, Thomas' exegesis is 'schematised' not to 'the mind of the church' or to philosophical structures,[168] but to the revelation impressed upon Paul's intellect. Indeed, it is precisely this attention to the words of the apostle which Thomas deploys to counter exegetical tradition on 1 Thess. 4:16–17.[169] Thomas would not have understood the tension which Protestants hold between the Word of God and the church. For Thomas, every resource, ecclesiastical or philosophical, was to be taken captive unto Christ in the service of comprehending revelation.[170] In the exe-gesis we have examined Thomas strains hard to hear Paul *the apostle*'s insistence on the causality of the resurrection. We should expect nothing less. For Thomas the revelation which Paul was privileged to carry was essentially a cognitive, intellectual affair – a true perspective on the real-ity of things and events – and consequently Thomas' laboured attention to the causality of the resurrection is testament to the extent to which he is committed to the truth of the ideas which Paul articulates.[171]

This realism is perhaps the most striking aspect of Thomas' rich, multi-faceted, ceaselessly intra-textual exegesis. For Thomas, truth corresponds to reality, and to understand the truth of a text is to be conformed to the 'reality signified' by the text's mode of signifying.[172] For Thomas, truth finds a place in our intellect when our mind conforms itself to the thing which it is attempting to apprehend,[173] and correspondingly that which Scripture makes known (*res significata*) is to be treated with the utmost seriousness and attention. 'Truthful' exegesis must be conformed to pre-cisely what the apostle Paul makes known in Scripture, and it is for this reason that Thomas follows through so lovingly the *causality* of Jesus' resurrection, the basis of Paul's astonishing revelation.

Out of this studied attention to the text arises the immensely potent contribution on Christ's instrumentality. Thomas' use of instrumentality

[168] Torrance, 'Scientific Hermeneutics', 289.   [169] *Lectio* IV.II.103.
[170] *ST* 1a q. 1 a. 5 ad 2.   [171] Cf. *ST* 1a q. 1 a. 8 ad 2.   [172] *ST* 1a q. 39 a. 4 re.
[173] *SCG* I.16.1 re. Cited in B. D. Marshall, *Christology in Conflict: The Identity of a Saviour in Rahner and Barth* (Oxford: Basil Blackwell, 1987), p. 197, n. 54.

ascribes to the person of Christ a real role in our resurrection. The promise of our resurrection lies in the power held within Christ's humanity united to the Word of life, for 'the Word made flesh revives our bodies'.[174] Thomas' stress on the instrumental *humanity* of Christ allows that humanity to be saving precisely because every act of this humanity is absorbed within the saving power and will of God himself. There is, in Christ, 'the power of the divinity united in Him'.[175] This way of articulating the relationship between Christ's divinity and humanity is laden with eschatological fullness, for Thomas articulates a way of understanding the abiding power of Christ's risen body 'united to the Word of life' ('uniti verbo vitae').[176] Linking eschatology to a rigorous Christology, Thomas points to an overflowing of this communion of power, an effusion which Paul articulates as the resurrection of the dead, and Thomas understands as 'efficient causality'.

Christ's instrumental humanity thus embraces both the first cause (i.e. God) and the effects desired by the first cause (i.e. the general resurrection). Everything achieved by virtue of this instrument, suffused as it is by the divine power,[177] participates now in the saving will of God. Thomas' theological exegesis thus allows Christ's resurrection to be *itself* the foretaste of our resurrection, for the resurrection of Christ is now part of God's power:

> it [Christ's resurrection] is the cause of our resurrection insofar as *it works* by the divine power (quod est causa resurrectionis nostrae secundum quod *operatur* in virtute divina).[178]

Thomas' thinking on the resurrection's cause and causality is, as commentators have noted,[179] a meditation faithful to Paul's teaching. In Thomas' thinking the resurrection is restored as a dynamic, active power, willing our future salvation. Paul, too, was intoxicated with the God who raised Jesus from the dead (1 Thess. 1:10), and with the belief that there was now, through 'the power of his [Christ's] resurrection' (Phil. 3:10), the 'hope of salvation . . . through our Lord Jesus Christ' (1 Thess. 5:9–10). Both Paul and Thomas hold in unresolved tension what it is precisely that raises us from the dead. In 1 Thess. 4:13–18, Paul points to three active causes: God, through Jesus, who will bring with him the dead,

---

[174] *Lectio* IV.II.95; Duffy, *Commentary*, p. 35.   [175] *Lectio* IV.II.95; my translation.
[176] *Lectio* IV.II.95; Duffy, *Commentary*, p. 35.
[177] *ST* 1a2ae q. 112 a. 1 ad 1; 3a q. 19 a. 1 ad 1.
[178] *Lectio* IV.II.98; my translation (my italics).
[179] E.g. G. Sabra, *Thomas Aquinas' Vision of the Church: Fundamentals of an Ecumenical Ecclesiology* (Mainz: Matthias-Grünewald-Verlag, 1987), p. 93.

and the resurrection itself, which points 'in this way' (4:14) to the mode of our future salvation. Thomas, faithful to Paul, also leaves intertwined the three causes of the resurrection of the dead: Christ's resurrection itself,[180] Christ himself[181] and the divine power of the God 'who raises the dead'.[182] For both Thomas and Paul, what raises us from the dead, and promises us conformity to Christ, is *both* the same power that raised Christ from the dead *and* the resurrection of Christ as an effective power for all those 'in Christ'.

Thomas' contribution to exegetical method, and his relationship with historical criticism, is just as interesting as his more explicitly theological contribution. For Thomas, Paul's intentions are always forged wholly from within the words and literal reference of the text,[183] not from any historical-critical reconstruction. Thomas' relentless division of the text, a method that exposes its anatomy, evidences this studied attention to the object under scrutiny. Paul's intention is to be revered precisely because of his status – as one who is an apostle – and not because of a general presumption that texts mean what their authors intended, a fateful conflation of the meaning of the words with a putative, reconstructed *historical* reference. Thomas' interest in the literal sense of Scripture was not an attempt to work from a reconstructed intention to the meaning of the words (as with the tendencies critiqued in Part I), but an attempt to take seriously the signification of the words *themselves* as words over which the ultimate author, God, held providential control.[184]

Thomas' suggestive canonical exegesis arises from this commitment to God's providence. The irrepressible canonical conversation which Thomas conducts with the text is quite alien to contemporary scholarly notions that a text's meaning is historically fixed, and not to be related to diverse passages written at different times and in different contexts. Certainly aware of the literary differences to be found within the canon,[185] Thomas promotes the idea that there is a providential aspect to Scripture's meaning.[186] Dismissed by the unsympathetic as mere proof texting, Thomas' exegetical method is a lot more interesting than such curt dismissals might suggest. For Thomas there is a truth stretching across the whole of Scripture, precisely because Scripture possesses a prophetic momentum. Biblical authors are imperfect instruments moved by the

---

[180] *Lectio* IV.II.98.   [181] *Ibid.*   [182] *Lectio* IV.II.99; Duffy, *Commentary*, p. 38.
[183] B. S. Smalley, *The Gospels in the Schools* (London: Hambledon Press, 1985), p. 265.
[184] *ST* Ia q. 1 a. 10 re.
[185] Psalms, *Prooemium*. See Torrell, *Saint Thomas*, pp. 259–60.
[186] Stump, 'Revelation and Biblical Exegesis', pp. 178f.

principal power, God.[187] Consequently, there is the capacity for texts to exercise a prophetic function (even if the actual authors of the prophetic texts were unaware of this movement),[188] for God knows all things in their causality.[189] Thomas would have been baffled by being accused of a-historicism by modern scholars, for the God who holds providential control over time and causes knows everything, and everything which Scripture speaks of, in its precise causality, as happening in time and through events.

From this active understanding of God as the cause of everything Thomas deploys Scripture as a vast echo chamber with the capacity to explore, tease out and stretch Paul's words.[190] The texts cited by Thomas, more than mere proof texts or decorative additions, witness to his committed fidelity to the entirety of Scripture, and the remarkable extent to which he has adopted Scripture in his own vocabulary.[191]

Thomas' reading of 1 Thessalonians, in particular his exegesis of 1 Thess. 4:13–18, is a reading that is at every stage straining forward to an understanding of what the text is saying in reality. For Thomas, indeed, there was an intensity to be attained in the conflation of reading and understanding:

> 'Understanding' implies a certain intimate knowing; to understand, *intelligere*, is as it were to read within, *intus legere*. This is evident when you consider the difference between intelligence and sense. For sense-knowledge is engaged with external empirical qualities, whereas intellective knowledge *penetrates* as far as the essence of a thing . . . what a thing really is (quod quid est). Now there are many degrees of reality, as it were inside it, to which a man's knowledge should reach. For under its accidents lies the substantial nature of a thing, under words lies what they signify, under likenesses and figures lies the truth which is represented.[192]

---

[187] *ST* 2a2ae q. 173 a. 4 re.   [188] *Ibid.*   [189] *ST* 1a q. 14 a. 13 re.

[190] See, for example, *Lectio* II.I.24, where the meaning of the word 'vain' is opened up to a number of possibilities by reference to the canon.

[191] W. G. B. M. Valkenberg, *Words of the Living God: Place and Function of Holy Scripture in the Theology of St Thomas Aquinas* (Leuven: Peeters, 2000), p. 131.

[192] *ST* 2a2ae q. 8 a. 1 re (my italics).

3

JOHN CALVIN AND 1 THESSALONIANS

Introduction

John Calvin's theological thinking and study of Scripture enjoyed an organic relationship, the two aspects of Calvin's thinking developing reciprocally. For Calvin the touchstone for all doctrine was Scripture itself, and theology was only ever an aid to purer understanding of the Word. Calvin's frequently cited preface to his 1559 *Institutes* definitively indicates that his theology pivoted around 'right reading' of Scripture:

> it has been my purpose in this labour to prepare and instruct candidates in sacred theology for the reading of the divine Word, in order that they may be able both to have easy access to it and to advance in it without stumbling . . . If, after this road has, as it were, been paved, I shall publish any interpretations of Scripture, I shall always condense them, because I shall have no need to undertake long doctrinal discussions . . . In this way the Godly reader will be spared great annoyance and boredom, provided he approach Scripture armed with a knowledge of the present work.[1]

Calvin's life project was to expound the Bible's clear message. His first Biblical commentary was a commentary on Romans published in 1540, written during a productive sojourn in Strasbourg between 1539 and 1541. Six years later, he published his commentary on the Corinthian correspondence, and in 1548, commentaries on Galatians and 1 and 2 Timothy; in 1549, commentaries on Hebrews and Titus were completed. In 1551, he published his commentary on 1 and 2 Thessalonians.

In line with our reading of Thomas, we shall endeavour to undertake a close examination of Calvin's reading of 1 Thessalonians. This will involve us in examining *how* Calvin reads the Scriptural text, exposing

---

[1] J. Calvin, *Institutes of the Christian Religion*, tr. F. L. Battles, ed. J. T. McNeill (Philadelphia: Westminster Press, 1960), pp. 4–5.

the hermeneutical decisions he makes as he interprets (section 1). Despite Calvin's reluctance to set out his interpretative decisions, no exegete is devoid of a hermeneutical system, and it will be our business to unfold Calvin's exegetical methods and strategies. The above reference from the *Institutes* reveals that it will be faithful to Calvin to turn to this source for occasional illumination. Calvin's other Biblical commentaries will be referred to where they promise to be helpful. Calvin's hermeneutical system will be broken down by examining his attention to the text (section 1.1), to the canon (section 1.2) and to Patristic sources (section 1.3).

From this grounding, we shall be equipped to examine *what* Calvin says the text says, before turning to Calvin's wider corpus to illuminate our reflections (section 2). We shall conclude by reflecting on what contribution this voice of tradition, as we have heard it in Calvin's commentary on 1 Thessalonians, is likely to make to our reading in Part III (section 3).

1 The hermeneutical principles of Calvin's 1 Thessalonians commentary

1.1 Attention to the text

Calvin's sustained attention to the text itself, with what the text says in its very wording, is often observed. Karl Barth enthuses in relation to Calvin's exegesis:

> We can learn from Calvin what it means to stay close to the text, to focus with tense attention on what is actually there. Everything else *derives* from this. But it has to derive from *this*.[2]

Calvin was a hermeneut of the Holy Spirit. In this regard, as Barth recognised, Calvin is ultimately fascinated not with the text itself, but with the Spirit of God speaking through the text. Properly read, the words of the prophets and apostles are the instruments through which believers may acquire the illumination of the Spirit.[3] Calvin's desire is to penetrate so deeply into the text that he enables its ability to speak to us now:

> We are in the first century but we are equally in the sixteenth. We hear Paul, and we also hear Calvin. The voices merge into one another so that we can hardly distinguish them, and we get

---

[2] K. Barth, *The Theology of John Calvin*, tr. G. W. Bromiley (Grand Rapids: Eerdmans, 1995), p. 389 (italics in the original).

[3] Calvin, *Institutes*, I.ix.3.

some sense of the truth of the saying that the Spirit who spoke by the prophets must penetrate into our hearts.[4]

For Calvin the words of Paul are but the 'instrument' of the Spirit of God,[5] and it is precisely with and through the text that we must seek God's will. To discern the mind and the intention of the author, a frequent concern throughout Calvin's commentary, is to discern the mind of the Spirit, the author's real source of inspiration. The point of connection, the extent to which we can discern the author's intention in our present context of faith, is determined by the extent to which the Holy Spirit is active in the heart and mind of the individual interpreter. The Spirit's office is to assure us of Scripture's divine provenance.[6]

Accordingly, when Calvin states boldly 'Those, therefore, who conclude from this that it is souls which sleep, lack understanding',[7] understanding is something always rooted in faith. Illumined by the Holy Spirit the elect can see and understand what should be plain to all.[8] 'Understanding' is rooted in the reader's foundation in the movement of the same Spirit who inspired the author in the past and inspires readers now, and so is able to help the reader discern the Word of God *within* the words of the text. The authority of the Word is, for Calvin, indissolubly bound to the Spirit's activity within the life of the individual believer.[9] This understanding however, should not be understood purely as a mental apprehension, for the truth of Christianity 'is received only when it possesses the whole soul, and finds a seat and resting place in the inmost affection of the heart',[10] which, as Calvin elucidates, is 'the innermost part of the soul'.[11]

For Calvin the authority of Scripture resides in the secret testimony of the Spirit reassuring us that Scripture is from heaven.[12] Striking away any interpretative authority that the church might assume, Calvin thus turns to a strikingly individualistic doctrine. It is the individual's faith that affirms Paul's authority, and not any church that claims to be connected with the same Spirit of inspiration. Calvin's apparent focus on the intention of the author is, in this perspective, an insight into his view of Biblical inspiration, how the Holy Spirit transformed mere human words into 'oracles of God'.[13] In this way, for Calvin the literal sense *is* the spiritual sense, for the meaning of the Bible is the meaning ultimately 'intended'

---

[4] Barth, *Theology of John Calvin*, p. 392.   [5] *Comm. 1 Thess. 5:20.*
[6] H. J. Forstman, 'Coherence and Incoherence in the Theology of John Calvin', in J. H. Leith, ed., *Calvin Studies III* (Davidson: Davidson College, 1986), p. 51.
[7] *Comm. 1 Thess. 4:13.*   [8] *Comm. 2 Tim. 3:16.*   [9] Calvin, *Institutes*, I.viii.13.
[10] *Ibid.*, III.vi.4 (see also I.v.9; III.ii.36).   [11] *Comm. 1 Thess. 3:13.*
[12] Calvin, *Institutes*, I.vii.4.   [13] *Ibid.*, IV.vii.9.

by the Spirit.[14] Calvin's emphasis on the Holy Spirit is always pointing us not so much towards Paul as author of 1 Thessalonians as towards God as Author, an insight correctly apprehended only through faith.

Calvin's emphasis on 'authorial intention', from this explicitly theological perspective, is rooted in a conviction that God is Scripture's ultimate Author.[15] Calvin's emphasis on authorial intention is faithfully pre-critical,[16] formed from within the movement of the Spirit's activity, the dictation of the Biblical authors, and the faith of the individual reader.[17]

Calvin's profound seriousness with regard to the Scriptural text had its foundations in his humanist education. It is well known that Calvin was an accomplished humanist, publishing an erudite commentary on Seneca's *De Clementia* at twenty-three. With his conversion, possibly as early as a year later, Calvin filtered his considerable humanist learning through his increasingly Reformed perspective.

Where we associate 'humanism' now with the fostering of ethical values independently from any ecclesial or metaphysical contribution, the humanism of Calvin's era was by no means an extra-ecclesial movement, but principally a cultural and educational movement with origins in the Italian Renaissance.[18] In its most general form, humanism revered the mastery of the classical languages of Greek, Hebrew and Latin, and admired the style found in classical writings. In their elevation of rhetoric, humanists self-consciously opposed scholastic modes of knowledge. The clarion call of humanism was a return to the original sources (*ad fontes*) and a clearing away of what was perceived to be misguided scholastic thought.

Basil Hall outlines three distinguishing marks of Biblical humanism,[19] a movement, it should be noted, not restricted to the Reformers. Indeed, humanism was enthusiastically supported by figures such as Cardinal Sadoleto (to whom we shall shortly turn). First, Biblical humanists endeavoured to master Greek, Hebrew and Latin with the purpose of expositing the Bible more rigorously than their scholastic predecessors had done. Secondly, returning to the Bible was seen as the route out of

---

[14] K. Greene-McCreight, 'Ad Litteram: Understandings of the Plain Sense of Scripture in the Exegesis of Augustine, Calvin and Barth of Genesis 1–3', unpublished Ph.D. thesis, Yale University, 1994, 248.

[15] Calvin, *Institutes*, I.vii.4.   [16] See excursus 1 below.

[17] Calvin, *Institutes*, I.viii.13, I.ix.2.

[18] N. Mann, 'The Origins of Humanism', in J. Kraye, ed., *The Cambridge Companion to Renaissance Humanism* (Cambridge: Cambridge University Press, 1996), pp. 1–19.

[19] B. Hall, 'Calvin and Biblical Humanism', in R. C. Gamble, ed., *Influences upon Calvin and Discussion of the 1559 Institutes* (New York: Garland Press, 1992), pp. 59–60.

the current intellectual and moral malaise afflicting the church. A return to the straightforward message of the Word of God was the antidote to excessive allegorising. And thirdly, renewed energy was applied to establishing the most accurate Biblical text. Textual criticism was thus a major facet of Biblical humanism,[20] and sixteenth-century France was a major centre for one of the key facets of humanism: philology.

Calvin's personal heritage in Biblical humanism was extensive. Wolmar, Cop, Olivétan, Cordier (Calvin's teacher of Latin and French at Paris, to whom Calvin dedicated his 1 Thessalonians commentary), Alciati and Bucer were all prominent humanists who either through their teaching or friendship played a part in Calvin's mastery of the apparatus of humanism. From his brief but nonetheless influential legal training at Bourges, Calvin had learned much of the technique of moving past the gloss to the most original form of the text.[21]

Calvin's humanist background is evident throughout his commentary on 1 Thessalonians, and François Wendel would seem to be accurate in evincing that Calvin's conversion clearly did not result in a repudiation of his humanist learning.[22] Reading as a linguist, Calvin also reads the text as a Reformed theologian, one whose close reading of the text indicates his conviction that all of Scripture is inspired by the Spirit.[23] Approaching the text as inspired by God, with its authors as instruments, Calvin scrutinises the text as closely as possible to gain access to 'the pure Word of God'.[24] Reading from Colines' Greek New Testament, an edition based on Erasmus' work and the Polyglot,[25] he frequently draws attention both to linguistic idioms and text-critical issues pertaining to 1 Thessalonians.[26] He thus demonstrates the humanist drive to equate purity with origins.

Calvin's disciplined reading fixes attention on Paul's words so that, through these words, we may know what Paul 'connotes' ('significat'),[27] 'with what purpose' he speaks ('quorsum')[28] and what his 'mind'

---

[20] Perhaps the most famous father of this revived textual criticism was Lorenzo Valla (1405–57).

[21] B. Hall, *John Calvin: Humanist and Theologian* (London: The Historical Association, 1956), p. 34.

[22] F. Wendel, *Calvin: The Origins and Development of his Religious Thought*, tr. P. Mairet (London: Collins, 1963), p. 33.

[23] E. A. Dowey, *The Knowledge of God in Calvin's Theology* (revised edn; Grand Rapids: Eerdmans, 1994), p. 99.

[24] *Comm. 1 Thess. 2:13.*

[25] T. H. L. Parker, *Calvin's New Testament Commentaries* (London: SCM, 1971), pp. 106–9.

[26] *Comm. 1 Thess. 1:4, 7; 2:5, 7, 12, 13, 20; 3:1; 4:6, 8, 9, 10, 15, 16; 5:4, 8, 9, 13, 22.*

[27] *Comm. 1 Thess 5:15; CO 52:173.*

[28] *CO 52:140 (on 1 Thess. 1:2); my translation.*

('mentem') is.[29] Exact rendering of the words used by the apostle Paul is a way of reading him faithfully, and so preventing 'any unnecessary change in the Greek wording used by Paul'.[30] At 4:15, Calvin states that with the phrase 'we that are alive', Paul is 'using the present tense in place of the future in accordance with Hebrew usage', and then in commenting on the next verse remarks on the use of κελεύσματος.[31] So too, in commenting on 5:8 and 5:9 Calvin displays a keen interest in the classical languages and their use. One of the humanists' philologically driven concerns was that language both be understood properly and be interpreted correctly. Calvin accordingly shows an awareness that περιποίησις can be interpreted as both 'enjoyment' and 'acquisition' (he translates it as 'obtaining').[32]

Context was important to humanists in determining whether or not a word was translated correctly: a word's context in the wider passage determines how we should translate it. This could serve as a means of closing down meaning and settling interpretative debates, as in Calvin's discussion of 1 Thess. 2:7.[33] Once a certain word is tied down to a grammatical or historical context (or of course both), the endless potential of words as signs pointing to yet more things beyond is broken down. Thus, Calvin translates the same imperative form – παρακαλεῖτε – in 4:18 and 5:11 in different ways according to its literary context. In 4:18 he translates it as 'Comfort' and in 5:11 as 'Exhort', explaining his rationale thus:

> This is the same word which we found at the end of the previous chapter, and which we translated *comfort*, because the context required it. The same meaning would also suit the present passage quite well. The subjects which he has discussed previously afford material for both, comfort as well as exhortation.[34]

Aside from philological concerns there were rhetorical interests: the identification and categorisation of language in the *particular context* in which it was being used. Commenting on 1 Thess. 5:3, Calvin picks up on Paul's comparison of the 'sudden destruction' with the labour of 'a woman with

---

[29] *CO* 52:165 (on 1 Thess. 4:13); my translation.

[30] *Comm. 1 Thess.* 1:7. Interestingly, at *Comm. 1 Thess.* 2:13 Calvin seems so confident that he has accessed Paul's meaning that he *adds* to the text 'I have, therefore, had no hesitation in inserting the particle *ut*, which helped to make the meaning more clear.'

[31] *Comm. 1 Thess.* 4:16. [32] *Comm. 1 Thess.* 5:9.

[33] *Comm. 1 Thess.* 2:7; *CO* 52:148: 'Some interpret this to mean, *when we might have been a burden*, i.e. might have caused you expense. The context, however, requires (sed contextus postulat) that τὸ βαρύ should be taken to mean *authority*.' This trait is also evident at *Comm. 1 Thess.* 2:12.

[34] *Comm. 1 Thess.* 5:11.

child'.[35] Calvin passes further comments on Paul's metaphorical reference to the faith of the Thessalonians,[36] his self-comparision to a nurse,[37] the thief in the night, the pregnant woman,[38] night and day,[39] sleep and drunkenness,[40] and quenching the Spirit.[41] Calvin's attention to rhetoric alerts him to when Paul is deploying 'another argument' ('altero argumento'),[42] and when he is merely developing arguments.[43] So too does Calvin betray his keen attention to Paul's varying use of language when he makes reference to the different uses of words relating to armoury in Eph. 6:14 and 1 Thess. 5:8.[44]

Central to Calvin's exegesis were the principles of clarity and brevity,[45] qualities that distinguished humanists from prolix scholastics. This desire for a purer writing style was not just a humanist endeavour forged in opposition to the perceived verbosity of scholasticism but, in its own right, a mode of reading the text closely with absolute faithfulness. In the dedication of the Romans commentary these principles of brevity are set out with the most candour:

> Both of us [Simon Gryaneus and Calvin] felt that lucid brevity constituted the particular virtue of an interpreter . . . Our desire, therefore, was that someone might be found, out of the number of those who have at the present day proposed to further the cause of theology in this kind of task, who would not only study to be comprehensible, but also try not to detain his readers too much with long and wordy commentaries.[46]

The motivations for this brevity were rooted in Calvin's attitude that the exegete should clothe himself with humility before the Word of God, for Scripture's true meaning was always the most elementary one.[47] To 'turn the meaning of Scripture around without due care' is 'presumptuous' and even 'blasphemous'.[48] Attention to Paul's words, and the clear mediation of those words to the church, means that for Calvin there is no scope for hidden or obscure meanings. The most important task facing an exegete is not the endless play of words, but the simple unfolding of the author's mind. Calvin's exegesis comes from the pen of somebody cultivating a

---

[35] For Calvin's attention to this kind of language see W. J. Bouwsma, *John Calvin: A Sixteenth Century Portrait* (New York: Oxford University Press, 1988), p. 125.
[36] *Comm. 1 Thess. 1:8.*   [37] *Comm. 1 Thess. 2:8.*   [38] Both *Comm. 1 Thess. 5:3.*
[39] *Comm. 1 Thess. 5:4.*   [40] *Comm. 1 Thess. 5:6.*   [41] *Comm. 1 Thess. 5:19.*
[42] *Comm. 1 Thess. 5:8; CO* 52:170.
[43] *Comm. 1 Thess. 2:1; 5:9.*   [44] *Comm. 1 Thess. 5:8.*
[45] See F. W. Farrar, 'Calvin as an Expositor', *The Expositor* 7 (2nd series, 1884), 433–4.
[46] *Comm. Rom.* (dedication).   [47] *Comm. Gal. 4:22.*   [48] *Comm. Rom.* (dedication).

writing style that aims to present the truth directly to the reader.[49] Faced with multiple meanings for 'trump' in 1 Thess. 4:16, Calvin curtly states that 'I will leave it to others to debate in finer detail the meaning of the word *trump*.'[50] Likewise Calvin is scornful of those scholars who play around with explanations of the different names of the armour in 1 Thess. 5:8, complaining that such endeavours are 'pointless' ('frustra').[51] This clarity, and corresponding suspicion of prolixity, is sprinkled throughout the commentary. Commenting on 1 Thess. 5:10, Calvin acknowledges the arguments about what kind of 'sleeping' Paul is referring to, but jumps over quickly to what he regards 'is essential' ('summa est').[52] It is important to note here that it is Calvin who makes the interpretative decisions, for it is he who shuts off the potential for an abundance of meaning by declaring, in a seemingly arbitrary manner, what is 'pointless' or 'essential'.

The purpose of Paul, as one inspired by the Holy Spirit, is discerned from within the very contours of the text. As we have seen, attention to 'the Greek wording used by Paul' is attention not just to what 'he is saying',[53] but to what God's Spirit is saying through Paul. Although it is right to indicate the importance of historical context to Calvin's exegesis,[54] there is restraint in the amount of historical detail discussed in his commentary. Even where historical information is discussed, it does little to distract him from his principal task,[55] which is to 'explain Paul's way of thinking' ('explicat Pauli mentem').[56]

Calvin's exegesis is, however, marked by a curious (and pregnant) tension. Close study of the Biblical languages in their context had impressed upon him that Paul's words were not the words of his age, but of 'that age',[57] and that the text contained echoes of the times of Epicurus and Diogenes the Cynic.[58] Calvin the humanist knew that language was context-bound to some degree.[59] What is revealed in Scripture is limited and defined by its historical provenance. Thus, we should not ask of the text questions Paul was not intending to answer – such as the fate of

---

[49] T. F. Torrance, *The Hermeneutics of John Calvin* (Edinburgh: T. & T. Clark, 1988), p. 188.

[50] *Comm. 1 Thess. 4:16*. Cf. *Comm. 1 Cor. 15:52*.

[51] *Comm. 1 Thess. 5:8*; *CO* 52:170.

[52] *CO* 52:171 (on 1 Thess. 5:10); my translation.   [53] *Comm. 1 Thess. 1:7*.

[54] See, e.g., D. L. Puckett, *John Calvin's Exegesis of the Old Testament* (Louisville: Westminster John Knox Press, 1995), pp. 69–70.

[55] *Comm. 1 Thess. 1:9*.   [56] *Comm. 1 Thess. 5:22*; *CO* 52:178.

[57] *Comm. 1 Thess. 1:3*.   [58] *Comm. 1 Thess. 1:9*.

[59] See *Comm. Jn. 6:32*; *Comm. Jer. 50:18*, where the meaning of the text is closely bound to historical considerations.

unbelievers – for 1 Thessalonians is a text whose meaning is limited by 'what suited his [Paul's] present purpose' ('quod praesenti instituto congruebat').[60] We see here an awareness of the difference between then and now, elucidated more fully elsewhere:

> the servants of God should teach nothing which they have not learned from him, still, according to the diversity of the times, they have had diverse ways of learning. But the present order differs very much from what existed in former times.[61]

Despite this historical sensitivity to the text, Calvin holds his historical-grammatical tendencies in tension with a conviction that, as an apostle, God called Paul 'according to His own good pleasure'.[62] The author of 1 Thessalonians is a 'superhuman' model for all pastors,[63] whose 'sacred breast' is ablaze with the love of God.[64] Echoing his words in the *Institutes* that apostles are 'sure and genuine scribes of the Holy Spirit',[65] as a 'holy apostle' Paul has 'learned by revelation all the secrets of the kingdom'.[66] God commands us by 'the voice of Paul' himself,[67] and consequently speaks with 'the mouth of Paul' as his instrument.[68] The inspiration of Paul's words is not overly mechanical, however – throughout the process of inspiration Paul retains his individual style:

> It is no objection that the article is put between the pronoun ὑμῶν and the noun ἔργου. We frequently find this in Paul.[69]

Calvin's comments on 1 Thess. 4:13f. provide some insight into this tensive aspect of his exegetical hermeneutics. He begins by setting out the contextual background within the Thessalonian church, reflecting that 'it is unlikely that blasphemers had destroyed the hope of the resurrection among the Thessalonians, as had happened at Corinth', and moving on to consider that the members may have retained some of their old superstitions concerning the dead. As if realising the risk of digression, Calvin switches to 'the main thing (summa) . . . that we must not grieve inordinately for the dead, because we are all to be raised again'.[70] Calvin's interest in the text is more than an interest in its linguistic form, or its historical context. These are mere props to understanding the Word that God is communicating through Scripture.

---

[60] *Comm. 1 Thess. 4:14; CO* 52:165. See also *Comm. 1 Thess. 4:16.*
[61] Calvin, *Institutes*, IV.viii.5.   [62] *Comm. 1 Thess. 2:4.*   [63] *Comm. 1 Thess. 2:9.*
[64] *Comm. 1 Thess. 3:8.*   [65] Calvin, *Institutes*, IV.viii.9.
[66] *Comm. 1 Thess. 3:5; 4:15.*
[67] *Comm. 1 Thess. 5:19.*   [68] *Comm. 1 Thess. 5:21.*
[69] *Comm. 1 Thess. 1:3.* Also *Comm. 1 Thess. 3:6.*
[70] *Comm. 1 Thess. 4:13; CO* 52:164.

Calvin's attention to the text is dependent upon the relationship he constructs between the Word and the Holy Spirit. It is the Spirit's interaction with the Biblical author, and our connection with that same Spirit, which keeps Calvin's Biblical understanding intratextually generated. For Calvin the meaning is always to be found within the text, not in any extratextual details spinning away from the text. The author's inspired intention acts as the legitimate restraint on all subsequent interpretation, a meaning arrived at through brevity. It is here that Calvin locates the firmness and clarity of Scripture, to the exclusion of any subsequent, successive lives which the words of Scripture may come to enjoy through the Spirit's continuing activity in the church. Determined attention to the intention of God as Author through the instrument of the human author was the means by which Calvin ensured 'pure and faithful instruction in the Word . . . free from all taint or deception'.[71] Calvin's theology thereby seems to turn the Holy Spirit into an entity of history, at one moment inspiring authors in a context-bound way, and at the next moment allowing readers access to that historically limited intent or purpose. Viewed in this regard, the following words of Calvin on the Holy Spirit's activity seem particularly striking:

> he [the Spirit] would have us recognize him in his own image, which he has stamped upon the Scriptures. He is the Author of Scripture: he cannot vary and differ from himself. Hence *he must remain just as he once revealed himself there.*[72]

1.2   Attention to the canon

We turn now to Calvin's use of Scripture to exposit 1 Thessalonians. One of the most striking differences in comparison with Thomas' commentary on 1 Thessalonians is the restraint with which Calvin cites from the rest of the Biblical canon. Exegeting the eighty-nine verses of 1 Thessalonians, Calvin cites only forty-one Scriptural references, which works out at less than one Scriptural reference for every two verses. As we saw, in his commentary on 1 Thessalonians Thomas managed some 340 Scriptural citations, just below four citations for every verse.

Closer examination reveals more restraint. Calvin's preference seems to be to explain Paul by Paul, rather than by the whole of the canon. Of the forty-one Scriptural references or direct citations, the vast majority are either from the Pauline corpus, or from Luke's narration of Paul's

[71] *Comm. 1 Thess. 2:3.*   [72] Calvin, *Institutes*, I.ix.2 (my italics).

activity in Acts.[73] Some thirty (73 per cent) out of the forty-one Scriptural references are from Pauline epistles or from Acts. This is an interesting hermeneutical decision, revealing a preference for understanding the human authorship of Paul rather than turning to the whole of Scripture.

The following breakdown helps clarify Calvin's deployment of the canon:

(1) The explicative function of Paul's writings
One function of the canon is to explain what Paul says reticently or allusively in 1 Thessalonians by turning to what he says elsewhere in his corpus. Explaining Paul's purpose in referring to 'wrath' in 1 Thess. 2:16, Calvin understands it to mean 'the judgement of God', as in Rom. 4:15 and 12:19.[74] Further uses of understanding Paul by Paul (or by Luke's account of his missionary successes in Acts) are found throughout the commentary.[75] But so restrained is Calvin's method of explaining Paul by Paul that he even warns against harmonising 1 Thess. 5:8 with Eph. 6:14, because 'Paul's language here is different.'[76]

(2) The explicative function of the rest of the canon
In these instances what Paul says in 1 Thessalonians is explained with reference to what is said elsewhere in Scripture. No questions are asked about the suitability of this mode of explication, or the compatibility of the different texts. It is assumed that the words of David in the Psalms, or Christ in the Gospels, can explicate Paul's words in 1 Thessalonians. This is not, however, Calvin's favoured mode of explaining Paul.[77] One such instance is in explaining Paul's reference to imitation in 1 Thess. 1:6. Here Calvin aligns Paul with Moses, as personalities through whom God works 'as His instruments and servants', and through whom people come to see God's 'generosity', and so might imitate God by reciprocating God's gracious love for them.[78]

(3) The contesting witness of Scripture
In these instances the single, indivisible witness of Scripture to sound doctrine is only accepted after a tussle with passages that might contradict

---

[73] Calvin accepted the Pauline authorship of the Pastorals, Colossians and Ephesians. However, close reading of the text of Hebrews had convinced him that Paul did not write this epistle. For the purposes of this section we are working with the letters Calvin believed to have been written by Paul.

[74] *Comm. 1 Thess. 2:16.*

[75] *Comm. 1 Thess. 1:4, 9* (twice); *2:1, 4, 9* (twice), *11, 16, 18* (twice); *3:2, 10, 12; 4:1, 3, 14* (twice); *5:10, 15, 16, 20, 21* (twice).

[76] *Comm. 1 Thess. 5:8.*

[77] *Comm. 1 Thess. 1:9; 2:15; 3:2; 4:9; 5:3, 4, 16* (thrice), *23.*

[78] *Comm. 1 Thess. 1:6.*

what Paul says in 1 Thessalonians. For Calvin, if we perceived any contradiction in Scripture this was a problem with us as faulty readers, and not with Scripture itself.[79] Commenting on Paul's reference to the hindrance of Satan in 1 Thess. 2:18, Calvin juxtaposes Paul's reference to God preventing him from visiting Rome in Rom. 1:13. For Calvin 'both statements are true', and he harmonises them by allotting to Satan the ministry of hindrance, and to God the 'supreme authority to open up a way for us as often as he pleases'.[80] The other verse, 1 Thess. 4:16, where Calvin wrestles with the apparently contradictory 1 Cor. 15:36, will be discussed below (section 2.6). It suffices to say that Calvin allows for no contradiction, for the solution to the problem is 'easy' ('facilis').[81]

We saw a tensive quality in Calvin's close attention to the text; it is equally present in his reading of the canon. On the one hand, there is in Calvin a non-negotiable belief in the absolute unity of the canon. The Spirit of God which inspired Isa. 60:2 is the same Spirit that inspired 1 Thess. 5:4, and it is unquestionably legitimate to allow the two to interpret each other.[82] This unity in Scripture is obvious to all with the insight of God's Spirit:

> What wonderful confirmation ensues when, with keener study, we ponder the economy of the divine wisdom, so well ordered and disposed; the completely heavenly character of its doctrine, savoring of nothing earthly; the beautiful agreements of all the parts with one another.[83]

For Calvin the unity of Scriptures is found precisely in the realisation that Christ is its constant meaning,[84] from Genesis through to Revelation.[85]

The conviction that Scripture was a unified witness and that any possible contradiction within its pages could be met with an 'easy' solution[86] was held in unresolved tension with insights which Calvin drew from Renaissance humanism. First, Calvin believed that a passage's literary context within its time of delivery was a major aid to a passage's meaning.[87] Secondly, and in conjunction with this, he held that the writers of Scripture were teachers, who, like the best teachers, directed their words expertly to their time and context:

---

[79] R. C. Zachman, 'Gathering Meaning from the Context: Calvin's Exegetical Method', *JR* 82 (2002), 23–4.

[80] *Comm. 1 Thess. 2:18.*   [81] *Comm. 1 Thess. 4:16; CO* 52:167.

[82] *Comm. 1 Thess. 5:4.*   [83] Calvin, *Institutes,* I.viii.1.   [84] *Comm. Jn. 5:39.*

[85] Barth, *Theology of John Calvin,* p. 390.

[86] *Comm. 1 Thess. 4:16.*   [87] Calvin, *Institutes,* IV.xvi.23.

> It would be really a frigid way of teaching if the teachers did not determine carefully the needs of the times and what suits the people concerned, for in this regard nothing is more unbalanced than absolute balance.[88]

To be sure, Calvin is never in any doubt that, concerning 1 Thessalonians, 'it was the will of the Spirit of God to spread through all the church the teachings which He has given in this epistle'.[89] Despite this, Calvin's additional insight was that literary and historical context was an important determinant in adducing the meaning of a given Biblical text. Surely this conviction is evidenced by the relative paucity of canonical citations (certainly in comparison with Thomas), and the preference for explicating Paul by reference to Paul rather than the rest of the canon.

1.3   Calvin's use of the Fathers

Calvin had a profound respect for the Fathers. True to the humanist principle of *ad fontes*, he immersed himself in the writings of the early church, and the number of Patristic references grew considerably throughout his successive *Institutes*. The prolixity of medieval scholasticism was cast as a departure from the wisdom of the apostolic church and the Fathers:

> All the Fathers with one heart have abhorred and with one voice have detested the fact that God's Holy Word has been contaminated by the subtleties of sophists and involved in the squabbles of dialecticians . . . Why, if the Fathers were now brought back to life, and heard such a brawling art as these persons call speculative theology, there is nothing they would less suppose than that these folk were disputing about God![90]

There was, naturally, a polemical edge to Calvin's use of the Fathers. Immersing himself in the Fathers, and making frequent reference to them, he was consolidating his charge against the Roman Church that it was they, and not he, who had departed from the historic basis and unity of Christianity. This trait is very evident in his highly charged letter of 1539 to Cardinal Sadoleto. The Cardinal had taken advantage of Calvin's stay in Strasbourg to write to the Genevans, urging them to return to the Roman Catholic fold. As Calvin wrote in his rhetorical retort, the Reformers, far

---

[88] *Comm. Matt. 3:7.* Cited in W. J. Bouwsma, 'Calvinism as Renaissance Artifact', in T. George, ed., *Calvin and the Church: A Prism for Reform* (Louisville: Westminster John Knox Press, 1990), p. 38.
[89] *Comm. 1 Thess. 5:27.*   [90] Calvin, *Institutes*, p. 22.

from breaking up the church's unity, were retrieving from the 'ruins' of the present church the 'ancient form' of the church, the age of the apostles and great Fathers such as Augustine, Ambrose and Chrysostom.[91] The 'secret magic' and 'preposterous riddles' of scholasticism had polluted this purity.[92] The attack on the Roman Church could find support not just from a return to Scripture, but also from the teaching of the Fathers, *the very thing* Sadoleto and others accused Calvin of rending asunder:

> in attacking, breaking down, and destroying your [the Roman Church's] kingdom, we are armed not only with the energy of the Divine Word, but with the aid of the Holy Fathers also.[93]

Nevertheless, Calvin would not be Calvin if he had not insisted that any authority the Fathers and councils held was always subordinate to Christ and the Word. Our trust in the Gospel must not 'depend on human authority', but solely and always 'on the known and certain truth of God . . . the pure Word of God' ('purum Dei sermonem').[94] Interpreters must guard against the invasion of any authority other than the unadorned Word. True authority lay solely with the Word, and any notion of this authority proper to the Word being transferred to the Fathers could not be tolerated,

> For although we hold that the Word of God alone lies beyond the sphere of our judgement, and that Fathers and Councils are of authority only in so far as they accord with the rule of the Word, we still give to Councils and Fathers such rank and honor as it is meet for them to hold, under Christ.[95]

Moreover, despite Calvin's respect for the Fathers, it would work against his stated aim of 'lucid brevity' to turn his Scriptural commentaries into exegetical battlefields.[96] In general, he avoids sparring with previous Biblical interpreters, or indeed citing them at all – he is aware that his commentaries (unlike his *Institutes*) are meant to be genuinely accessible.

In the course of our commentary, Calvin makes reference to relatively few exegetical predecessors: Ambrose,[97] Augustine,[98] Chrysostom[99] and

---

[91] J. Calvin, 'Calvin's Reply to Sadoleto', in *A Reformation Debate: Sadoleto's Letter to the Genevans and Calvin's Reply*, tr. H. Beveridge, ed. J. C. Olin (New York: Harper and Row, 1966), p. 62.

[92] *Ibid.*, p. 65.   [93] *Ibid.*, p. 73.   [94] *Comm. 1 Thess. 2:13; CO* 52:151.

[95] Calvin, 'Calvin's Reply', p. 92.   [96] *Comm. Rom.* (dedication).

[97] *Comm. 1 Thess. 5:22.*   [98] *Comm. 1 Thess. 4:16.*

[99] *Comm. 1 Thess. 1:4* (twice); *4:6; 5:18, 22.*

Origen.[100] This, in itself, reminds us that his simple, straightforward exegesis was directed towards the building up of all the church. As far as possible, Calvin the commentator resolved to do nothing other than 'to unfold the mind of the writer whom he has undertaken to expound'.[101] Calvin's preface to his 1557 commentary on the Psalms neatly outlines his interpretative principles:

> I have not only observed throughout a simple style of teaching, but in order to be removed the farther from all ostentation, I have also generally abstained from refuting the opinions of others, although this presented a more favourable opportunity for plausible display, and of acquiring the applause of those who shall favour my book with a perusal. I have never touched upon opposite opinions, unless there was reason to fear, that by being silent . . . I might leave my readers in doubt and perplexity . . . I have felt nothing to be of more importance than to have a regard to the edification of the Church.[102]

Calvin's desire for brevity certainly seems behind the reticence with which he cites the Fathers in his 1 Thessalonians commentary. It is also interesting that the Fathers whom he does cite there, Origen excepted, are amongst the ones who come in for the highest praise in the reply to Cardinal Sadoleto:

> place, I pray, before your eyes, that ancient form of the Church, such as their writings prove it to have been in the age of Chrysostom and Basil, among the Greeks, and of Cyprian, Ambrose, and Augustine, among the Latins; after so doing contemplate the ruins of that Church, as now surviving amongst yourselves.[103]

Despite Calvin's stated esteem for Chrysostom, Ambrose and Augustine, his use of these three reveals an exegetical independence. Of the five references to Chrysostom in the 1 Thessalonians commentary, only one is unambiguously favourable.[104] In the other references, it is implied that Chrysostom's exegesis is too parsimonious,[105] that it is 'too forced',[106] that Paul's words 'have a fuller meaning' ('pleniorem sensum') than Chrysostom allowed,[107] and that he has failed to 'explain Paul's way of

---

[100] *Comm. 1 Thess. 4:17.*   [101] *Comm. Rom.* (dedication).
[102] *Comm. Psalms* (preface).   [103] Calvin, 'Calvin's Reply', p. 62.
[104] The first reference in *Comm. 1 Thess. 1:4.*
[105] The second reference in *Comm. 1 Thess. 1:4.*
[106] *Comm. 1 Thess. 4:6.*   [107] *Comm. 1 Thess. 5:18; CO* 52:175.

thinking'.[108] This is perhaps all the more surprising given Calvin's undisputed high regard for Chrysostom's exegetical principles.[109] Ambrose, along with Chrysostom, is equally criticised for failing to grasp Paul's 'meaning'.[110]

The single reference to Augustine (discussed in section 2.6 below) equally implies a detached criticism. Augustine's concerns over the possible contradiction between 1 Thess. 4:16 and 1 Cor. 15:36 arise because he has trouble understanding how those alive at Jesus' return can 'rise again'.[111] Once again we must recall that Calvin had an exceedingly high regard for Augustine. Nevertheless, in Calvin's dismissal of Augustine's extended struggle over the harmonisation of 1 Thess. 4:16 and 1 Cor. 15:36 – 'the solution is easy'[112] – we can hear echoes of criticisms levelled at Augustine elsewhere by Calvin.[113]

The last Father to discuss is Origen, who is perhaps not surprisingly dealt with very negatively. Origen's exegesis is an 'aberration' ('deliria') and 'too horrible to speak of'.[114]

One cannot draw any general conclusions about Calvin's method of using the Fathers from the micro-perspective that is the 1 Thessalonians commentary. What we can say, with what we do have, is that he demonstrates a drive to stick to the text, free from protracted debates. Where he does draw on the Patristic heritage, it is usually to demonstrate his independence from it. For Calvin, it is the Word's authority that tests the contribution of the historical church, not the Patristic inheritance which tests or validates the Word.

2   Eschatology and Calvin's reading of 1 Thessalonians

An examination of Calvin's treatment of eschatology in 1 Thessalonians might seem unpromising. His fame, after all, is not based on his eschatological thinking.[115] This is perhaps surprising, since for many interpreters the Reformation injected a new sense of dynamism into history in place

---

[108] *Comm. 1 Thess. 5:22.*

[109] See I. Hazlett, 'Calvin's Latin Preface to his Proposed French Edition of Chrysostom's Homilies: Translation and Commentary', in J. Kirk, ed., *Humanism and Reform: The Church in Europe, England, and Scotland, 1400–1643* (Oxford: Blackwell, 1991), pp. 129–50.

[110] *Comm. 1 Thess. 5:22.*   [111] *Comm. 1 Thess. 4:16.*   [112] *Comm. 1 Thess. 4:16.*

[113] *Comm. Jer. 28: 7–9; Comm. Ex. 7:22.* Both cited by Puckett, *John Calvin's Exegesis,* p. 74, n.16.

[114] *Comm. 1 Thess. 4:17; CO* 52:167. This is a mild rebuke of Origen in comparison with his other comments in *Comm. Gen. 2:8; 21:12; Comm. 2 Cor. 3:6.*

[115] D. E. Holwerda, 'Eschatology and History: A Look at Calvin's Eschatological Vision', in R. C. Gamble, ed., *Calvin's Theology, Theology Proper, Eschatology* (New York: Garland Publishing, 1992), p. 130.

of a moribund scholasticism. Just as it is possible to read the Reformation as a movement charged with an eschatological momentum,[116] so too is eschatology a prominent theme of 1 Thessalonians, and in Calvin's reading of the text.

Reading Calvin's commentary closely, with an eye on allusions developed more fully elsewhere in his work, we shall see that it is a work saturated with an eschatological vision. With this eschatological theme running throughout the commentary it will be necessary to distinguish the various threads woven through the commentary. I propose, then, a six-fold way to understand Calvin's reading of the eschatology of 1 Thessalonians: faith as eschatological (section 2.1); a dualism between this world and the next (section 2.2); an emphasis on the hidennness of the future (section 2.3); a belief in the immortality of the soul (section 2.4); an opposition to Chiliasm (section 2.5); and the universal transformation (section 2.6). This exploration of Calvin's reading of the text will equip us in our evaluative stage (§3).

2.1   Faith as eschatological

For Calvin, faith is a progressive assimilation into the knowledge and love of God, a movement of which God is in full charge. Faith is bound and defined by its *end* in God's will and love, a ceaselessly progressive momentum 'under the direction of the Holy Spirit'.[117] This theme of an eschatological faith, a faith orientated towards its end, runs throughout the commentary.

Faith, running its whole course, is surrounded by God, both at its beginning and at its end: 'God, as he begins our salvation by calling us, accomplishes it by forming our hearts to obey Him.'[118] Faith can only reach its victorious end in and with God because 'there is no perfection among men'.[119] Our salvation is something begun by Christ, for on us 'Christ has begun to shine by the faith of His Gospel.'[120] The faith of those who believe in Christ is nothing less than 'a progress in godliness',[121] a progress for which it is *God* who 'has bestowed superlative gifts upon us for the purpose of perfecting what He has begun'.[122] Calvin depicts faith as a constant forward expansion, true conversion being nothing less than an 'advance in godliness'.[123] It is God who enjoys the position of

---

[116] T. F. Torrance, 'The Eschatology of the Reformation', in T. F. Torrance and J. K. S. Reid, eds., *Eschatology* (*SJT* Occasional Papers No. 2; Edinburgh: Oliver and Boyd, 1957), p. 39.

[117] *Comm. 1 Thess. 5:20.*   [118] *Comm. 1 Thess. 1:6.*   [119] *Comm. 1 Thess. 4:10.*

[120] *Comm. 1 Thess. 5:4.*   [121] *Comm. 1 Thess. 3:5.*   [122] *Comm. 1 Thess. 1:2.*

[123] *Comm. 1 Thess. 1:9.*

being the 'sole author' of the 'whole renewal' of humanity.[124] Although 'our salvation is based on *God*'s free adoption of us',[125] and any increase in our love for one another is 'from God alone',[126] believers do have a responsibility to 'fan more vigorously the sparks which God has kindled in them by daily progress'.[127]

Faith in Christ, the believer's continual progress,[128] is thus extending towards its perfection, an apex over which God holds authority. The ceaseless running towards our victory has as its point of aim God himself,[129] and believers must run this race with 'perseverance'.[130] It is God who will decide when the fruits of our faith's progress are fully ripe and mature, for only at this stage will Christ return to the world to assume his 'judgement seat':[131]

> Paul, however, does not explain the nature or the extent of the holiness of believers in this world, but desires that it may be increased until it reaches its perfection. For this reason he says *at the coming of our Lord*, meaning that the completion of what our Lord is now beginning in us is being delayed until that time.[132]

Upon assuming his judgement seat, Christ will face two different camps. On the one side he will face those whose lives radiate a faith that has constantly sought 'to stretch forward to further progress'.[133] Moving under the direction of God, this faith has reached its full ripeness. The deeds of others, however, extend to heaven in a different way. The deeds of the evil – Calvin has in mind the Jews who Paul states are impeding the gospel's path – are as eschatological as the faithful pursuits of the godly. They too will find their end in God:

> This is why the punishment of the ungodly is often postponed – it is because their acts of ungodliness are so to speak not yet ripe.[134]

---

[124] *Comm. 1 Thess. 5:23.* See H. Quistorp, *Calvin's Doctrine of the Last Things*, tr. H. Knight (London: Lutterworth Press, 1955), p. 33.
[125] *Comm. 1 Thess. 2:12* (my italics). [126] *Comm. 1 Thess. 3:12.*
[127] *Comm. 1 Thess. 5:19.* Thus at *Comm. 1 Thess. 2:12*, Calvin juxtaposes the tension between call and response, that 'our salvation is based on God's free adoption of us . . . It now remains for us to respond to God's call, i.e. to show ourselves to be such children to Him as He is a Father to us.'
[128] *Comm. 1 Thess. 4:1, 10.* [129] *Comm. 1 Thess. 2:19.* [130] *Comm. 1 Thess. 1:2.*
[131] *Comm. 1 Thess. 4:16.* [132] *Comm. 1 Thess. 3:13.* [133] *Comm. 1 Thess. 4:1.*
[134] *Comm. 1 Thess. 2:16.*

2.2   The dualism between this world and the next

One way to sustain this relentless progress into godliness is to obtain a renewed perspective on the world. Calvin is well known for his pessimistic view of what can be attained from this world and from the state of our humanity,[135] and in his commentary on 1 Thessalonians he maintains a consistent dualism between the glories of the next world and the worthlessness of this world to which we are exiled.[136]

The world which we inhabit is continually interrupted by Satan's wily interferences, a distinctively apocalyptic note that runs throughout the commentary.[137] For Calvin, 'the life of Christians is like a perpetual warfare, because Satan does not cease to cause us trouble or to be filled with hatred towards us'.[138] The Christian's faith is based on a hope that there is a better world than this one in which we are marooned.[139] Despite the evidently barren nature of this world,[140] Christians hope in 'things not seen',[141] a faith waiting 'until we behold it in full':[142]

> Intent on the hope of the manifestation of Christ they [Christians] are to despise all other things, and armed with patience are to rise superior both to wearisome delay and all the temptations of the world.[143]

Unless we are secured and sustained by the hope of eternal life, we shall find ourselves drawn to the world.[144] This hope of an everlasting life itself stands radically apart from the world's understanding of death as 'the final destruction', an attitude resulting from a worldly arrogance that 'anything that is taken out of the world is lost'.[145] Calvin draws a parallel between this faith we have in God and the total separation between heaven and earth. As he remarks in his Philippians commentary, to be dead to the world is to be alive to Jesus.[146] One cannot have both the world and heaven; the eschatological decision must be made. Consequently, our hope in God's saving will 'is as far removed from conjecture as heaven is from the earth'.[147] As he or she trudges through the worldliness of

---

[135] *Comm. 1 Thess. 1:8.* R. W. Battenhouse, 'The Doctrine of Man in Calvin and in Renaissance Platonism', *Journal of the History of Ideas* 9 (1948), 462, usefully modifies Calvin's pessimism, and reminds us that the inverse of Calvin's apparent pessimism is an obvious optimism at what humanity should be.

[136] Calvin, *Institutes*, III.ix.4.

[137] *Comm. 1 Thess. 1:1, 8; 2:14, 18; 3:2, 5, 11; 5:8, 13, 27.*   [138] *Comm. 1 Thess. 5:8.*

[139] Faith and hope thus operate as virtual synonyms in Calvin's thought: *Institutes*, III.ii.42.

[140] Calvin, *Institutes*, III.ix.2.   [141] *Comm. 1 Thess. 1:9.*   [142] *Comm. 1 Thess. 4:16.*

[143] *Comm. 1 Thess. 1:3.*   [144] *Comm. 1 Thess. 1:9.*   [145] *Comm. 1 Thess. 4:13.*

[146] *Comm. Phil. 3:20.*   [147] *Comm. 1 Thess. 2:13.*

the world, the believer's inevitable weariness is allayed by 'the hope of Christ's coming', marking our 'final redemption'.[148] At this climactic stage, what is 'hidden' to the eyes of the flesh, and is now ours only as part of 'the secret delights of the spiritual life',[149] will be broadcast universally. What we are waiting for in hope is the decisive and culminating resurrection of the dead,[150] the point at which the whole man is called into eternal life with God.[151] Armed with this knowledge, the Christian should not grieve over the dead in the same way that non-believers do, for we 'depart from the world in order finally to be gathered into the kingdom of God'.[152]

The Christian, whose life in Christ provides a new hope for his or her ultimate end, has new spectacles through which to see the world properly. Placing all our hope in God and Christ, we shall see that there is 'nothing in the world to bear us up'.[153] As those who have been 'rescued' from the world's darkness,[154] the children of light (5:5) live in a world endowed with a keen sense of 'spiritual sobriety'.[155] Removed from the cares and attractions of this world, the Christian's 'whole mind' is now directed to the coming again of Christ.[156] To regard the world correctly is to view it through the perspective of its end, as something wretched we pass through on the way to something far more glorious. A life shaped by meditation on the future allows the whole of the Christian life to be viewed through the prism of this end.[157]

2.3   The obscurity of the future

Linked to Calvin's extreme pessimism about what the world can offer us by way of hope for the future is a consistent emphasis on the obscurity of the future. There are absolutely no resources in the world that can offer us any shape or principle for the timing of Christ's return. Just as the realm of God is far removed from the realm of human beings, so we cannot expect to find any clues in this world as to when Christ will return. Equally, this obscurity of the future is rooted in the characterisation of faith as eschatological in scope and direction (see section 2.1 above). We must be content with the 'brief glimpse of the magnificent and venerable

---

[148] *Comm. 1 Thess 1:9.*
[149] *Comm. 1 Thess. 1:9.* Cf. *Comm. 1 Thess. 5:3; Comm. 1 Cor. 15:21–2.*
[150] *Comm. 1 Cor. 15:18, 19.*   [151] *Comm. 1 Thess. 1:9; 5:23.*
[152] *Comm. 1 Thess. 4:13.*   [153] *Comm. 1 Thess. 1:10.*
[154] *Comm. 1 Thess. 5:4.*   [155] *Comm. 1 Thess. 5:6.*   [156] *Comm. 1 Thess. 1:9.*
[157] H. O. Oberman, '*Initia Calvini*: The Matrix of Calvin's Reformation', in W. H. Neuser, ed., *Calvinus Sacrae Scripturae Professor* (Grand Rapids: Eerdmans, 1994), p. 126.

appearance of the judge' given in Paul's letter,[158] for 'the meaning of that deliverance will be made plain on the last day'.[159] Just as God is in charge of our progress into full perfection, and as we await the clarification of what is now 'incredible',[160] so too we should not presume to look for signs of the time in the world around us.[161]

Christians must know that it is 'foolish to want to determine the time from presages and portents',[162] and instead must patiently await the return of Christ without the aid of hints or predictions. Indeed, it is for this very reason that Paul, who knew by a 'special revelation' that Christ would not come in his lifetime, implies he will still be alive at Christ's return:

> His purpose in doing this is to arouse the Thessalonians to wait
> for it, and to keep all the godly in suspense, so that they may not
> promise themselves some particular time.[163]

Whether or not Calvin is reacting against the fanaticism and various Spiritual enthusiasms of his time,[164] he evidently *is* keen that 1 Thessalonians is read with restraint. Consequently he emphasises what he regards as the central thrust of 1 Thess. 5:1–11, that excessive investigation into times and portents is 'a curious and unprofitable inquiry'.[165] This obscurity of the future is likewise developed in connection with what Calvin says about the symbolic language of 1 Thessalonians. There is a meaning of Scripture whose fullness is properly reserved. Calvin is evidently keen that we should banish our stupid imaginations[166] and keep the focus on 'spiritual sobriety';[167] the text of 1 Thessalonians will then not become a foil for the indulgence of our curiosity.[168]

2.4   The immortality of the soul

In parts of his commentary Calvin is clearly struggling against two exegetical groups. One group are those Anabaptists who advocated the doctrine of 'soul sleep', against whom Calvin pushed for the immortality of the soul; the other group are Enthusiastic Chiliasts, against whom Calvin asserts Christ's eternal reign (see section 2.5 below). The term 'Anabaptism' is in actual fact a less than satisfactory term to encompass a wide diversity of 'Radical Reformation' movements. It is disputed just how well acquainted Calvin was with the whole sweep of those

---

[158] *Comm. 1 Thess. 4:16.*   [159] *Comm. 1 Thess. 1:9.*   [160] *Comm. 1 Thess. 4:15.*
[161] Quistorp, *Calvin's Doctrine*, p. 114.   [162] *Comm. 1 Thess. 5:2.*
[163] *Comm. 1 Thess. 4:15.*   [164] Quistorp, *Calvin's Doctrine*, p. 113.
[165] *Comm. 1 Thess. 5:1.*   [166] Calvin, *Institutes*, I.xiii.1.
[167] *Comm. 1 Thess. 5:6.*   [168] *Comm. 1 Thess. 4:15.*

advocating some form of 'soul sleep', for while some held that the soul fell into a state of slumber at death to be revived at the resurrection of the body (pyschosomnolence), others held that the soul died with the body, only to be completely recovered with the resurrection of the body (thanatopsychism).

The particular problem in 1 Thess. 4:13f. is that when Paul talks of those who have fallen asleep in the Lord, he does not clarify whether he is referring to sleeping souls or sleeping bodies. For Calvin, however, there is no ambiguity:

> The reference, however, is not to the soul but to the body, for the dead body rests in a tomb as on a bed, until God raises the person up. Those, therefore, who conclude from this that it is souls which sleep, lack understanding.[169]

For Calvin the body sleeps, as though on a bed, and it is a gross misunderstanding to claim that the reference is to sleeping souls. It is the part of us that is perishable that withers away at our 'appointed death',[170] and sleeping 'as on a bed' it awaits its summoning arousal. The human person, animated by his or her soul, is to look upon the body as 'the house in which he dwells'.[171] After the 'prison house of the body' has died, the immortal and created essence of the soul remains in God's full stewardship.[172] When the text thus refers to our state of slumber it cannot be referring to the soul, for as Calvin indicates later in this commentary, the soul is 'the immortal spirit which dwells in his body'.[173] Calvin's brevity at this point of his commentary is all the clearer when juxtaposed with his denunciations of the 'cancer' that was the error about the sleeping soul in his 1542 anti-Anabaptist work *Psychopannychia*.[174] In the context of this 1 Thessalonians commentary, Calvin squared directly with those who read 1 Thess. 4:13 as a reference to 'soul sleep'. Contrary to this, Calvin was keen to place our death and resurrection in exact conformity to Jesus' death and resurrection, the model of our future. To believe that souls might sleep upon our death would imply that the soul of Jesus had been gripped by sleep.[175] Calvin wrestled with what he saw as the folly of soul sleep throughout his writings, as evidenced in the typically rhetorical plea from the *Institutes*:

---

[169] *Comm. 1 Thess. 4:13.*   [170] *Comm. 1 Thess. 2:16.*   [171] *Comm. 1 Thess. 4:3.*
[172] Calvin, *Institutes*, I.xv.2.   [173] *Comm. 1 Thess. 5:23.*
[174] J. Calvin, 'Psychopannychia', in *Tracts and Treatises in Defence of the Reformed Faith*, vol. III, tr. H. Beveridge, ed. T. F. Torrance (Edinburgh: Oliver and Boyd, 1958), p. 415.
[175] *Ibid.*, p. 458.

> Shall we say that souls rest in the graves, that from there they may
> hearken to Christ? Shall we not say rather that at his command
> bodies will be restored to the vigor which they had lost?[176]

We do not need here to explore the extent to which Calvin is being faithful
to the Biblical message of the resurrection of the dead, or whether he is
importing into his exegesis remnants of classical philosophy, a debate
prominent in recent Calvin studies.[177] Some have argued that he operates
with an un-Christian and Platonic dualism. From the perspective of this
commentary, however, the dualism with which Calvin is most clearly
operating is that between spirit and flesh:

> let us learn to fear the vengeance of God which is hidden to
> the eye of flesh, and take our rest in the secret delights of the
> spiritual life.[178]

In this brief commentary Calvin does indeed refer to the body as the
soul's dwelling place; similarly, in the *Institutes* the body is sometimes
understood as a 'prison'.[179] Likewise, he refers cryptically to the mission of the church as 'the eternal salvation of souls'.[180] He manifestly
stands closer to the Platonic understanding of the soul, as opposed to the
Aristotelian conception.[181] What would appear to be crucial for Calvin
is that our fleshly existence in the body is something awaiting its own
redemption through immortality. The soul is thus 'freed' from the body,
not because of an imposition of a Platonic dualism, but because our bodily
existence, as Calvin sees it, is weighed down by our fleshly, corrupt existence.[182] Far from setting body and soul against each other, he alludes
to their essentially holistic salvation. Only when God raises the 'man'
('hominem') up from his tomb[183] is our body's integrity restored to us
in full.[184] Our bodily resurrection marks, for Calvin, the disposal of our
body's 'quality',[185] the shedding of that fleshly part of us which is corrupt and a 'defilement'.[186] Eternal life, the 'final resurrection' that will
free us from the flesh's 'impelling force',[187] is thus the restoration of *the*

---

[176] Calvin, *Institutes*, III.xxv.7.

[177] See C. Partee, 'Soul and Body in Anthropology', in *Calvin and Classical Philosophy*
(Leiden: E. J. Brill, 1977), pp. 51–65.

[178] *Comm. 1 Thess. 1:9.*   [179] Calvin, *Institutes*, III.vi.5, ix.4.

[180] *Comm. 1 Thess. 5:12.*   [181] Calvin, *Institutes*, I.v.5, 11.

[182] Calvin, 'Psychopannychia', p. 443.

[183] *CO* 52:164; my translation (on 1 Thess. 4:13).

[184] Calvin, *Institutes*, I.xv.4   [185] *Comm. 1 Thess. 4:16.*

[186] *Comm. 1 Thess. 4:3.* See also *Comm. 1 Cor. 15:50.*

[187] *Comm. 1 Thess. 4:15; 1:6.*

whole of the individual. Expositing Paul's reference to the 'spirit and soul and body' in 1 Thess. 5:23, Calvin articulates a holistic approach to our salvation, reminding us that 'Paul . . . commits to God the keeping of the whole man with all its parts.'[188]

2.5   Calvin's opposition to Chiliasm

The second school of thought which Calvin denudes of any standing is that which he appears to associate with Origen: Chiliasm.[189] Calvin's exegesis of 4:17 is set out in opposition to 'the aberrations of Origen and of the Chialists'.[190] Calvin identifies with Origen the teaching (based on Rev. 20:1–7) that believers would live with Christ in a yet to be renewed earth for the limited time span of a thousand years. This is an interpretation to which Calvin is vigorously opposed, not least because it would mean that Christ was limited to reigning for only a thousand years, which 'is too horrible to speak of'.[191] In limiting our lives with Christ to only a thousand years, such foolish interpretations degrade Christ, for it is clear that 'believers must live with Christ for as long as He himself will exist'.[192] Christ's life and believers' lives now intertwined, to speak of one is to speak of the other, and so to degrade the hope of our lives is to drag down the glory of Christ, as Calvin indicates in his brief refutation of Chiliasm in the *Institutes*:

> Those who assign the children of God a thousand years in which to enjoy the inheritance of the life to come do not realize how much reproach they are casting upon Christ and his Kingdom.[193]

Believers thus should look forward to nothing but the eternal kingdom, 'the promise of eternal life with Him'.[194] Christ has defeated death and so lives eternally. Christians must believe that this same power, which Jesus enjoys in union with God, will be communicated to them,[195] is indeed already at work in them,[196] and will call them into eternity. The manifestation of Christ's glory being far greater than our childish imaginations,

---

[188] *Comm. 1 Thess. 5:23.*

[189] This is curious, since it is well attested that Origen resisted millenarianism. See C. E. Hill, *Regnum Caelorum: Patterns of Future Hope in Early Christianity* (Oxford: Clarendon Press, 1992), pp. 127–41 *inter alia*. It is interesting that in *Institutes*, III.xxv.5, the only other place where Calvin combats Chiliasm, Origen is not mentioned.

[190] *Comm. 1 Thess. 4:17.*   [191] *Ibid.*   [192] *Ibid.*

[193] Calvin, *Institutes*, III.xxv.5. See Quistorp, *Calvin's Doctrine*, pp. 158–62, for discussion of Chiliasm and Calvin.

[194] *Comm. 1 Thess. 4:17.*   [195] *Comm. 1 Thess. 3:11.*   [196] *Comm. 1 Thess. 2:13.*

Christ's reign points to a time 'when sin is blotted out, death swallowed up, and everlasting life fully restored!'.[197]

2.6   The universal transformation

In his remarks on 4:16–17 Calvin engages directly with the exegesis of Augustine. For Calvin, the sudden change when we are taken up into the clouds will be 'like death', for when the living are taken up, the destruction of their 'flesh' will suffice as a 'kind of death' ('mortis species').[198] Thus both the living and the dead shall rise into the presence of Christ, and there need be no contradiction with Paul's statement in 1 Cor. 15:36 that a seed cannot grow again unless it dies.

Augustine is not so easily reconciled to these possible tensions in Paul's thinking. In *The City of God*, XX, a section explicitly mentioned by Calvin, Augustine wrestles with the apparent problem – are those who will be found alive upon Jesus' return never to experience death? Augustine considers the possibility that while we are being carried through the air, the living pass with 'wondrous swiftness' from death to immortality.[199] For Augustine, it is not an option merely to state that 'it is impossible for them to die and to come to life again while they are being borne aloft through the air'.[200] He focuses on the clouds, or the air in which we shall meet Jesus. For Augustine, Paul's statement that 'we shall ever be with the Lord' (4:17) is a statement that expresses our state of eternal life in union with Jesus. In such a state we shall have 'everlasting bodies', and so be with Jesus Christ 'everywhere'.[201] Logically, therefore, there can be no possibility that it is the air in which we are to remain for ever.

Augustine's concern is the contradiction-free unity of Scripture's witness. Nevertheless, the words of Paul in 1 Cor. 15:22, 'That which thou sowest is not quickened, except it die', are difficult to reconcile with those of Paul in 1 Thessalonians, unless there is some form of death. For Augustine, if men are to rise to the new life of immortality, then in some way they will have had to 'return to the earth by dying'.[202] For not only is the integrity of Paul's words in 1 Corinthians in jeopardy, but so too is the very post-Fall punishment of Genesis: that 'Dust thou art, and unto dust shalt thou return' (Gen. 3:19). Augustine thinks he is faced with the possibility that 'we shall have to confess that those whom Christ will find still in their bodies when He comes are not included in the words of

---

[197] Calvin, *Institutes*, III.xxv.5.   [198] *Comm. 1 Thess. 4:16*; *CO* 52:167.
[199] Augustine, *City of God*, XX/20.   [200] *Ibid.*   [201] *Ibid.*   [202] *Ibid.*

the apostle and of Genesis. For, being caught up in the clouds, they are certainly not "sown", since regardless of whether they undergo no death at all or die for a little moment in the air, they neither go into the earth nor return to it.'[203]

Augustine gets out of this apparent impasse by appealing to 1 Cor. 15:51, which, in its clear reference to πάντες, refers to a change in the state of 'all'. Focusing on the transformation that will be experienced by 'all', Augustine returns to his earlier supposition and states that there would seem to be no difficulty in holding that as we are caught up, even the living will experience a short 'sleep'. Augustine's appeal is that if we can believe in the miracle of the resurrection of the dead, we can surely believe that in the ascent through the air, those still in their bodies will pass swiftly from mortality to immortality. But the question still remains: how does Augustine reconcile this 'sowing' in the air with the clear teaching of Genesis that 'Dust thou art, and unto dust shalt thou return'? For Augustine this need not mean that when we die our bodies have to return to the earth; it can be understood as essentially meaning 'When you lose your life, you will return to what you were before you received life.'[204] Thus wherever we die (in the air or on earth) and whenever we die, we cannot but help return to the form in which we were before we received life. Perhaps aware of his somewhat contorted reasoning – arising from the apparent contradictions in 1 Thessalonians 4 and 1 Corinthians 15 – Augustine concludes his exposition with the thought that

> with our inadequate powers of reasoning, we can only guess at how this is to come to pass; and we shall not be able to know until after it has happened.[205]

Augustine's prime concern is Scripture's unity, and that what it says in one place cannot be contradicted in another. In this sense he reads like a much more canonically concerned reader than Calvin would appear at first reading.[206]

Calvin notes the 'great difficulty' Augustine has with this passage, and states, with perhaps not totally uncharacteristic immodesty, that the solution is 'easy'.[207] Augustine's wrestling with this text operates as a foil to Calvin's conviction that the meaning of Scripture is clear and obvious. Its meaning need not be in doubt, for those of faith know that Scripture's piercing brightness is its perspicuous quality. For Calvin, moreover, the

---

[203] *Ibid.* [204] *Ibid.* [205] *Ibid.*

[206] See excursus 2 below for Augustine's further exegesis of these passages.

[207] *Comm. 1 Thess. 4:16.* This confidence is found elsewhere: see *Institutes*, III.xxv.8.

authority of the Fathers was always *functional* and *pragmatic*: should they clutter up the path to discovering the mind of the author, they could always be neatly cast aside.

In effect, Calvin appeals to another verse from the Pauline corpus: that it is the corruptible flesh that will be transformed in the act of being caught up is clear from the reference of 2 Cor. 5:4, that 'what is mortal may be swallowed up by life'. This will be a 'kind of death',[208] a death which, as Calvin implies, and makes clear elsewhere in the commentary, will not necessitate a separation of body and soul.[209] Turning to his own metaphorical reading of death, Calvin appears to poke fun at Augustine's literal rendering of the creed which speaks of Jesus being judge of 'the dead and of the living', a reading which leads to Augustine's wandering confusions.[210] If, like Calvin, he had concentrated on the destruction of the flesh at the general resurrection, then he would have seen that while the dead put off the substance for a space of time, the living will rise to put off nothing but the quality (in that they will rise with the same body, but will enjoy incorruptibility whereas before they had been subject to corruption).[211] Those still alive at Christ's return will then have their corruptible flesh transformed suddenly and directly by Christ's 'power',[212] and will not have to undergo any state in which their body slumbers.

For Calvin, the return of Christ will communicate definitively and conclusively to all believers – dead and alive – the salvation he has already achieved within himself. Thus Calvin writes that salvation is something already 'acquired for us by Christ',[213] for even now 'Christ by His death has delivered us from the wrath of God.'[214] Believers, however, await that glory which Christ enjoys now, for it was for this reason that Jesus rose from the dead. United to Christ as 'Head',[215] those who are members of Christ's body can be assured of their final resurrection. To be sure, through the Spirit who dwells in us, this wondrous exchange which Christ initiated is already in process, for 'those who are ingrafted into Christ by faith share death in common with him, in order that they may share with Him in life'.[216] Believers, therefore, are to place their hope in the universal resurrection, at which point our corrupt flesh will be revived and we shall become sharers in his glory.[217] Only with the resurrection of the dead will the quality of our 'greatly corrupted nature' be put off, so that we

---

[208] *Comm. 1 Thess. 4:16.*   [209] *Ibid.*   [210] *Ibid.*   [211] *Ibid.*   [212] *Ibid.*

[213] *Comm. 1 Thess. 5:9.*   [214] *Comm. 1 Thess. 1:9.*   [215] *Comm. 1 Thess. 4:18.*

[216] *Comm. 1 Thess. 4:14.* So also *Comm. 1 Thess. 5:10,* 'we are passing from death into life'.

[217] *Comm. 1 Thess. 2:19.*

can receive our 'final redemption'.[218] Christ's return therefore points to
the full effect of his resurrection, the enfolding of his believers within his
power,[219] the extension 'to the whole body of the Church [of] the fruit
and effect of that power which He displayed in Himself'.[220]

3 Conclusions

It is time to take our leave of the concluding image in Part I – that of
pressing the text forward into a ceaselessly progressive momentum – and
to conclude with some thoughts about how Calvin is likely to affect an
expansive reading of 1 Thessalonians.

Calvin's reading of the text is based on a resolve to pay attention to
nothing but the words,[221] an earnest desire to stay very close to the text
at all times. I agree that any interpretation of 1 Thessalonians must be
accountable and responsible to what is there in the text, but would disagree with how Calvin mixes the literal sense with the spiritual sense.
For Calvin, the literal sense *is* the spiritual sense, and this singularity is
attained by the faithful individual who reads the text for its inner, spiritual meaning. It is the *single, undisputed* meaning of the text that is its
penetrating quality,[222] and hence at various points in the commentary we
witnessed Calvin shutting down meaning and closing down any option
of ambiguity. There is little scope in Calvin's hermeneutics for the depth
of Scripture's meaning and referent, rather a shrill insistence that the
faithful individual alone can grasp Scripture's uncomplicated, unadorned
message. Cutting itself off from any dependence on the church's collective memory, the singularity of the text's meaning, the attempt to grasp
Paul's Spirit-inspired mind, would before long become intermeshed in the
historical-critical drive for the reconstructed author's intention, the fateful move extensively critiqued in chapter 1. In the course of this chapter,
attention has frequently been drawn to the tense nature of Calvin's exegesis, and it is clear that in his use of humanist techniques of reading, his
deployment of the canon and his employment of tradition he stands very
much on the cusp of modernity.

Running against Calvin's desire for 'spiritual sobriety'[223] is my belief
that connecting the text with the whole Spirit-led tradition of the church
exposes the infinitely contestable meaning of the text to its ultimate depth.
Whilst I concur with Calvin's serious reading of the text, I ultimately

---

[218] *Comm. 1 Thess. 1:9.* Calvin refers pessimistically to our fleshly existence in *Comm.
1 Thess. 1:6, 9; 4:3; 5:19.*
[219] *Comm. 1 Thess. 5:10.*   [220] *Comm. 1 Thess. 1:10.*   [221] *Comm. 2 Cor. 10:12.*
[222] *Comm. Isa. 45:19.*   [223] *Comm. 1 Thess. 5:6.*

disagree about how we can claim to 'hold Paul's meaning'.[224] Holding Paul's meaning, for this study, will be predicated on the assumption that the text itself is a bearer of plurivocality, not univocality. Crucially, however, I would hold that this multiplicity of meaning is not something imposed on the text, but is *proposed* by the text's witness, and *supported* by tradition (not least Calvin's commentary!). Equally, I would be keen to display the potential of a reading that exposed itself to the richness of the canonical conversation, a possibility which Calvin is reluctant to countenance (no doubt out of fears that Scripture's all-important simplicity might be lost). Calvin's highly individualistic understanding of the relationship between the believer and Scripture, coupled with his fondness for exegetical clarity, leaves us very uneasy in relation to his seemingly arbitrary pleas about what is the 'main point',[225] what is 'essential'[226] and what is 'pointless'.[227] In these important ways I disagree with Calvin as to how we encounter 'the pure Word of God'.[228]

To turn now to Calvin's theology, as opposed to his hermeneutics, he maintains a most impressive dialectic between the transcendence of the future and salvation as a principle already at work in the world. Here, much more than in his distracted reflections on the soul and the body, Calvin is being faithful to Paul's driving concern, that salvation is both something achieved and at work (5:9–10) and something that will manifest itself in a mode outside our expectations (5:2). This notion of an eschatological faith, a faith already sharing in the life of the risen Christ and orientated towards the full sharing of his glory, is a theological insight that I will be keen to develop in Part III. Central to Paul's concern is that the Thessalonians must see the dead as they really are, 'passing from death into life'.[229] This faith in the climactic resurrection of the dead, the triumphant outworking of God's power to all the 'members of Christ', is,[230] as Calvin recognises, faith in that which is as yet unseen and seemingly impossible in the eyes of the world. In his stress on the future's transcendence Calvin points to faith in the apparently impossible becoming possible, an insight at the very heart of the resurrection hope:

> Eternal life is promised to us, but it is promised to the dead; we are told of the resurrection of the blessed, but meantime we are involved in corruption; we are declared to be just, and sin dwells within us; we hear that we are blessed, but meantime we are overwhelmed by untold miseries . . . God proclaims that He will come to us immediately, but seems to be deaf to our cries.[231]

[224] *CO* 52:165, 'Tenemus nunc Pauli mentem.'   [225] *Comm. 1 Thess. 4:13.*
[226] *Comm. 1 Thess. 5:10.*   [227] *Comm. 1 Thess. 5:8.*   [228] *Comm. 1 Thess. 2:13.*
[229] *Comm. 1 Thess. 5:10.*   [230] *Comm. 1 Thess. 4:18.*   [231] *Comm. Heb. 11:1.*

Excursus 1 – Calvin as a pre-modern exegete

The term 'pre-critical' is actually a less than satisfactory term used to describe the hermeneutical methods of exegetes like Thomas and John Calvin. The problem with this rather loaded term is its implication that there have been two periods that can be neatly compartmentalised as 'pre-critical' and 'critical'. As a result it ignores the inevitable overlap between these two periods. Augustine and Jerome raised textual issues, and Calvin was certainly aware of issues of authorship, disputing the Pauline authorship of Hebrews. Hence the reference to *pre-modern* readings of 1 Thessalonians in the title of this part of the book.

Thomas O'Loughlin has helpfully suggested that we focus less on categorising eras by *method* and more on what the exegete wants to *find* in his interpretation.[232] Where for 'modern' exegetes the texts of Scripture are part of a successive religious history, for 'pre-modern' exegetes the text is understood Christocentrically, and all exegesis is directed towards the understanding of Christ. In this sense Calvin would certainly appear to be 'pre-modern'. His method involved aspects which we might understand now as 'critical', but his end was clear:

> Christ cannot be properly known from anywhere but the Scriptures. And if that is so, it follows that the Scriptures should be read with the aim of finding Christ in them.[233]

Excursus 2 – Augustine on the tension between 1 Thess. 4:16–17 and 1 Corinthians 15

That a possible contradiction between Paul's teaching in 1 Thessalonians 4 and 1 Corinthians 15 continued to vex Augustine after *The City of God* is evident from the 'Eight Questions of Dulcitius' (c. 422).[234] Here Augustine is responding to the third query of Dulcitius, 'whether those who are lifted up in the clouds will be delivered unto death, unless, perchance, we should accept this change as a substitute for death?'.[235] Augustine dwells first on the literal meaning of the text, 'that certain ones, when the Lord comes at the end of the world and there is to be the resurrection of the dead, will not die, but, found living, will be changed suddenly into that immortality which is given to the other saints'.[236] But

---

[232] T. O'Loughlin, 'Christ and the Scriptures: The Chasm between Modern and Pre-Modern Exegesis', *The Month* 31 (1998), 475–85.

[233] *Comm. Jn.* 5:39.

[234] Augustine, 'Eight Questions of Dulcitius', in *Saint Augustine: Treatises on Various Subjects*, ed. R. J. Deferrari, tr. M. S. Muldowney et al. (FOC 16; Washington: Catholic University of America Press, 1952), pp. 427–66.

[235] *Ibid.*, p. 446.　　[236] *Ibid.*, p. 447.

no sooner has he clarified this than he seems dissatisfied with it, wrestling with his belief that all must die before they are resurrected, and holding out for the learned men who could convince him of another meaning in the face of that which 'the words themselves seem to cry out'.[237] If, at the return of Christ, that which the texts appear to cry out is verified (that those who are alive will not experience death), Augustine surmises, we shall have to return to the canonical texts which would seem to suggest otherwise. But Augustine is so troubled by Paul's apparent teaching in 1 Thess. 4:16–17 that he concludes by imploring Dulcitius to send him anything he has read on the subject.[238]

---

[237] *Ibid.*, p. 448.   [238] *Ibid.*

4

CONCLUSION TO PART II

Three centuries separating them and emerging from divergent confessional traditions, Thomas Aquinas and John Calvin are rarely studied within the same volume. Notwithstanding this novelty, it is worth recalling that our turn to these pre-modern voices arose from the critique mounted in chapter 1 of recent historical-critical treatment of 1 Thessalonians. Focus on 1 Thessalonians' history of interpretation was inspired by the conviction that God's revelation in Christ is a dynamic process, revealed in time and through the tradition of the church's reading of Scripture. We hoped that from Part II we might both learn new things about the reality generating 1 Thessalonians and recover exegetical methods we could deploy in Part III of the monograph.

Before launching into Part III it is necessary, in this short section, to reflect comparatively on *how* both Thomas and Calvin read the profundity of 1 Thessalonians. At the back of our minds, as we do so, will be the programmatic critiques set out in Part I. We shall then examine to what extent together they have exposed the witness of the text, or its ultimate reality, as a route into the task of Part III.

Attention to the text

For both Thomas and Calvin the text, and what its actual words say, holds an unassailably regnant position. There are, however, a number of differences in the way that Thomas and Calvin read the words of the text, as words of Scripture.

For Thomas the words of Paul in 1 Thessalonians are understood by reference to words from both Paul's other writings *and* the whole of the rest of the canon. As argued, this openness to the resonance of the canon is founded on a conviction that Scripture's meaning is ultimately grounded in divine providence. Calvin's reading differs in that there is much more attention to the philological and linguistic aspects of the letter (a feature entirely missing from Thomas' reading), a drive which encourages reading the human authors of the Bible as literary personalities. It requires little imagination to see the link between the historical-critical project's separation of the form and content of Scripture, and Calvin's dual stress on 'spiritual sobriety',[1] and attention to the 'mind' of the author.[2] Since he stresses the literary features of the *individual* letter, there is in Calvin the genesis of the Bible's fragmentation into a library of unrelated, historically situated books. This is a development hinted at by his notable reluctance to relate 1 Thessalonians to the rest of the canon.

Calvin's measure and restraint, not least in his use of the canon, is intriguing when compared to the fecundity of providential meaning which Thomas encourages with his understanding of the canon as a vast echo chamber. As alluded to above, Calvin's push for 'the single true sense of the text'[3] was fateful, and stands uneasily beside the vision articulated in Part I of a text whose fullness of meaning is ceaselessly progressive. Calvin was inherently suspicious of those who talked of Scripture's meaning being hidden or difficult to obtain,[4] as for him the purity of Scripture's meaning was discerned through attention to the author's inspired mind. Thomas, in contrast, allows for a certain 'excess of meaning' to break out through his wide use of the canon. This is a method that sits more comfortably with the ceaselessly expansive reading outlined in Part I. Nevertheless, it is worth noting that Thomas and Calvin share a preference for understanding Paul by Paul, and this is a trait I plan to mirror equally in Part III.

To clarify, for both Thomas and Calvin there is no Stendahlian distinction between what the text meant and what it means now. For both Thomas and Calvin, what it meant *is* what it means, and vice versa. Neither read the text as sources (as seen in the discussion of J. A. D. Weima in chapter 1 above), and both, in their own ways, read the text as a record of Paul's apostolic witness. Nevertheless, Calvin lays the foundations for the reading of Biblical texts as historical texts, an assumption that before we state what a Biblical text means, we must begin by reconstructing what it meant. First, as already noted, there is the separation of 1 Thessalonians from its canonical context, a prejudice that reveals a preference for reading the text as situated in its historical context of production. Secondly, there is the fondness for reading 1 Thessalonians in its Greek

---

[1] *Comm. 1 Thess. 5:6.*   [2] *Comm. 1 Thess. 4:13.*

[3] B. S. Childs, 'The *Sensus Literalis* of Scripture: An Ancient and Modern Problem', in H. Doner, R. Hanhart and R. Smend, eds., *Bëitrage zur Alttestamentlichen Theologie: Festschrift für Walther Zimmerli zum 70. Geburtstag* (Göttingen: Vandenhoeck and Ruprecht, 1977), p. 87.

[4] *Comm. 1 Peter* (dedication).

original and the noted sensitivity to linguistic idioms. The cry of *ad fontes*, whilst at one level representing a rebuff of the Roman Church Vulgate, further emphasised the reading of Biblical texts as historical texts. As we saw in James Dunn's defence of historical criticism, attention to Greek and Hebrew can easily be aligned with a conviction that to understand the meaning of a text, or the intention of its author (often conflated), is to appreciate that the text's historical context provides the normative reference point for the text's contemporary meaning.[5]

I am not claiming that Calvin was himself a mature historical-critical scholar. His evident Patristic literacy, for example, is striking. Likewise, for both Thomas and Calvin there is an unassailable conviction that Scripture cannot contradict itself. Nevertheless, in relation to Calvin, much more than can be said for Thomas, there is an uncomfortably close relationship between his exegetical method and the historical criticism identified and critiqued in Part I. Kicking away tradition's role as an organic link between text and church, and counselling a 'spiritual sobriety',[6] Calvin's enthusiasm for the 'mind of the author' easily and without much effort became the quest of historical criticism.[7] It requires little imagination to discern the trajectory linking the Reformation 'sola Scriptura' principle with the Enlightenment and historical-critical projects that swept away the notion of the Bible as a treasury of meaning in favour of the quest for a single, determinate meaning.[8]

Theological contribution

The *results* of Thomas' and Calvin's exegesis make for an equally interesting comparison. As we saw, Calvin's reading of 1 Thessalonians is heavily eschatological, a reading that infiltrates every level of his exegesis of the letter. He reads it, not by individually examining pericopes in isolation from each other, but by being gripped by that which Paul was gripped by – God's eschatological triumph in Christ – and following that through in every part of his reading. As argued in the conclusions to chapter 3, Calvin's eschatology – both its transcendence and its outworking in the world already – is immensely fruitful.

---

[5] Dunn, 'Historical Text', p. 347.   [6] *Comm. 1 Thess. 5:6.*

[7] *Comm. Rom.* (dedication). For the links between modern historical scholarship and the humanism in which, as we saw, Calvin was so proficient see D. R. Kelley, *Foundations of Modern Historical Scholarship: Language, Law and History in the French Renaissance* (New York: Columbia University Press, 1970).

[8] A. Louth, *Discerning the Mystery: An Essay on the Nature of Theology* (Oxford: Clarendon Press, 1983), pp. 96–101.

Thomas' contribution to a theological reading of 1 Thessalonians is distinct, though one we intend to utilise no less keenly. Motivated by the conviction that what Paul communicates is really true, Thomas follows through with utter seriousness Paul's remarkable witness of 1 Thess. 4:14, and in so doing points to a way of combining eschatology, soteriology and Christology. Such theological rigour is worth trying to follow in Part III.

Thomas' and Calvin's readings thus complement each other. We draw from Thomas the desire to understand theologically – as much as it is possible to dare to understand Paul's revelation – the central claim of 1 Thess. 4:13–18. But likewise we draw from Calvin the willingness and desire that this insight must be conformed to the whole of 1 Thessalonians, as a revelation into God's saving will that can be related to all of 1 Thessalonians, even as it lies at its centre. For those like Gerald Shepphard, the results of Calvin's reading of 1 Thessalonians demonstrate his commitment to the 'scope' of Biblical books, an interpretative move which faithfully relates the disparate parts of the text to the literary theme or argument of the whole text.[9]

We should be careful, however, not to end on a note which uncritically valorises either Thomas' or Calvin's commentaries. There is in both of their commentaries a marked stress on the immortality of the soul, an emphasis which, although held in tension with an emphasis on bodily resurrection, some would see as a remarkably *un*-Pauline drive. Likewise, there are aspects of both Thomas' and Calvin's comments on the reaction of the Jews to the Gospel which we would be happy to leave in their respective centuries.[10]

Overwhelmingly, however, turning to Thomas and Calvin in reaction to the ossifying tendencies of historical criticism has provided fertile new methods of reading 1 Thessalonians. In distinction from interpreters like J. D. G. Dunn, both Thomas and Calvin have endeavoured to keep the text and its subject matter bound together, and both (in their different ways) read this subject matter as God's eschatological triumph in Christ. Although in many ways, Calvin reads like a midwife to historical criticism, his reading of the text, just like Thomas', is governed more by its subject matter than by judgements about its historical context. Their readings have helped us to see new ways to deploy the canon, to turn

---

[9] G. T. Shepphard, 'Between Reformation and Modern Commentary: The Perception of the Scope of Biblical Books', in *A Commentary – Galatians, William Perkins*, ed. G. T. Shepphard (New York: Pilgrim Press, 1989), pp. xlviii–lxxvii.

[10] *Lectio* II.II.46–8; *Comm. 1 Thess. 2:14–16.*

to the Fathers when they act as guardians of the Word, to seek with full earnestness the driving force of Paul's conviction, and to read with utmost seriousness the apex of Paul's revelation which he makes known in 1 Thess. 4:13f.: that Christ holds dominion over death. This seriousness with which Thomas and Calvin read Paul's eschatological witness will provide the impetus for the reading of 1 Thessalonians proposed in Part III.

PART III

A proposed reading of 1 Thessalonians

5

DEATH AND RESURRECTION IN 1 THESSALONIANS

Introduction

Were it not for the insights accrued from both Thomas' and Calvin's commentaries on 1 Thessalonians, it would be difficult to discern what interpretative strategies should be prioritised in this proposed theological interpretation of 1 Thessalonians. Calvin evidenced the importance and vitality of an eschatological vision, a vision loyal to the whole of 1 Thessalonians, operating with a tension between the transcendence of the future and salvation as a principle already at work in the world. We saw in Thomas' commentary the potential of a Christological sensitivity to the exegesis of the resurrection's causality charted by the apostle Paul in 1 Thess. 4:14.

Standing in this corporate endeavour to understand Paul, like Thomas we shall want to wrestle with the causality of Christ's resurrection, about how the One who died and rose for us is the pledge of our future salvation. And echoing Calvin, we shall be keen to develop a mode of reading which has at its core Paul's own eschatological witness, but demonstrates that the resurrection of the dead not only comprises the 'crown of the whole Epistle, but also provides the clue to its meaning, from which place light is shed on the whole, and it becomes intelligible, not outwardly, but inwardly, as a unity'.[1]

Critical fidelity to Thomas' and Calvin's exegetical insights, using their readings as tools in our own conceptual expansion of Paul's witness, implies that a number of things can be expected in this chapter's method *and* focus. An attempt will be made to integrate and display a combined loyalty to Paul and to the canon; to deploy Christian tradition where it acts as servant to unfold Paul's teaching; to read the entirety of 1 Thessalonians around what both Thomas and Calvin believe to be at its heart, its eschatological subject matter; and to investigate how a focus

---

[1] K. Barth, *The Resurrection of the Dead*, tr. H. J. Stenning (London: Hodder and Stoughton, 1933), p. 11.

on Christ can recapture the force of Paul's witness. The mode of reading we shall develop in this chapter deliberately stands in contrast to the historical-critical readings critiqued in chapter 1.

Our theological reading of 1 Thessalonians will have at its centre the attempt to make sense of Paul's witness in 1 Thess. 4:14, 'For since we believe that Jesus died and rose again, even so, through Jesus, God will bring with him those who have died' (εἰ γὰρ πιστεύομεν ὅτι Ἰησοῦς ἀπέθανεν καὶ ἀνέστη, οὕτως καὶ ὁ θεὸς τοὺς κοιμηθέντας διὰ τοῦ Ἰησοῦ ἄξει σὺν αὐτῷ).

The prime loyalty is to the text itself, and the understanding of this text *through* the canon, Paul's corpus in particular. Such a hermeneutical decision is likely to attract the suspicion of Biblical scholars with a preference for carving up the canon and allotting specific pieces of it to reconstructed periods of religious history. For many historical critics, even the mere act of interpreting 1 Thessalonians with the assistance of the remaining Pauline *Hauptbriefe* would represent an unjustifiable trespass on the hallowed ground of historical particularity. Our persistence in reading the canon to help us understand 1 Thessalonians does not, however, merely arise out of a naïve cheerfulness that the hermeneutical strategies of the pre-modern era can be neatly transposed into our time. A quite specific theological justification can be advanced for the kind of reading deployed in the course of this chapter.

Paul writes, as consistently stressed above, as a witness to revelation, willing us to perceive what he perceives more clearly than we do. In other words, the unavoidable humanity of Paul, his particular advice to specific Christian communities, is the miraculous instrument of God's Word.[2] Wholly in line with this dogmatic location of Paul's role is a confident articulation of Scripture's *ontological* status. Scripture is a unified witness to God's saving will, and is read correctly when viewed as a collection of texts set apart by God for these saving purposes. This is what the canon, to put it boldly, *is*: texts appropriated by God so that we may know his will for all of humanity. Such an approach, as John Webster forcefully articulates,[3] undoubtedly represents a considerable assault on the dominance of immanent, historicising and political readings of the canon. So familiar are we with such readings of the canon that talk of the canon in specific relationship to *God*'s purposes seems bizarre and alien. This is essentially a theological and spiritual malaise, for it is theologians

---

[2] G. C. Berkouwer, *Holy Scripture*, tr. J. B. Rogers (Grand Rapids: Eerdmans, 1975), p. 203.
[3] J. B. Webster, 'The Dogmatic Location of the Canon', in *Word and Church: Essays in Christian Dogmatics* (Edinburgh: T. & T. Clark, 2001), pp. 9–46.

who have neglected their duty to demonstrate that the miracle of grace operates through and with Scripture's patent humanity, not in spite of it.

In terms of interpretative practice, the doctrine of the canon reminds us that sensitivity to the uniqueness of each Biblical author's voice must be properly balanced by a willingness to read each Biblical voice in company with the other voices.[4] As an instance of dogmatics, such a practice is simply done before it is apologetically justified. The principal office of *theological* exegesis, at least in this particular setting, is to make known the outworkings of an approach that takes seriously Scripture's ultimate reality, that its being is in the saving activity of God.

If theological exegesis is undertaken in dialogue with the canon, so too does it turn to those readers of Scripture whose insights are the classical backdrop for the church's articulation of the Gospel. The theological dialogue partners we engage with in this chapter will incorporate selected Fathers of the East and West up to John Damascene's death in 749 CE; Thomas Aquinas; the medieval Byzantine theologian Gregory Palamas (1296–1359); John Calvin; Karl Rahner; Karl Barth; and contemporary Orthodox theologians. There is a deliberate eclecticism to the range of voices I aim to draw upon here, with representatives from the Roman Catholic, Orthodox, Anglican, Reformed and Byzantine traditions and the Patristic period all making appearances at points in this chapter. The purpose of drawing on these disparate voices is not to reduce or belittle the very real differences amongst them, but to attempt to bring the richness of Christian tradition (insofar as this chapter can represent it) into conversation with 1 Thessalonians, and so to expose to ever greater depth the witness or ultimate content of this text.

The persistent refrain of this chapter, that attention to the work of God in Christ has the capacity to unravel Paul's meaning, might sound neo-Patristic. In this sense I *am* saying that Christ is the central mystery of this text, a theme prominent in Calvin's exegesis and one that can be traced back to Patristic meditation on the ultimate meaning of Scripture.[5]

To put it simply, the reading of 1 Thessalonians which follows will be 'around Christ',[6] a task that implies both seeking the whole meaning of Christ within Scripture *and* treating the person and work of Christ

---

[4] See O. Weber, *Foundations of Dogmatics*, vol. I, tr. D. L. Guder (Grand Rapids: Eerdmans, 1981), p. 268.

[5] See the exposition of Cyril of Alexandria's Christ-ruled reading of Scripture in R. L. Wilken, 'St. Cyril of Alexandria: The Mystery of Christ in the Bible', *Pro Ecclesia* 4 (1995), 454–78.

[6] R. Williams, 'Reading the Bible', in *Open to Judgement* (London: Darton, Longman and Todd, 1994), p. 160.

with rigour (insofar as it is patently crucial to know more about the person around whom we are reading the text). Understanding the text and understanding Christ are thus radically reinforcing components of our attempt to do 'theology exegetically and exegesis theologically'.[7]

It is now necessary to set out something of what the exegesis will actually look like. In section 1, the interfaces between eschatological assertions and hermeneutics will be identified. These reflections will provide an initial foundation for articulating eschatological assertions about Christ, the central motif of the exegesis.

In section 2, Paul's contribution will be examined, and some of the parameters in which he must be placed will be set out. There will be a critique of those who would marginalise the creeds in 1 Thessalonians of most import to us (section 2.1), and whilst it will be held that Paul displays no interest in the ontological aspects of Christology, it will be argued that 1 Thessalonians presents in primordial form a strong, saving relationship inherent between God and Jesus (section 2.2).

Slowly equipping ourselves textually, theologically and hermeneutically, in section 3 we shall seek to learn more of Christ's saving work, as expressed in the apostolic attestation that Christ died 'for us' (1 Thess. 5:10). Three perspectives will be offered from which to view the richness of God in Christ's salvific death, and the section will conclude with the image of Christ's wondrous exchange (section 3.3), an image that can both account for the depths of Christ's death and prepare us for the theological exposition of our future resurrection.

The fourth section, in which we examine eschatological participation and promise in 1 Thessalonians, forms the climax to the claim that 1 Thessalonians is capable of considerable depth if we risk exposing it to theological thinking. Section 4.1 will set out a tentative survey of images which Paul and the Fathers deployed to grapple with the mystery and meaning of the divine–human encounter in Jesus, and suggest that a similar commitment to the inexhaustibility of images might help us in the task of understanding Paul's teaching. We shall explore a number of eschatological images present in 1 Thessalonians: images of faith, love and hope (section 4.2); of light and prayer (section 4.3); of the 'dead in Christ' (section 4.4); of 'sleeping' Christians (section 4.5); and of the parousia itself (section 4.6). These images, all present within the text of 1 Thessalonians, will be exploited, stretched and mined to make as much theological sense as possible of Paul's teaching in 1 Thess. 4:14: that

---

[7] R. L. Wilken, 'Exegesis and the History of Theology: Reflections on the Adam-Christ Typology in Cyril of Alexandria', *CH* 35 (1966), 155.

those who believe in the death and resurrection of Jesus can be assured that, through God, they will be incorporated within the same power.

1   Eschatology and hermeneutics

The exegetical, theological and imaginative task ahead of us is inescapably hermeneutical. It is above all an exposition of how and where the grace in Christ is to be articulated and experienced now. In this way the unavoidable particularity of the eschatological admonitions of 1 Thessalonians is to be read. The Thessalonians' experience of grace must point us towards understanding how we can trace similar experiences of grace in our hope for the future.

Axiomatic for any theological treatment of eschatology is the conviction that Jesus' future salvific significance is *not* something reserved for one historical space in time, but is true of Christ in all times. This claim has two central insights. First, the promise of Christ's future is always experienced as expanding out of time's various passages and into the promise of eternity. Secondly, and as a direct implication of the previous statement, insofar as a theological exposition of Biblical eschatology locates itself in the future as grace experienced through Christ today, it is a hermeneutical *faux pas* to locate a theology of eschatological grace exclusively through an archaeological project of historical recovery and authorial intention. Such an approach would in reality undermine the necessarily theological (and imaginative) task of articulating the future out of the promise of Christ's grace experienced in the present. These two assertions merit further explication.

Historical commentators often point to Paul's purpose, a purpose helpfully delimited by what he does *not* choose to say. His intention is stated clearly in 1 Thess. 4:13 – Paul the pastor does not want the Thessalonians to grieve for those who are dead as though death has defeated the purposes of God, and so his words are those of pastoral reassurance.[8]

The historical context of this eschatological discourse is therefore not *how* the dead are to be raised, but whether the already dead are to be included in the resurrection heralded by the return of Christ. Will the dead miss out on that glorious resurrection? Paul's answer is a resounding 'No'. There is little talk of the nature of the resurrection itself, merely a pastorally direct reassurance that the dead will not be exempt from the general resurrection. Moreover, although this passage touches on our notions of

[8] E. J. Richard, *First and Second Thessalonians* (SP; Collegeville: Liturgical Press, 1995), p. 248.

the general resurrection (and certainly was read thus by Thomas),[9] there is no mention of the universal judgement as at 2 Cor. 5:10. Paul's words are fixed on responding to a communal concern – grief that the dead will miss out on the general resurrection – with talk of collective eschatology, 'we will be with the Lord forever' (4:17).

Paul's words in 1 Thessalonians are directed and frustratingly (for some) focused. Paul is *not* writing for the benefit of systematic theological reflection. As an occasional piece of literature, the letter contains little of what we would seek answers for in a comprehensive treatment of life beyond death. There is, for example, little evidence of interest in the fate of non-believers (see 1:9–10). Paul's words are addressed to grieving believers.

A theological exposition begins by acknowledging that in no situation since its first distribution, and certainly not since it was canonised, has the authority of this letter entirely matched Paul's original intention. The letter's authority has been deemed to lie somewhere other than in this irretrievable historical intent – in that which, through the apostle Paul, it communicates, rather than some putative situation it was written to meet. The text's mysterious authority is thus located courtesy of a deliberate hermeneutical switch, not in the incongruity of an irretrievable historical context of delivery, but more in the congruity of the insights generated and sustained by the realities of which the text speaks.

Our theological project thus poses a deliberate hermeneutical challenge. In order to understand that which 1 Thessalonians timelessly communicates the parallels we seek are not the historical, lexical and archaeological parallels favoured by historical critics. Rather, if we are to treat what Paul is really talking about as revelation, as that which as claimed in chapter 1 is ceaselessly profound, we should expect to find resources within the church's widest theological tradition illuminating and expansive. Ultimately this is the fruit of prioritising the subject matter and reality which the text conveys.

Although the *Sitz im Leben* of Paul's words is not the prime concern here, it cannot be cast aside too glibly. For the *Sitz im Leben* of all eschatological assertions *represents the futurity of Christ's grace experienced in the present*. It is this grace that links together in a mysterious continuity the first recipients of 1 Thessalonians and all subsequent readers (Thomas and Calvin included). What unites all readers and hearers of this text is the grace experienced in the present as eschatological hope and promise. In this sense the seemingly relentless passage of time, measured

---

[9] *Lectio* IV.II.103.

by human reckoning, is as nothing compared to the grace experienced in the eschatological moment, the grace experienced as the interpretation of our *past* selves and the anticipation of our *futures* in extramundane communion. In this theological perspective – which has as its nucleus our futures in God – there is less need to turn to some putative historical context as a locus of authority. The ultimate authority which unites all readers of 1 Thessalonians through time is the revelation that our futures lie in Christ. It is this grace of Christ which is the centre of authority behind all eschatological assertions. Or, as Barth recognised, to speak of eschatology, in all times, is to speak of Christ:

> There is not a single eschatological statement even in the New Testament which allows us to ignore this One. His death, resurrection and coming again are the basis of absolutely everything that is to be said about man and his future, end and goal in God. If this gives way, everything collapses with it.[10]

The signal essay of the Jesuit theologian Karl Rahner (1904–84), 'The Hermeneutics of Eschatological Assertions', provides much of the hermeneutical sophistication our project requires at this stage.

Rahner argues that we should quite rightly inquire into the *Sitz im Leben* of the Scriptural eschatological pronouncements, aware that in so doing we are dealing with the stuff of 'primordial revelation', of which anything subsequent is 'derivative and explanatory'.[11] Nevertheless, if we want to talk dogmatically of eschatology, we must recall that it must remain talk of *that which is future*.[12] (There is then something curiously ironic about discussion of Biblical eschatology which remains purely on the archaeological level.) Talking of that which is future is a necessarily risky task epistemologically, not least because in the present there is always an important part of the future which is hidden in darkness and obscurity. Eschatology is talk of the future from the basis of the present, a future that is known now only as mystery, as hidden. What God reveals is precisely this – that the future is not to be known predictively.[13] This hidden quality of the future is more than obvious and platitudinous – it is the very basis of hope.[14]

<hr />

[10] *CD* III/2, pp. 623–4.

[11] K. Rahner, 'The Hermeneutics of Eschatological Assertions', in *Theological Investigations*, vol. IV, tr. K. Smyth (London: Darton, Longman and Todd, 1966), p. 325.

[12] *Ibid.*, p. 326. Also on that page is Rahner's critique of the existentialism associated with Rudolf Bultmann. Eschatology which remains on the level of talking about the 'here and now' is 'theologically unacceptable'.

[13] *Ibid.*, p. 329.   [14] *Ibid.*

Talking of the future in the present implicates us in a dialectical process, a location in a present properly orientated towards the mystery of the future, the understanding of the present in such a manner that knowledge of the future necessarily '*grows out of it*'.[15] Just as the Thessalonian Christians were caught up in the process of understanding their eschatological futures in their *now*, so too in our now are we to talk of our futures in Christ. Knowledge of eschatology is necessarily, therefore, knowledge of how *this* present can itself be seen as possessing eschatological promise, a bringing into creative tension present and future, experience and promise. Eschatology always involves talking about more than the present. But so too is our talk of the future (insofar as it can be articulated) shaped by our eschatological existence in the present.

For Rahner, it is the (eternal) experience of Christ's grace which unites the seemingly divergent context of the Thessalonians and what we are to say eschatologically now. (Rahner nowhere mentions the Thessalonian Christians – I am deducing this from what he does say about the hermeneutics of eschatological assertions.) In this sense, there is no ontological difference between the eschatological assertions of Paul to the Thessalonians and what we are to say dogmatically now. What 1 Thessalonians makes known theologically we too say now – that although the grace of Christ is experienced immanently, it remains a future we can articulate only as that which is 'impenetrable' and 'uncontrollable' (cf. 1 Thess. 5:2).[16] For both the Thessalonian Christians and for us now, the truth remains the same: eschatology is the forward expansion of the grace of Christ experienced in the present. Anything that is said eschatologically, at any time, always emanates from the experience of Christ's grace and 'derives from the assertion about the salvific action of God in his grace on actual man'.[17] For Peter Phan, therefore, this is the centre of Rahner's argument,[18] that the *Sitze im Leben* of all eschatological statements are essentially the same, 'the experience of God's salvific action *on ourselves* in Christ'.[19] Thus, at all times, in all places, the future is experienced as 'a reality which has achieved power to influence the present itself and in that sense has become the real'.[20]

At this early stage, Rahner's hermeneutics provide us with three maxims. There is, first, a reminder that the task of interpreting Biblical

---

[15] *Ibid.*, p. 331.   [16] *Ibid.*, p. 333.   [17] *Ibid.*, p. 338.

[18] P. C. Phan, *Eternity in Time: A Study of Karl Rahner's Eschatology* (Selinsgrove: Susquehanna University Press, 1988), p. 71.

[19] Rahner, 'The Hermeneutics', p. 336 (italics in the original).

[20] K. Rahner, 'The Question of the Future', in *Theological Investigations*, vol. XII, tr. D. Bourke (London: Darton, Longman and Todd, 1974), p. 184.

eschatology is one of 'almost unmanageable complexity', testified not least by Rahner's intricate argument.[21] The right to be heard speaking about the future of God, and our roles within that future, is earned by slow, patient labour. Secondly, there is in Rahner's hermeneutics a recognition of the contribution of historical-critical pursuits, but a location of these pursuits within a theological framework which casts such pursuits aright, as well as pushing us to realise that the hermeneutics of eschatological assertions is at all times a theologically charged task.[22] Thirdly, there is a potent reminder that any eschatological assertions we see fit to make now remain always as 'a retrospective interpretation of the old, not a new and better assertion which replaces the old'.[23] In this sense we are *not* engaged in the task of replacing or duplicating the eschatology of the Paul of 1 Thessalonians, but *participating* in the movement of the same experience of eschatological grace.

One of the implications for our endeavour is that to speak on the basis of 1 Thessalonians' eschatology is not an exercise in retrieval. It is not an exercise in arguing for what Paul meant or even primarily what he intended when he wrote this or that. It is rather an exercise of discerning what can be said on the basis of this text of our futures, from our location in the eschatological present that is Christ's grace experienced as salvific presence. It is a thinking alongside and with Paul, a level of thinking sustained by the same grace of Christ which unites Paul and all subsequent interpreters.

The focus of our study will be on the worlds of understanding which the apostle Paul points us towards; this exploration will be offered as an amplification of the realities to which the revelation of 1 Thessalonians points. The intention of reading of 1 Thessalonians in this way, with Rahner's hermeneutical manifesto in mind, is to dwell not so much on putative circumstances lying behind the text as on the new realities proposed and sustained by attention to the text itself.

The concentration on the revelatory subject matter of the text – on the *realities* which the text encourages the theologian to begin to understand – is a frequent theme in Karl Rahner. Although he does not explicitly say that he is talking about 1 Thess. 4:13f., there can be little doubt what sections of Paul's literary output are in his mind when he writes,

> We do not need to be afraid that we will depart from the teaching of St Paul, if we do not rack our brains too much about how the dead will hear the sound of the archangel's trumpet and how

[21] Phan, *Eternity in Time*, p. 68.   [22] *Ibid.*
[23] Rahner, 'The Hermeneutics', p. 345.

this harmonises with the sending out of the many angels or with the resuscitating voice of the Lord himself, which we are told about in his own eschatological discourse. We can regard this text as an image and yet be terrified by what it truly means to convey both to the people of these days and to us today: the all-powerfulness of God over the dead, who even when dead cannot escape him; indeed, we may conjecture that God in his omnipotence, just because he is all-powerful and never in danger of being rivalled, will give even the created forces of the world a share in the work of the consummation of the dead into the life beyond all death.[24]

Mindful of Rahner's protestations, and of theology's requirement to be open to the mystery of God's salvific will, we shall seek to keep distinct the symbol from the symbolised, the mode of signification from that which is ultimately being signified. Our driving interest will be to explore the potency of the images contained within 1 Thessalonians, images pointing to God's all-powerful hold over death.

2   Paul's contribution

2.1   The integrity of Paul's contribution

A large part of what Christianity has to say about death and the dead and their futures is to be found in the deceptively simple creed of 1 Thess. 4:14, 'we believe that Jesus died and rose'. The One who died and rose, as the One who converted the world to God, is the 'living' God's (1:9) response of grace to the reality of death as a power. The simplicity of the creed – that 'Jesus died and rose' – should not mask the profound truth held within the God who united Jesus' death to his resurrection. Just as the One who died 'for us' (5:10) died 'for our sins' (1 Cor. 15:3), so too is this saving power only made manifest by his resurrected state: 'If Christ has not been raised . . . you are still in your sins' (1 Cor. 15:17).[25] In rising, or as Paul characteristically prefers, being risen from the dead *by* God (1:10), the saving work of Christ is now lifted up into the expanse of God, and his saving work on the cross is given ultimate significance and vindication *through* the resurrection.[26]

---

[24] K. Rahner, 'The Resurrection of the Body', in *Theological Investigations* 2, tr. K.-H. Kruger (London: Darton, Longman and Todd, 1963), p. 210.

[25] For this effective unity of salvation see C. B. Cousar, *A Theology of the Cross: The Death of Jesus in the Pauline Letters* (Minneapolis: Fortress Press, 1990), p. 96.

[26] Cf. K. Rahner, *Foundations of Christian Faith*, tr. W. V. Dych (London: Darton, Longman and Todd, 1978), p. 266.

Before any theological advances are attempted, it is necessary to recognise that in Paul's creed-like statements – 'Jesus died and rose' (4:14) and Jesus 'died for us' (5:10) – Biblical scholars see evidence of pre-existing Christian formulae, primordial examples of a Christian creed.[27] Ernst Käsemann, in his work on the death of Jesus in Paul's thought, dismisses such inherited liturgical tradition as inadequate guides to Paul's radical, cross-centred thought-world.[28] For Käsemann, such inherited, ecclesially bound statements offer little help in understanding the radical nature of Jesus' death *on a cross*. Although Käsemann is amongst the most important Pauline theologians of last century and one is reluctant to treat his work with anything but the highest respect, there is much to be said for Charles Cousar's argument that it is legitimate to judge Paul on the final form of his epistles. It is therefore acceptable to include pre-existing formulae as part of Paul's intended communication.[29] As Paul is both receiver and moulder of the tradition in which he stands, the kerygmatic statements that Jesus 'died and rose' or that Jesus 'died for us' cannot be as easily relegated as Käsemann would like.

Paul's theological contribution, it is correctly noted by New Testament scholars, is not an ontological Christology.[30] His prime contribution is that of a *functional* Christology, and it is to that voice we must listen in our wider discussion of the salvific work of Christ made known in his death 'for us'. Correspondingly, in 1 Thessalonians Paul spends little time on the means by which Christ saves and is more concerned with the effects of this death 'for us'. Jesus 'died for us, so that whether we are alive or dead, we may live together with him' (ἀποθανόντος ὑπὲρ ἡμῶν, ἵνα εἴτε γρηγορῶμεν εἴτε καθεύδωμεν ἅμα σὺν αὐτῷ ζήσωμεν, 5:10).[31] Paying attention to 5:10b, Kenneth Grayston is no doubt correct to assert that the closest parallel in Paul's thought is Rom. 14:9:[32]

> For to this end Christ died and lived again, so that he might be Lord of both the dead and the living.

In dying 'for us', and vanquishing death's sting through his resurrection, Christ now stands as Lord of a community of believers incorporating both

---

[27] E.g. M. Hengel, *The Atonement: The Origins of the Doctrine in the New Testament*, tr. J. Bowden (London: SCM, 1981), p. 37.
[28] E. Käsemann, 'The Saving Significance of the Death of Jesus in Paul', in *Perspectives on Paul*, tr. M. Kohl (London: SPCK, 1969), pp. 37, 45.
[29] Cousar, *A Theology of the Cross*, p. 17.
[30] E.g. M. D. Hooker, 'Chalcedon and the New Testament', in S. Coakley and D. Pailin, eds., *The Making and Remaking of Christian Doctrine: Essays in Honour of Maurice Wiles* (Oxford: Clarendon Press, 1993), p. 87.
[31] See excursus 3 below.
[32] K. Grayston, *Dying, We Live: A New Enquiry into the Death of Christ in the New Testament* (London: Darton, Longman and Todd, 1990), pp. 14–16.

the dead and the living. Whether we are now dead or alive, we are with the One who has died and been raised from the dead by God.

2.2   The saving work of God in Christ

If the claim that Jesus died 'for us' is of any abiding soteriological worth, it is a claim that inseparably involves God in the work of Jesus. Jesus saves because what Jesus is doing 'for us' is bound up with what God is doing 'for us', in the form of the One who is wholly human and wholly divine without confusion and with complete unity. Jesus dies 'for us' on the basis of this *internal* relationship between the Father and the Son, both enjoying the very same properties and essence. Unless we can say both that this human who died on the cross was fully divine and that this God who is said to be on the cross is fully human, we cannot say that this death is fully saving.[33] Although, as conceded above, Paul is not concerned with the ontological interests of Patristic Christology, 1 Thessalonians does point, in a primordial form, to a strong salvific relationship inherent *between* God and Christ.

At points in the letter Paul can use the terms 'God' and 'Christ' almost interchangeably, as if referring to the same person. Just as the 'church of the Thessalonians' is 'in God the Father' (1:1),[34] so too are the Christian communities in Judaea 'churches of God *in* Christ Jesus' (2:14).[35] Cyril of Alexandria, for whom the unity between God and Christ could hardly be over-emphasised, likewise noted approvingly that in 1 Thess. 1:8; 2:1– 2, 9, 13 Paul unquestioningly alternates between 'gospel of God' and 'gospel of Christ'. For Cyril, this stood as apostolic proof that Christ is called God, and hence that for Paul, Jesus is wholly divine:

> Does he not clearly refer to his preaching of Christ as the 'gospel of God' and 'the word of God'?[36]

Similarly, just as later in the letter Paul talks of the dead 'in Christ' (4:16), so too is this a relationship initially enjoyed by God. Paul alludes to the

---

[33] K. Tanner, *Jesus, Humanity and the Trinity: A Brief Systematic Theology* (Edinburgh: T. & T. Clark, 2001), p. 32.

[34] Here I favour the incorporative sense of the dative (ἐν θεῷ πατρί) as opposed to the instrumental sense argued for by Best, *A Commentary*, p. 62.

[35] It should be noted that this is a verse whose authenticity is disputed, and the literature is predictably voluminous. Still, *Conflict*, pp. 24–45, provides a good overview of the debate, whilst arguing for Pauline authenticity.

[36] Cyril of Alexandria, 'Scholia on the Incarnation of the Only Begotten', §§21–3. Translated in J. A. McGuckin, *St. Cyril of Alexandria: The Christological Controversy, its History, Theology, and Texts* (Leiden: E. J. Brill, 1994), p. 314.

self-expression of God in the person of Christ when he writes of 'the will of God *in* Christ Jesus' (5:18). This is an intriguingly early example of a strikingly high claim for the person of Jesus. It is then quite logical that Paul expects God to execute his saving work 'though Jesus' (4:14),[37] for Jesus is God's very 'Son' (1:10).

God and Jesus are united partners in the work of salvation, a feature of this letter which, we have seen, was recognised from the earliest times. Athanasius, writing on 1 Thess. 3:11 in the midst of his Anti-Arian discourse, asserts that here Paul is keen to emphasise the unity of the Father and Son. In using the third person singular – κατευθύναι – rather than the third person plural,[38] Paul indicates that there are not two people working the grace to direct Paul to the Thessalonians, but the Father working *through* the Son:

> For one and the same grace is from the Father in the Son, as the light of the sun and of the radiance is one, and as the sun's illumination is effected through the radiance.[39]

We need not restrict ourselves to ancient luminaries. The Eastern Orthodox Biblical scholar Paul Tarazi equally reads this unexpected form of the verb as proof that Paul regarded God and Jesus 'as one source of the same action, though the one is not the other'.[40]

This involvement of God within Jesus' saving work is developed in other parts of the Pauline corpus. As Charles Cousar demonstrates, the prepositional phrase found in 1 Thess. 5:10 (ὑπὲρ ἡμῶν) is echoed in Rom. 5:6–8,[41] a passage whose theme is that the work and person of Jesus are the means by which God reveals his love (the phrase 'for us' is located twice in Rom. 5:8 by means of εἰς ἡμᾶς). As Cousar notes, and we can rightly expand, Rom. 5:8 displays a 'striking closeness' of activity between God and Christ,[42] a reciprocity brought out by the mirroring in these verses of the 'for us' phrase. God proves or demonstrates (συνίστησιν) his love 'for us' by the death of Christ, who died 'for us'. God reveals in Christ his love for the 'ungodly' (Rom. 5:6), and Christ's

---

[37] The closest parallel to this is Rom. 5:21, 'just as sin exercised dominion in death, so grace might also exercise dominion through justification leading to eternal life through Jesus Christ our Lord.'

[38] Κατευθύναι is in the third person singular of the aorist optative. If Paul had wished to say 'May they direct', he would have used the form κατευθύναιεν.

[39] Athanasius, 'Four Discourses against the Arians', III.xxv.11, in *NPNF*[2] IV, tr. J. H. Newman (Edinburgh: T. & T. Clark, 1891).

[40] P. N. Tarazi, *1 Thessalonians: A Commentary* (Crestwood: Saint Vladimir's Seminary Press, 1982), p. 130.

[41] Cousar, *A Theology of the Cross*, p. 44.   [42] *Ibid.*, p. 45.

act on the cross is a revelation of the nature and being of God. Thus Jesus' act refers beyond itself to the salvific will and desire of God himself. This reciprocity between God and his Son is in accord with Gal. 1:4, where Christ is the One 'who gave himself for (ὑπέρ) our sins to deliver us from the present evil age, according to the will of God our Father'. Precisely because God's will works itself 'through Jesus' (4:14), Paul can understand Jesus' death both as his own giving (Gal. 2:20) *and* as the giving of God (Rom. 8:32).

It therefore seems legitimate to read Paul's statement that Jesus 'died for us' as essentially a claim about God's involvement in the death of the person of Jesus. The claim that this One, Jesus, died 'for us' is thus only intelligible insofar as we establish what it means to say that God was involved in this death. To be sure, this is where Paul's contribution needs to be supplemented: although God in Christ is Saviour for Paul, he spends little time on *how* these two natures meet and interrelate.

The problems surrounding the attestation of Jesus' divinity all the way to his death are legion. If, in the Word becoming incarnate, 'all that is the Father's, is the Son's',[43] how can the 'living' God (1:9) take on that which is not God: mortality and the appearance of eternal extinction? How can the immutable God apparently take on the things of temporality: birth and life's extinction, death?[44] How can God retain the saving capacity – as God – within the act which is, on first reading, the clothing in the arch-contradiction of God himself: death? Such condundrums are related to the wider task of incarnational theology, of explaining how God remains God in bodily form, whilst managing to take on enough humanity for it to be possible to see his death as truly 'for us'.

In the midst of this debate our theological interests are *relatively* specific (though they necessarily feed off the debate which these ancient questions and discussions have fostered): in seeking a theological reading of 1 Thessalonians, what sense does it make to say that Jesus 'died for us'? It is in pursuit of answering that question, to which we now turn, that we shall progress to a deeper understanding of 1 Thess. 4:14.

3   God's grace in dying 'for us'

Beginning to unravel the theological potential of a text which speaks of Jesus dying 'for us' (ὑπὲρ ἡμῶν, 5:10), we start with the impossibility

---

[43] Athanasius, 'Four Discourses against the Arians', III.xxiii.4.

[44] In relation to these questions see the discussion of Theodore of Mopsuestia and Nestorianism in J. Meyendorff, 'Christ's Humanity: The Paschal Mystery', *SVTQ* 31(1987), 8. Kenoticism is another response to the difficulties of talking of God dying on the cross. In this perspective there is a risk of Jesus being only human on the cross, not full of the life of the divine: see *ibid.*, 14–15.

made reality. On the cross the incarnate deity takes on all that is against his nature: death and extinction. Jesus' death is 'for us' precisely because as the Word incarnate Jesus is *not* death, and his taking on that which is not his is an expression of God's salvific desire to live in renewed communion with humanity. This death is experienced and believed in as a death 'for us', the mysterious act by which God remains God even in taking on death, and in so doing extends his love to *every aspect* of our humanity in order to bring it back to life in the living God.

Such preliminary reflections remind us that the primordial creed, Jesus died 'for us', is an attestation that Jesus' death was a death that spilled out of its own limited frame of reference, and in its *precise* character as death, is relevant 'for us'. That in Christ, the human and divine natures meet as God's initiative to restore creation is an exposition of the nascent Christian realisation that the One who 'died and rose' is the One who was acting 'for us'. The God who acted in and through Christ died 'for us' in a manner typical of a God who wills not to be God in isolation, but God firmly in relationship with created humanity.[45]

At its most elementary, the *pro nobis* claims of Christian faith are attestations in a God who desires to live in relationship with creation, even if that means restoring the relationship which our sin has rent asunder.[46] God is a creator irrepressibly involved with his creation.

The Christian confession of faith is that all the darkness of death has been taken on fully and freely assumed into the light that is the life of the incarnate God. But more, Christ's death is a death whose effects are 'for us': it is a death which makes sense of *all* our deaths precisely because he has died 'for all' (2 Cor. 5:15). The death in time of Jesus, as the Lord of all time, therefore becomes a death for all time, for all who seek to understand more of death's nature. The death of Christ, whilst at one level representing the death of a brigand on a Roman cross, is a death which is, totally independently from our claims on the cross, a death 'for us', a death which appropriated in faith can begin the process of unravelling the divine potential of our deaths (and lives). Jesus' death on a cross enables our deaths to be taken up into the life of the triune God. The creed that Christ 'died for us' is an exposition that the whole of humanity's being, even unto death, has been taken up into the loving self-expression of God made known in Christ.

The views presented in the New Testament, and in subsequent theological reflection on exactly *how* Jesus' death is redemptive, are notoriously

---

[45] *CD* IV/1, p. 7.

[46] *Ibid.*, pp. 53–4. See also K. Barth, 'The Humanity of God', in *The Humanity of God*, tr. J. Newton Thomas (London: Collins, 1961), p. 46.

pluriform, and a whole plethora of images have been and are deployed in order to make sense of the saving significance of the death of Jesus. This dazzling kaleidoscope of perspectives (which I shall attempt to bring into some kind of collective focus) is itself evidence of the numerous ways in which Christian communities have perceived themselves to be redeemed. In the same way that we cannot restrict eschatology by making it a predictive exercise, so too we cannot expect to talk of any *one* way in which Jesus is Saviour. Working with a number of salvific images, I shall ensure that we do not box in the mystery of the salvation made known by God in Christ, but remain open to the scope of redemption broadcast in Jesus' death 'for us'.

Keen to retain the integrity of the different conversants I plan to engage with, I propose three intertwined and mutually interpretative ways in which to interpret and understand the formula Jesus died 'for us'. First, Jesus' death 'for us' is a demonstration of God's radically *complete* grace (section 3.1). In this sense, the priority of God's loving manifestation in Christ is absolute and undisputed, an important reminder in the face of the theology which will be developed later. Secondly, Jesus' death discloses God's radical love (section 3.2), manifested in the 'us' for whom Christ died. Thirdly, the death of the Son ignites God's radical exchange made known in the Incarnate Son (section 3.3). It is this final image of redemption which most adequately prepares us for our reading of the resurrection of the dead (section 4). It is important to recall that none of these models are complete in themselves, but standing together they grapple with the mystery of the One whose death is 'for us'.

3.1   The radically complete grace of God

In dying 'for us', God in Christ does for us what we could not do for ourselves unaided. Jesus dying 'for us' is gift and grace on our behalf, as something *already* fully complete before we even begin our approach of faith because the reconciliation between God and humanity has its roots *within the person of Jesus Christ*. Salvation, in this perspective, is a profoundly ontological event.[47] Taking on death 'for us', so to absorb it into the life and source of the One who 'died and rose', God defeats death's power of eternal extinction once and for all. Whilst giving himself over to death completely, God never stops being God in this act of expunging death's dominion.[48] That God takes on all that is not God, whilst never

---

[47] T. F. Torrance, *The Trinitarian Faith: The Evangelical Theology of the Ancient Catholic Church* (Edinburgh: T. & T. Clark, 1988), p. 158.

[48] *CD* IV/1, p. 185.

ceasing to be God, is part of the mystery of the claim that Jesus died 'for us', namely that this One's death is of benefit to all humanity. In this sense, dying 'for us', taking our death into the life of the living God, is a claim for what is done in the human Jesus, that in the saving cross 'sin and death have been assumed by the One, the Word, who cannot be conquered by them'.[49]

Christ's death is an act whose salvific potency and communicative will are radically independent of any claims which we might lay on it by way of imposition. In this way, Jesus' death is a prevenient act of God through which he expresses his eternal desire that we live in fellowship with him. God initiates this process, taking on humanity to the point of death and so allowing all humanity to share in the life of the divine. Christ's death as an act of grace is, by definition, an act independent of any claims which humanity may wish to make for it by means of restriction. God's Word, at work in us (2:13), is thus a Word of cruciform service directed to us, an offence against any model where grace ends up as a mirror of *our* needs and desires.[50]

Dying 'for us' is an act of God in Jesus' complete freedom, a freedom to be God even when dead in the human form of his Son. The salvific potency of this death 'for us' is so complete that we need not think our faith can complement it or boost its power. Whatever our response, we cannot hope to supplement the potency of what 'has taken place fully *in* Him'.[51]

Jesus' full identification with us in our mortal existence can be seen in two events that occur before his own physical death. First of all, Jesus is the One who weeps at the death of his friend Lazarus in John 11 'out of compassion for all humanity, not bewailing Lazarus only, but understanding that which happens to all, that the whole of humanity is made subject to death, having justly fallen under so great a penalty'.[52] Secondly, Jesus is the One who appears to shrink from his own death in Gethsemane. Jesus' death is 'for us' because it is part of the identity of the One who travelled with us in grief, the fear of death, and even death itself. The soteriological significance of Jesus' saving identification and union with our humanity, and our mortality, cannot be overstated. Weeping at the death of Lazarus, and seeming to shrink from his own death in Gethsemane, unless

---

[49] Tanner, *Jesus*, p. 29.

[50] R. Williams, *Resurrection* (London: Darton, Longman and Todd, 1982), p. 80.

[51] *CD* IV/1, p. 230 (my italics).

[52] Cyril of Alexandria, *Commentary on the Gospel According to S. John*, VII (on Jn. 11:36–7), various translators (London: Walter Smith, 1885).

He had felt dread, human nature could not have been free from dread; unless He had experienced grief, there could never have been any deliverance from grief . . . The affections of His flesh were aroused, not that they might have the upper hand as they do indeed in us, but in order that when aroused they might be thoroughly subdued by the power of the Word dwelling in the flesh, the nature of man thus undergoing a change for the better.[53]

In this sense the raising of Lazarus is part of the progressive unfolding of what is revealed in the course of Jesus' ministry: Jesus is taking all the things of humanity and lifting them into the life of the 'living' God.[54] God, in Christ, is giving to humanity the gifts of his divine life.[55] What is revealed in the One who died 'for us' is crucially (literally) linked to the One who throughout his ministry rebelled against death's dominion: in assuming all that is death, Christ, as the One whose humanity is united to the living Word, transforms death into life.[56] In the One who raised Lazarus from the dead, and who died 'for us', death itself becomes something 'for us'. In dying 'for us', gifting *to us* the pattern of his life which had trampled down death, Jesus crosses over death's boundary 'for us' so that we may live in his company 'forever' (4:17).

God in Christ is doing more than joining us in fellowship in our deaths, for he is also decisively communicating the properties of God to death itself, enabling his death to be truly 'for us'. All of death is totally transfigured by the grace of God in Christ. Death, previously an ugly manifestation of our sin, becomes the means by which God reveals his abundant grace; what to us is empty and bereft of hope is transformed, through God's fullness, into a signal of hope.[57]

The difference that Christ's death makes, and the reason why it is 'for us', is that his voluntary death was one not compelled by any deficiency in himself, but solely through the love of God in Christ.[58] As the Son of the 'living God' (1:9), he simply did not *have* to die, but in choosing to die, and so save humanity through his death, he gains power over death itself, and he offers this power to all. At all times this death 'for us' was

[53] *Ibid.*, VIII (on Jn. 12:28).

[54] For this strand of Alexandrian Christology, that in Jesus' human ministry God is progressively gifting to humanity the goodness of God himself, see Tanner, *Jesus*, p. 27.

[55] Gregory of Nyssa, 'An Address on Religious Instruction', in *Christology of the Later Fathers*, tr. and ed. E. R. Hardy in collaboration with C. C. Richardson (London: SCM, 1954), §12.

[56] *CD* III/2, p. 600.

[57] K. Rahner, *On the Theology of Death*, tr. C. H. Henkey (Freiburg: Herder, 1961), p. 78.

[58] G. Florovsky, 'The Lamb of God', *SJT* 4 (1951), 25.

a death over which Christ had complete dominion, something that is not true for us: 'the death did not happen because of the birth, but on the contrary the birth was accepted for the sake of the death'.[59] Throughout, God in Christ remained in complete dominion over death – his victory over death's force was (and will be) assured.

In the figure of Christ our salvation is thus radically complete; for those willing to hear, the whole of our salvation is to be found in the saving work of Christ. God is thus both subject and object, actor and author, reconciler and reconciled in this divine drama of redemption, a drama in whose outworking we become players by receiving that which has already been achieved by God in Christ: 'reconciliation' and an 'overflowing of grace' (Rom. 5:11, 17). This is to read seriously the sense in which Jesus died *'for* us'.

3.2   The radical love of God

In dying 'for us' God reveals his nature to be loving, precisely because he died 'for *us*'. Experiencing death in itself, Christ endured the full intramundane and extramundane horrors of death. He knows what it was to die in pain, fear and loneliness. Jesus knows what it is to approach death with fear: 'Father, if you are willing, remove this cup from me' (Lk. 22:42), and in the darkness which seems to negate the possibility of God's presence, 'My God, my God, why have you forsaken me?' (Mk. 15:34). Jesus' death is a death that is apparently no stranger to the opacity of God's presence. So complete is God in Jesus' identification with creation that he experiences death in the extremities of its metaphysical horrors. God's love is revealed in the radical extension into this 'far country', and death is quite literally the farthest he could have gone for us.[60] God's love makes known the advent of God into the very depths of humanity's darkness, his healing desire that, in all its ambiguities, he would make our condition his own.

God's love in dying 'for us' is all the more astonishing given that this was a place that should have been ours. In this sense, Jesus' death 'for us' was a death *in our place*. There is a need to recognise and grapple with this vicarious aspect to Jesus' death and the venerable history of exegesis from which it emerges. Certainly the idea of Christ's substitutionary death is a prominent theme in Paul (e.g. Gal. 3:13), but there is

---

[59] Gregory of Nyssa, *The Catechetical Oration*, §32, tr. J. H. Srawley (London: SPCK, 1917).

[60] For the original use of the phrase 'far country' see *CD* IV/1, pp. 157–210.

also considerable evidence for its popularity with the Eastern Fathers.[61] Such an emphasis on Christ's work on the cross need not be seen as a threat to the saving significance of Christ's person. The two should properly be seen in concert, with Christ's substitutionary role on the cross being best understood through an apprehension of the nature of Christ's person. Thus Christ's death 'for us' is understood from the perspective of his person, of who Christ was and is.

If we consider properly the 'us' for whom Christ died, it is hard to escape reading 1 Thess. 5:10 as conveying a sense of vicarious representation, an 'on behalf of' or an 'in place of' action. God in Christ was one with us in every sense – apart from our sin – but nevertheless 'Christ died for our sins' (1 Cor. 15:3).[62] Not waiting for us, God in Christ died for us as sinners (Rom. 5:6–8), and so shows that he goes before us and acts preveniently in releasing us from death's hold. Christ dies 'for us' so that humanity may recapture the sense of communion with the divine lost because of sin. Being perfect, and unblemished by sin, *in Christ* God reconciles the world to himself (2 Cor. 5:19).[63] God in Christ, taking up a substitutionary role in our salvation, therefore has universal implications, and it is for this reason that Paul can say that Christ 'died for all' (2 Cor. 5:14).[64] This was something that was ours to do, but we were doomed to futility because 'a sinner cannot justify a sinner'.[65] In this sense, Anselm was correct to remind us that only a God-man could save us, for only God can defeat death, and only one who is fully human can die in solidarity with us. Karl Barth, writing on the use of the prepositions ἀντί, ὑπέρ (the preposition used in 1 Thess. 5:10) and περί in the New Testament treatment of Jesus' death, comments that

---

[61] L. Koen, *The Saving Passion: Incarnational and Soteriological Thought in Cyril of Alexandria's Commentary on the Gospel According to St. John* (Uppsala: Acta Universitatis Upsaliensis, 1991), p. 124, n. 6, notes the frequency with which ὑπὲρ ἡμῶν is used by Greek Fathers in a substitutionary sense. Athanasius deployed the phrase in such a way 150 times; Basil 70 times; Gregory of Nyssa 70 times; and Gregory of Nazianzus some 35 times.

[62] Hengel, *The Atonement*, p. 36, proposes that wherever we see ὑπὲρ ἡμῶν we should understand it as a reference to the forgiveness of sins.

[63] For G. Aulén, *Christus Victor*, tr. A. G. Hebert (London: SPCK, 1931), p. 72, *this* is the 'classic' view of the atonement, that 'God is at once the author and the object of the reconciliation; He is reconciled in the act of reconciling the world to Himself.'

[64] Cf. J. D. G. Dunn, 'Paul's Understanding of the Death of Jesus as Sacrifice', in S. W. Sykes, ed., *Sacrifice and Redemption: Durham Essays in Theology* (Cambridge: Cambridge University Press, 1991), p. 51.

[65] Anselm of Canterbury, 'Why God Became Man', I.xxiii, tr. E. R. Fairweather, in *A Scholastic Miscellany: Anselm to Ockham* (London: SCM, 1956).

They cannot be understood if we do not see that in general these
prepositions speak of a place which ought to be ours, that we
ought to have taken this place, that we have been taken from it,
that it is occupied by another, that this other acts in this place as
only He can, in our cause and interest.[66]

While some recent thought has shied away from 'substitutionary' understandings of God's love on the cross, Paul's thought, it would seem,
supposes a strong relationship between Jesus' death and the reality of sin
in the world. Driven by the love of Christ (2 Cor. 5:14), God in Christ's
death is vitally linked to the reality of sin in the world, and the need for
those sins to be slain decisively, for 'the death he died, he died to sin,
once for all' (Rom. 6:10).

The Son of God taking on death is expressive of God's love because
it is a totally gratuitous act – other than for our salvation, there is and
was no need for Jesus to die. Jesus was completely sinless. He enjoys
fully the gifts of life within the fellowship of the Trinity already, and he
had no need to die and rise again. Jesus, in his very being, has never
stopped enjoying the fruits of immortality. He took on the sin of humanity as his own, and in so dying for our sins died 'for us'.[67] To be sure,
we must avoid the excesses of sacrificial understandings of Jesus' death.
His salvific death is 'for us' chiefly because he is the Word become
flesh, not because he is an innocent offering made *to* God. What takes
place here happens from within the ontological union of the human and
divine natures in the person of Jesus Christ.[68] At all times Jesus' acts
were an expression from within the economic will and love of God
himself – there is no point at which we can say 'this was Jesus' and
'this was God', for at every stage, 'Christ is of God' (Χριστὸς δὲ θεοῦ,
1 Cor. 3:23).

What Christ did, in recalling us from death to life, was an act of love
towards humanity, an act from which he had nothing to gain,[69] other than
our continuing communion within the life of God. His willingness to die
for us, and so make possible the gift of life with him (5:10), is purely the
desire of love. It was God in Christ who lovingly took on the horror of
death on the cross (healing the world from within, not from without as

---

[66] *CD* IV/1, p. 230.   [67] *Ibid.*, pp. 232–5.

[68] Cyril of Alexandria, *On the Unity of Christ*, tr. J. A. McGuckin (Crestwood: Saint
Vladimir's Seminary Press, 1995), pp. 59–60. See also Torrance, *The Trinitarian Faith*,
p. 168.

[69] On this paragraph see Gregory of Nyssa, 'An Address on Religious Instruction', §32.

Barth says),[70] who died 'for us' precisely so that with the power of sin slain we might enjoy communion with God once more. Dying vicariously 'for us', God in Christ extending out to us became our sin so that we might become the righteousness of God (2 Cor. 5:21). Thus in 2 Cor. 5:21 Paul uses this same phrase – ὑπὲρ ἡμῶν – in a passage where it is promised that what God was doing for the world in the reconciling ministry of Christ was 'not counting their trespasses'.[71] The vicarious aspect of Jesus' death, in Paul's thought connected with sin, seems hard to deny when one considers the intimate connection Paul constructs between Christ's death and 'our trespasses' (Rom. 4:25, παραπτώματα ἡμῶν). God is, it seems, doing something in economic unity with Christ which deals with our sins through his Son's death.

The emphasis is properly put on the radical and gratuitous freedom of God's love, the love which wills to bring the fullness of the divine life into ever closer communion with humanity. Vocabulary must be found to talk of our creaturely dependence – made known in the creator who dies 'for us' – whilst avoiding a perspective which talks more of the wretchedness of humanity than the gratuitous grace of God. The love of God, God being transcendent, is simply not dependent on the depravity of man. What is revealed in the God who dies 'for us' is precisely this overwhelmingly loving will. The New Testament scholar Ernst Käsemann articulates crisply what Christ's death represents in Paul's thought:

> What he is establishing is our incapacity to achieve salvation for ourselves. Salvation is always open to us without our doing anything for it – as a gift according to Rom 3:24, and as Rom 5:6ff. stresses with immense emotion, before we have fulfilled the will of God. It is only the love of our creator which saves.[72]

3.3   The radical exchange of God

Eastern Christianity has traditionally been wary of the excesses of vicarious understandings of Jesus' death and keen to retain the unity of God in Christ; penal understandings of Jesus' death 'for us' have often been suspected of subordinating Christ's role to that of an intermediary.[73] In

---

[70] *CD* IV/1, p. 237.   [71] Cousar, *A Theology of the Cross*, p. 80.

[72] Käsemann, 'The Saving Significance', p. 39.

[73] The actual picture is less polarised than stereotypes might suggest. Augustine talks of deification in 'On the Trinity', IV.ii, in *Basic Writings of Saint Augustine*, vol. II, tr. A. W. Haddan, ed. W. J. Oates, revd W. G. T. Shedd (New York: Random House, 1948). Likewise, John Damascene, 'Exposition of the Orthodox Faith', III.xxvii, discloses a discernible juridical slant in an Eastern thinker.

Orthodoxy the emphasis is put more on the death which the living God in Christ defeated, and less on the sin for which Christ 'paid' a debt.[74] Christ is Saviour because God in Christ assumes every part of our humanity, from birth to death. The saving capacity of the cross is that it is a witness to God's loving union with us in flesh. For the Eastern Fathers (and hence for Orthodox theology), the cross is salvific because what happens there is illustrative of the whole of the Word's incarnate existence: the salvific unity of divinity and humanity. John Breck, a contemporary Orthodox theologian, is not being glib when he insists that 'the Greek fathers were more concerned with *who* died on the cross than with the question of why that form of death was necessary'.[75]

The virtues of this approach are that it is able to claim that death is now wrapped up within the identity of the Christian God. God has experienced death, his solidarity with humanity extending even to our darkest hour. Athanasius refers to this two-fold saving power of God in Christ when he speaks of 'two marvels' taking place on the cross. In the meeting of God in Christ with all humanity 'the death of all was accomplished in the Lord's body', and so too 'death and corruption were wholly done away by reason of the Word that was united with it'.[76]

In this final exploration of Jesus' death 'for us' we shall seek something of a synthesis. Whilst incorporating elements of vicarious readings of Jesus' death, readings which take seriously who exactly is this 'us' for whom Jesus died, we shall explore more deeply the death represented by God in flesh participating in all the things of humanity and so redeeming them by lifting us up into his life.

To recapitulate: in dying, Jesus takes on that which is not his, death. Moreover, Jesus himself has nothing to gain from his death; the gain is all on our side. The language of 'interchange' has its uses here, although it has its limitations: it is the grace of God, acting through Jesus, that always remains in a state of primacy. The grace of God in Christ overwhelms any retributive schemes we might imagine God works with – that just

---

[74] For the Greek Fathers the problem with humanity was not so much sin, but our inescapable death, which was a barrier to deification (θέωσις) and hence everlasting union with God. Much of this was rooted in divergent Latin and Greek interpretations of Rom. 5:12. For the Latin Fathers, beginning with Tertullian and Cyprian and consolidated with Augustine, humanity's predicament for which we needed redemption was *inherited* guilt, for which death was a penalty.

[75] J. Breck, 'Divine Initiative: Salvation in Orthodox Theology', in J. Meyendorff and R. Tobias, eds., *Salvation in Christ: A Lutheran–Orthodox Dialogue* (Minneapolis: Augsburg Press, 1992), p. 115.

[76] Athanasius, 'On the Incarnation of the Word', §20, in *NPNF²* IV, tr. A. Robertson (Edinburgh: T. & T. Clark, 1891).

might still be alluded to in the term 'interchange' – for Christ is a gift which confounds any system in which we might dare to conceptualise and contain God.

Rom. 5:12–21 is the capital text for understanding just how the grace of God topples over the scales of just retribution. The abundance of grace is God's response to the piling up of our 'many trespasses' (Rom. 5:16), for the grace of God 'overflowed' (ὑπερεπερίσσευσεν, Rom. 5:20), submerging any sins which we had increased. Rom. 5:12–21 therefore charts the inevitability of God's victory of grace, the same inevitability, we might add, which God holds over all the dead. Although many have died as a result of Adam's sin, God's response is 'much more' (πολλῷ μᾶλλον, Rom. 5:15): it is the 'gift' (δωρεά, Rom. 5:15) of Jesus Christ.[77] Death's temporary victory over the man 'in Adam' is as nothing compared to the victory over death declared in the man Jesus Christ. It is no longer death that reigns; the dominion once enjoyed by death has been responded to by that which is 'much more' (Rom. 5:17): the abundance of grace and the gift of righteousness, our reception of which allows *us* to reign in life 'through the one man Jesus Christ' (Rom. 5:17). This exchange powered by God's abundant grace is dramatic – it is no longer death that holds dominion over us, but *we ourselves enjoy dominion* in life, all of this being possible only through Jesus Christ. Barth articulates well the force of this passage when he writes 'It is the slaves of death that are to become the lords of life.'[78] To articulate it even more appropriately, we might recall that we only reign in life through the victory of Christ, itself a sign that it is now grace which reigns (Rom. 5:21). The sphere of Christ's grace allows no space for death to be Lord, for there is only one Lord whose works are assured ultimate victory, 'whether we are alive or dead' (1 Thess. 5:10).

This grace of God which tramples down death does not work on a predictable path of reward and retribution, for it is a grace that is always extending out to 'justify the ungodly' (Rom. 4:5), precisely because in dying 'for us' Jesus dies for the ungodly (Rom. 5:6). Such grace will always deflate our attempts to contain it in any one system or understanding. In refusing to be 'boxed in', the outworking of God's grace wriggles free of the legalistic mindset of the Anselmian perspective: 'the Atonement is not accomplished by strict fulfilment of the demands of justice, but in spite of them; God is not, indeed, unrighteous, but He transcends

---

[77] This phrase, πολλῷ μᾶλλον, is found four times in Romans: in 5:9, 10, 15 and 17.

[78] K. Barth, *Christ and Adam: Man and Humanity in Romans 5*, tr. T. A. Smail (*SJT* Occasional Papers No. 5; Edinburgh: Oliver and Boyd, 1956), p. 22.

the order of justice.'[79] More importantly, the grace of God affords little space for anything resembling a reciprocal process of exchange.[80] The 'reconciling exchange' which God makes known in Christ cannot but be unequal, because the promise of our incorporation within Christ's incorruption is made possible by the incorruptible Christ being fully united to all the corruption of humanity. There is little reciprocation in such grace.

Jesus does indeed communicate to us the life which resides in him, but there is nothing we bring to this exchange, at least not yet. It is God who is in charge of this process of salvation – he is the subject of the action, and it is sin-laden humanity which is the object of God's activity. Rom. 3:25 is often cited as a strong example of humanity being acted upon by the will of God's loving exchange. It is God who promotes Jesus as 'a sacrifice of atonement' (ἱλαστήριον) so as to wipe away the sins of humanity. So too in Rom. 8:32 is God the subject – it is he who did not withhold his own Son, but rather gave him up 'for all of us' (ὑπὲρ ἡμῶν πάντων).[81]

On the cross Jesus takes our place, taking on what is not his, but ours, and in so freeing us from the sting of death, *he* promises us eternal life. This is the exchange alluded to in 1 Thess. 5:10.[82] Jesus takes on our death and dies 'for us', and because the One who died is the One who 'died and rose', our death passes through the promise of the resurrection. Jesus takes on our death 'for us' and gives us in exchange the promise that he has initiated a process whose assured future is that 'we might come to life with him'.[83] We are transferred from death to life precisely *through* the One who died 'for us'. He takes on our death, and we take on his life, insofar as we live and die 'in Christ' (4:16). Participation and substitution – so often the playground for theological tussles – are, in Paul's mind, closely related. It is by Christ's radical substitution that we participate in his risen life. This is the same kind of unequal exchange we saw at work in Rom. 5:12–21. Just as the 'free gift' (χάρισμα) of Christ radically outweighs our trespass (Rom. 5:15a), so too our death, taken on by Christ

---

[79] Aulén, *Christus Victor*, p. 107.

[80] M. D. Hooker, 'Interchange and Atonement', *BJRL* 60 (1978), 462.

[81] Although Paul is convinced not that Christ is an honourable man whose death is of some general benefit, but rather that God is working in and through Christ's death, he should not be read in an overly enthusiastic Nicene sense. Hengel, *The Atonement*, p. 35, notes passages where Jesus is the active subject of his own death: Gal. 1:4; 2:20.

[82] See Hooker, 'Interchange and Atonement', 462–3.

[83] This translation of 1 Thess. 5:10b is offered by R. C. Tannehill, *Dying and Rising with Christ: A Study in Pauline Theology* (Berlin: Verlag Alfred Töpelmann, 1967), pp. 133–4. The aorist subjunctive ζήσωμεν is translated in an inceptive sense, to convey the punctiliar sense of the aorist tense.

'for us', is completely flattened by the grace of life eternal with Christ (4:17; 5:10). God, who communicates his will of salvation through Jesus Christ (5:9), makes known through his Son's death and resurrection, and the subsequent lives called to participate in this triumph, that he is the God of the living:

> The essential point is that Christ died in order that He might bestow upon us His life, which is eternal and unending. Again, there is nothing strange in the fact that he now declares that we live with Christ, since having entered by faith into the kingdom of Christ, we are passing from death into life.[84]

The 'for us' formula is thus only properly understood via a perspective which sees Jesus initiating a process where he takes on that which is not his, and gifts to us in exchange that which we did not deserve. *He* takes on that which is not his – *death* – so that *we* might enjoy that which was not ours – *life* with God in Christ. This notion of reconciling exchange runs throughout the Pauline corpus.[85] Jesus saves because he takes on 'the likeness of sinful flesh' (Rom. 8:3), precisely because like the humanity he was identifying with he was 'born of a woman' (Gal. 4:4). Jesus' death for us is part of his representative saving capacity – Christ's death achieves something 'for all' (2 Cor. 5:14). Taking on *our* poverty, Jesus bestows *his* riches on us (2 Cor. 8:9). *He* is born under the law, so that all those under the law might enjoy sonship, just as *he* is God's Son (Gal. 4:4–5).[86] So too, in Gal. 3:13, Christ becoming a curse 'for us' (ὑπὲρ ἡμῶν) is the means by which we are redeemed from the curse of the law we laboured under. In this divine economy of exchange, the setting aside of our sins plays a vital part. We become the righteousness of God through the One who acts for God, but equally by means of the setting aside of our sins.

---

[84] *Comm. 1 Thess. 5:10.*

[85] E. Käsemann, 'Some Thoughts on the Theme "The Doctrine of Reconciliation in the New Testament"', tr. C. E. Carlston and R. P. Scharlemann, in J. M. Robinson, ed., *The Future of our Religious Past: Essays in Honour of Rudolf Bultmann* (London: SCM, 1971), pp. 49–64, makes the role of reconciliation in Paul's thought completely subsidiary to what he sees as the centre of Paul's thought: justification. Käsemann's *modus operandi* is similar to his 1969 essay (discussed in section 2.1), and he relegates Rom. 5:10f. and 2 Cor. 5:18–21 to 'tradition that was handed down to him' (p. 52). Hence such verses are deemed unreliable indicators of Paul's thought, not least because they represent the first attempts to domesticate the gospel (i.e. insert it into the language of the church), Käsemann's disingenuity is astounding. Whilst inveighing against those who would use the text 'as a quarry for modern theories' (p. 59), he constructs a canon within a canon, a project driven by his theology that 'The church itself is always the greatest obstacle to its own mission' (p. 60).

[86] Dunn, 'Paul's Understanding', p. 47.

Taking on all our sin is a vital part of Jesus' divine act of taking on what is not his. This transfer is well expressed in 2 Cor. 5:21. 'For us' (ὑπὲρ ἡμῶν) the One who knows no sin is made sin so that 'in him' (ἐν αὐτῷ) we might become the 'righteousness of God'. The sinless One, by dying for us, thus transfers all the gifts of God to those who have strayed from God's goodness. These verses, from 2 Cor. 5:18–21, point to the importance of the setting aside of our sin, and yet also to what God is doing in Christ, so that we might enjoy the gifts (i.e. the righteousness) of God. There *is* a salvific 'will of God *in* Christ Jesus' (1 Thess. 5:18) which transactionalist notions of Jesus' death should not let us ignore. Rightly, both New Testament scholars and systematic theologians warn against over-stressing 'substitution' in Paul's thought, at the expense of God's abundant sharing of his gifts.[87]

Before we talk of substitution, or sacrifice, or judgement – a plurality which Christian tradition has discerned in the 'for us' formula – we must talk of that which the death of Christ ultimately reveals: the astonishing act of the divine towards and for us. What the death of Jesus makes known is that God desires us, he wants to live in peace with us (1:1), and he wills that we are delivered from eternal destruction (1:9–10; 5:9). All this he achieves in the unity of his salvific love in and through his Son, and it is this dynamic of divine action that is, prior to everything else, experienced in the Saviour who died 'for us'.

Jesus' death 'for us' is a making known the radical love and self-surrender of God. God, swallowing up our death of destruction, offers us in its place a death of hope, a death in which it is possible for us to see what has become of our dying because in this death God has made himself radically known *for us*.[88] The notion of a reconciling exchange relies upon Christ giving us something. He *gives* his death to us, precisely by taking on our death, so that the story of his death may become the story of each and every one who believes his death to be 'for us', and therefore 'for me' (Gal. 2:20). Recognising that on the cross Jesus plays some kind of substitutionary role need not be read in an exclusive sense – the wondrous exchange of God in Christ involves *us* in God's grace at every stage of Jesus' healing ministry. Our story now becomes part of his

---

[87] See I. U. Dalferth, 'Christ Died for Us: Reflections on the Sacrificial Language of Salvation', in S. W. Sykes, ed., *Sacrifice and Redemption: Durham Essays in Theology* (Cambridge: Cambridge University Press, 1991), p. 320, for a systematic theologian, and Hooker, 'Interchange and Atonement', for a Biblical scholar. Calvin powerfully outlines the 'wondrous exchange' which God reveals in Christ: *Institutes*, IV.xvii.2; *Comm. 2 Cor. 5:21*.

[88] Barth, *The Epistle to the Romans*, p. 160.

story, and his story of what he does with death becomes indispensable for understanding what our death will become in our story. In his dying 'for us' death and life are now fused together – in our lives we walk around with his life-giving death in us (2 Cor. 4:10), and in our deaths we are filled with the very life of God himself. Orientated towards the future, his death is 'for us', because we see in his death what will become 'for us' in our death. More than dying 'for us' in a substitutionary sense, in rising from this very same death, God assures us of Jesus' exemplary new humanity. The reconciling exchange is set to continue.

4   Eschatological participation and promise in 1 Thessalonians

4.1   Theological prolegomena

For Paul, a large part of salvation is in the future, a future in which we must place our hope. The reconciliation which we enjoy through Jesus' death on the cross is a completed action which lies in the past: 'we *were reconciled* to God through the death of his Son' (Rom. 5:10). The aorist passive κατηλλάγημεν implies a complete act whose effects are now complete. Allied to this reconciliation which we 'now' (νῦν, Rom. 5:11) enjoy with God is our future salvation, a salvation from 'the wrath of God' (Rom. 5:9) which *will* be delivered to us 'by his life' (Rom. 5:10).[89] In Paul's thought we are *already* reconciled to God by his cross, but our future salvation is something we wait for with hope, the hope which 'does not disappoint us' (Rom. 5:5). Salvation, for Paul, is tinged with eschatological expectation – it is the life of the Risen One who *will* save us from the coming wrath. Traces of what Paul plots in greater detail in Romans 5 can be seen in 1 Thessalonians. In 1 Thess. 1:10 it is claimed that it is precisely *as* the One who has risen from the dead that Jesus will rescue us from the 'approaching' (ἐρχομένης) wrath. God's election, our 'obtaining of salvation' (περιποίησιν σωτηρίας, 5:9) from this impending wrath, is made possible 'through (διά) our Lord Jesus Christ' (5:9).

Paul articulates here the basis of the hope, not enjoyed by the rest (4:13), and the reason for the injunction that the Thessalonians – and all those who grieve subsequently – are to adopt a distinctive approach to death. It is worth reminding ourselves of the grammatical movement of

---

[89] Paul uses the future passive σωθησόμεθα twice in the space of these two verses, Rom. 5:9–10.

Paul's pastorally directed logic in 4:14. Our conviction of the protasis – that Jesus has known death and known what it is to rise from the realm of death – leads to the comfort of the apodosis: that God, through Jesus, will bring with him those who are sleeping (κοιμηθέντας). The pattern of the life of Jesus – the One who has died and risen – is the guarantor, the pledge of our futures. The resurrection that was his will be ours also. What God has done for Jesus in raising him from the dead he will, through Jesus, do for those who believe. Paul is quite consistent in this belief right to his last letter: 'he who raised Christ from the dead will give life to your mortal bodies also' (Rom. 8:11). The Christian hope, hoping against futility, is that the *whole* of the dead, 'spirit and soul and body' (5:23), will arise to meet the returning Saviour.[90]

For Paul, Jesus' bodily resurrection and our bodily resurrection are linked in a grace of conformity (see Rom. 8:11; 2 Cor. 4:14; 1 Cor. 6:14; Phil. 3:10f.). Paul's revelation was that in Christ, and with his resurrection, it was possible to see evidence of a 'new creation' (2 Cor. 5:17). Correspondingly, Paul counsels the errant Corinthian Christians to be aware of what they are doing with their bodies, for, as he implies, the same power which raised Jesus will raise them up too: 'God raised the Lord and will also raise us by his power' (1 Cor. 6:14). For Paul, indeed, the name of Christ is synonymous with the 'power of God' (Χριστὸν θεοῦ δύναμιν, 1 Cor. 1:24). To believe in the narrative of the One who 'died' and then 'rose' is to believe that the world is now wrapped up in 'the power of his resurrection' (τὴν δύναμιν τῆς ἀναστάσεως αὐτοῦ, Phil. 3:10), that the world has no future, no place to return to, other than God. In Christ, the world now has a new boundary: not the day of *our* death, but the 'day of the Lord' (5:2) when the world and God's triumphant grace will gloriously converge.[91]

Paul realised that to talk of the principle of the resurrection working its way through the world is to enter the realm of images and symbols rather than the hope of literal representation. He describes Christ as the 'first fruits' of those who have fallen asleep (1 Cor. 15:20) and compares

---

[90] There simply is not space here to deal with the debate concerning the relationship between bodily identity and personal identity; nor is it as prominent an issue in 1 Thessalonians as it patently is in 1 Corinthians 15. Paul's notion of the holistic salvation of humanity is made clear in 1 Thess. 5:23. Perhaps the least glib response to this knotty debate is that 'in Christ' our whole identities are perfectly preserved until our bodily resurrection, when who we are in the light of Christ will be fully revealed. R. Williams, 'Nobody Knows Who I am Till Judgement Morning', in *On Christian Theology*, pp. 276–89, is a highly pregnant essay in this regard.

[91] Cf. K. Barth, *Epistle to the Philippians*, tr. J. W. Leitch (Louisville: Westminster John Knox Press, 2002), p. 18.

his return to a harvest (1 Cor. 15:23), when those who were 'sown in weakness' will be 'raised in power' (1 Cor. 15:43, ἐγείρεται ἐν δυνάμει). Like many of the Fathers grappling with the mystery of the world's transfiguration in Christ, Gregory of Nyssa possessed a catena of metaphors which echoed the Pauline conception of a world in the grip of a new power:

> as fire that lies in wood hidden below the surface is often unobserved by the senses of those who see, or even touch it, but is manifest when it blazes up, so too, at His death . . . He who, because He is the Lord of glory, despised that which is shame among men, having concealed, as it were, the flame of His life in His bodily nature, by the dispensation of His death, kindled and inflamed it once more by the power of His own Godhead, fostering into life that which had been brought to death, having infused with the infinity of His divine power that humble first-fruits of our nature.[92]

Just as in Christ's human life, God's very divinity was united to our fleshly humanity, so in our continuing fellowship with Christ, through the Spirit, we await our flaming up, the manifestation of what we are now becoming in Christ, despite the visible persistence of death. The much-vaunted cosmic dimension and scope of the Fathers of the East are easily matched by the Pauline confidence that for those 'in Christ, there is a new creation: everything old has passed away; see, everything has become new!' (2 Cor. 5:17):

> now, as then, He is equally in us . . . Then He mingled Himself with our nature, in order that by this mingling with the Divine Being our nature might become divine, being delivered from death . . . For His return from death becomes to this race of mortals the beginning of the return to immortal life.[93]

Just as the Word was hidden in Christ's flesh, so in our bodies there is an already present participation with Christ's risen flesh, and the triumph of this outworking will be, just as Jesus' was, at our bodily resurrection. Participating in the power of Christ's risen, triumphant life, we are assured that 'we will certainly be united with him in a resurrection like his' (Rom. 6:5). In another of Gregory's suggestive images, just as air pushed

---

[92] Gregory of Nyssa, 'Against Eunomius', V.5, tr. W. Moore and H. A. Wilson, in *NPNF²* V (Edinburgh: T. & T. Clark, 1892).
[93] Gregory of Nyssa, *The Catechetical Oration*, §25.

down into water always escapes back to the surface in a bubble, and as Jesus descending to his death rushed back to the surface (life), so in our deaths, like the air always caught up within the rising bubble, our bodily resurrection, in conformity with his, is assured.[94]

To turn to one of Cyril of Alexandria's favoured images, Christ's resurrected life inserted within the weakness of our bodies is like a hot piece of charcoal placed in a dry straw stack. In the same way that the charcoal would ignite the dry straw and spread fire throughout it, so too Jesus' resurrected life inserted within us through the Eucharist injects our mortal life with his risen power.[95] Alternatively, in the imagery so favoured by Thomas, just as through Jesus' touch of the leper the healing power of his divinity is communicated,[96] so through our communion with the 'fire' of Jesus' resurrected life is its inherent heat communicated to us.[97]

To return to the discussion at the beginning of this chapter, the assurance of our future resurrection is only ever confirmed and built up out of the present experience of grace.[98] Giving voice to our eschatological future, in this perspective, is not here a deductive exercise, but an exercise in tracing *the consequences* of the life we lead now through the graced experience 'in Christ' (4:16).[99] The 'in Christ' formula (explored in section 4.4) reminds us that for Paul salvation is all about being pulled into a relationship with the Saviour himself, a relationship which charts the believer's whole future. In dying 'for us' – in *all* the depths of its substitutionary and reconciling exchange value – Christ initiated a salvific process where God reaches out to us, and we return to God by participating, through the aid of the Spirit, in the life of the risen Christ. As we lead our lives 'in Christ' God now offers us the chance to live in the power of his risen life. For those of faith there is a new imperative at work, the need to consider ourselves 'dead to sin and alive to God in Christ Jesus' (Rom. 6:11).

We have now examined Paul's claim that Jesus 'died for us' in its rich multivocality, climaxing with the image of the reconciling exchange (section 3.3). This reconciling exchange, which is set to continue, will be known most fully with the resurrection of the dead, a doctrine which we have the best hope of exploring through images. Consolidating our reading of 1 Thessalonians, we shall turn now to a number of images within 1 Thessalonians which point to the resurrection of the dead: a community transfigured and transformed (section 4.2); images of light

---

[94] *Ibid.* Cf. Tanner, *Jesus*, p. 117.

[95] Cyril of Alexandria, 'Commentary on John', in *Cyril of Alexandria*, tr. N. Russell (London: Routledge, 2000), pp. 117–18.

[96] *Lectio* IV.II.95.   [97] Cf. *ST* 3a q. 56 a.1 re.

[98] Rahner, 'The Hermeneutics', p. 342.   [99] Tanner, *Jesus*, p. 104.

and prayer within 1 Thessalonians (section 4.3); the image of the 'dead in Christ' (section 4.4); the 'sleeping' Christians (section 4.5); and the image of the parousia itself (section 4.6).

4.2   Transfiguration and transformation in 1 Thessalonians

Paul's revelation in 1 Thessalonians can be related concisely: in Christ what it is to live and what it is to die are now totally reconfigured. The believer in Christ is distinguished by the triad of faith, love and hope: 'We always give thanks to God for all of you, constantly mentioning you in our prayers, remembering before our God and Father your work of faith and labour of love (ἀγάπης) and steadfastness of hope in our Lord Jesus Christ' (1:2–3). To enter into the community called together by God is to live out a faith making itself known through its own generative power (1:8); it is to live in a community where there is an abundance of sacrificial love extending to one another and all (3:12; 4:9–10; 5:13, 15); and it is to live with a hope that looks for the consummation of this world in the will of God (1:10; 2:12, 19; 3:13; 4:13–18; 5:4). Squeezing this triad of faith, love and hope into two items of metaphorical armour, and in a possible reference to Isa. 59:17, Paul refers to Christian life as equipped with 'a breastplate of faith and love and a helmet, the hope of salvation' (5:8). For Thomas such spiritual armoury safeguards our present wellbeing – 'the life of the Spirit in us . . . Christ, through whom the soul lives' – and ensures our salvation, 'the goal which we hope to attain'.[100] This 'hope of salvation' (ἐλπίδα σωτηρίας, 5:8) is thus the outworking of faith in God's salvific will, the will to attain 'salvation *through* our Lord Jesus Christ' (σωτηρίας διὰ τοῦ κυρίου ἡμῶν Ἰησοῦ Χριστοῦ, 5:9).

In an elementary sense, it is faith which adopts what is made known by God in Christ: the source of humanity's conversion to God. It is faith in the work of the One who has died and risen that calls forth a new obedience to love, and a hope that our futures are 'already seized and determined'.[101]

Paul's redrawing of what it is to live and to die is an image cast around Christ. The most important identity which the Thessalonian Christians have is their location *within* the saving purposes of God, an especially prominent theme in this epistle. This is a location which totally relativises any grief which the Thessalonians manifest over the supposed gulf that now separates the living from the dead. The Thessalonian Christians are part of a church which is '*in* God the Father and the Lord Jesus Christ'

---

[100] *Lectio* V.I.120; Duffy, *Commentary*, p. 46.   [101] *CD* IV/1, p. 116.

(1:1). The salvific 'word of God' has a power which has worked through the Thessalonians, '*in* you who believe' (2:13). In this verse Paul reveals everything which is happening pertaining to faith as the work of God and his Word. Despite all the tribulations which Paul knows they have suffered, they still 'stand firm *in* the Lord' (3:8). Just as Paul and his co-workers encourage them '*in* the Lord Jesus' (4:1), so likewise are those caring for them doing so '*in* the Lord' (5:12).

As Cyril of Alexandria noted, there is a reciprocity between being '*in* Christ' and being '*in* God', for the 'gospel of God' (2:9) *is* the 'gospel of Christ' (3:2) (section 4.4). The very source of the church itself is the work of 'God the Father and the Lord Jesus Christ' (1:1) interlocked. This revealing of God's will in the person of Jesus is indicated towards the end of the letter, where Paul talks of 'the will of God in Christ Jesus' (θεοῦ ἐν Χριστῷ Ἰησοῦ, 5:18). Just as believers live and die 'in Christ', so in a similar manner God expresses his will 'in Christ'. This is a relationship proper to God, but is ours insofar as we are gathered into the ἐκκλησία and brought into faith by the inspiration of the Holy Spirit.[102] The salvific narrative, heralded by the God who 'raised Jesus from the dead' (1:10) is thus only made part of the individual believer's lives by the activity of the Holy Spirit. The origins of faith lie not in our nature, but with the initiative of the Spirit of God.[103]

For Paul the Holy Spirit is a gift of God to the Thessalonians (4:8). It is the same Holy Spirit which Paul and his fellow missionaries have received (1:5), and gives them the strength that comes from being 'in God' (2:2). It is this Spirit that enables the Thessalonians, even in the midst of persecution, to receive God's Word 'with joy of the Holy Spirit' (μετὰ χαρᾶς πνεύματος ἁγίου, 1:6). The resilient faith of the Thessalonians – behind which lies the Holy Spirit's activity – is a recurrent theme in 1 Thessalonians. It was because the Thessalonian Christians received the Word with the 'joy of the Holy Spirit' that their faith has 'become known' (ἐξελήλυθεν, 1:8) throughout Macedonia, Achaia and beyond (1:7–8). Little wonder, then, that the Thessalonian converts are Paul's 'glory and joy' (2:20). Indeed, so vibrant is the Thessalonians' faith that it even enables Paul to 'live' (3:8), a flourish which reveals how faith is something built up (cf. 5:11) corporately. All the more vital, then, that what God has given (4:8) and is the cause of their joyful faith amidst persecution, the Holy Spirit, should not be quenched (5:19).

---

[102] The Hebrew roots of ἐκκλησία (referring to a community gathered together at God's calling) are picked up by commentators, on the assumption that Paul is consciously building upon them. See, amongst others, Tarazi, *1 Thessalonians*, pp. 22–6.

[103] *Comm. 1 Thess. 1:6.*

It is most likely that this same Holy Spirit was thought to be behind what Paul says in 1 Thess. 4:9 is 'God-taught' (θεοδίδακτοι) – 'brotherly love' (φιλαδελφίας) and 'the love of one another' (τὸ ἀγαπᾶν ἀλλήλους). The Christian life, a life not humanly devised but 'God-taught',[104] is to love and serve others – a dedication made known by Paul's giving of his very 'being' (ψυχάς) to the Thessalonian Christians (2:8). It was only because of the love Paul had for the Thessalonians that he offers to them not only that which he preaches, but his very self.[105] Paul's self-surrender to the Thessalonian Christians is its own imitation of the One who 'did not please himself' (Rom. 15:3), an early indication of the one who would later boast of becoming 'a slave to all' (1 Cor. 9:19).

A life of sacrificial love, giving to the point of one's very *being*, is a life of ultimate freedom, a life which in its moments and acts of love witnesses to that which is eternal and radically valid. Paul's life witnesses to that which *cannot die*,[106] a service which as Thomas implies by his use of John 10:11 has its origins in Christ's triumphant love: 'The good shepherd lays down his life for the sheep.'[107] This God-taught ἀγάπη is, as Maximus the Confessor says in his writing on deifying love, the Christian virtue through which God and humanity are brought into union.[108] The love which Paul hopes *the Lord* will help them increase and abound in for one another (ὑμᾶς δὲ ὁ κύριος πλεονάσαι καὶ περισσεύσαι τῇ ἀγάπῃ εἰς ἀλλήλους, 3:12) is for Maximus the means by which the world and its inhabitants are transfigured, and brought together as one, at the initiative of the One who out of the impulse of the divine love became human.[109] The love of the One who died 'for us', mirrored in the transfigured community which, taught by God, abounds in the same self-giving love, is the means by which God and his people are drawn ever closer in union.

In a world of mourning and 'darkness' (5:4), the sign of what we are to enjoy in the richness of divine life is therefore traced by who we are becoming *now* through the aid of the Spirit. As we expand in love for one another, 'more and more' (περισσεύειν μᾶλλον, 4:10), the principle of God's transforming grace can be seen to be at work in the life of the church: God *is* 'calling' us (5:24) and we '*are* sons of light and of the day' (5:5).

---

[104] Interestingly, the word θεοδίδακτος is a Pauline neologism.

[105] Best, *A Commentary*, p. 102.

[106] Cf. K. Rahner, 'The Life of the Dead', in *Theological Investigations*, vol. IV, tr. K. Smyth (London: Darton, Longman and Todd, 1966), pp. 348–9.

[107] *Lectio* II.I.34.

[108] Maximus the Confessor, 'Letter 2: On Love', in Louth, *Maximus*, p. 90.

[109] *Ibid.*, pp. 87–8.

4.3   Light and prayer in 1 Thessalonians

As Thomas recognised, 'light' is an exceedingly rich intra-textual Scriptural term.[110] Paul's description of the Thessalonians as 'sons (or children) of light' (5:5), mentioned in an eschatological context, affords us the opportunity to turn to the interpretations which 'light' enjoys in the mystical theology of Eastern Christianity. As we shall see, in Orthodox and Eastern Patristic interpretations of Jesus' transfiguration, 'light' possesses both an eschatological depth and an allusion to mystical progression.[111]

There is a close connection between the light of the transfiguration by which Christ's divinity was revealed, the light of which we are children now, and the parousia.[112] Such a deployment of the gospel transfiguration narratives and their pre-modern interpretation is notable for two reasons. First of all, in attempting to understand more sharply what Paul refers to only obliquely, we are turning to extra-Pauline canonical texts. Echoes of what Paul writes about are discerned in these non-Pauline texts, a resonance possible to detect only with the assistance of the Patristic heritage. Reference needs to be made here to the opening remarks in the introduction to this chapter. Whilst Biblical scholars are attuned to reading the Bible as a randomly compiled collection of texts, emanating from a medley of contexts and interests, one of the contributions that theological exegetes might hope to make is an ontological one – that Scripture *is*, in the purposes of God, a unified witness to the saving will of God. Secondly, in this use of the transfiguration we are confronting the contemporary lacuna in theological readings of the events of Jesus' human life. In both these instances our Christ-ruled reading of Paul comes to our aid, allowing us to trespass on ground often deemed unapproachable.

As at the transfiguration, when the disciples see Jesus as who he really is – as the One who is the very life and light of God himself – so the parousia, for us, marks the full disclosure, the definitive revelation of the life we are carrying within ourselves in this present age. The parousia, and the final judgement which Paul associates with it (3:13), is the definitive unveiling of who, in life, we are and were: the life 'in Christ' which lives by his light, awaiting the day when 'the just will shine like the sun' (Mt. 13:43). As the transfiguration revealed the ultimate reality of Jesus'

---

[110] *Lectio* V.I.115.

[111] V. Lossky, *The Mystical Theology of the Eastern Church*, various translators (Crestwood: Saint Vladimir's Seminary Press, 1976), pp. 217–35.

[112] Gregory Palamas, *The Triads*, II.iii.20, tr. N. Gendle (New York: Paulist Press, 1983).

life, revealing him as the One he truly was,[113] so it is necessary to say
that there is an end to the world which reveals, discloses, unveils *our*
ultimate reality, the 'light' by which we live. So too, as the disciples on
the mountain were bathed in the divine light of Jesus' 'inborn glory of
the Godhead',[114] when we attain the state of being 'with Jesus forever'
(4:17) we shall be inundated with the vision of the divine glory:[115]

> in the age to come *we shall always be with the Lord*, beholding
> Christ refulgent in the light of the Godhead.[116]

The 'day' to which we belong as 'sons of light' (5:5), this definitive
manifestation of our complete transfiguration by grace, is the end of what
is now a 'hidden, secret, invisible glory', and a disclosure of that which
is 'unfailingly glorious':[117]

> For what is our hope and joy and crown of glory – is it not you –
> before our Lord Jesus at his coming? For you yourselves are our
> glory and joy!   (2:19–20)

The light of the Spirit we are now (5:5), in our 'bodies' as Paul says
in 2 Cor. 4:6, is therefore a pledge of the eschatological light that will
dazzle and transform us, in a manner similar to the dazzling light which
revealed the true nature of Jesus' body on Mt Tabor.[118] United to God in
Christ's saving work, we already carry within ourselves that light which,
banishing all shadows and images, will reveal fully who we are becoming

---

[113] D. Rogich, 'Homily 34 of Saint Gregory Palamas', tr. D. Rogich, *GOTR* 33
(1988), §7.

[114] John Damascene, 'Homily on the Transfiguration of our Lord Jesus Christ by Saint
John of Damascus', tr. H. L. Weatherby, *GOTR* 32 (1987), §10.

[115] Palamas, *Triads*, III.i.10, citing Pseudo-Dionysius.

[116] John Damascene, 'Homily on the Transfiguration', §15 (my italics).

[117] Barth, *Epistle to the Philippians*, p. 78.

[118] The leaps made here are exactly those Gregory Palamas makes in *Triads*, III.iii.9:
'Similarly, the chosen disciples saw the essential and eternal beauty of God on Tabor . . .
the very formless form of the divine loveliness, which deifies man and makes him worthy
of personal converse with God; the very Kingdom of God, eternal and endless, the very
light beyond intellection and unapproachable, the heavenly and infinite light, out of time
and eternal, the light that makes immortality shine forth, the light which deifies those who
contemplate it. They indeed saw the same grace of the Spirit which would later dwell in
them . . . they contemplated that uncreated light which, even in the ages to come, will be
ceaselessly visible only to the saints.'
Earlier, Pseudo-Dionysius had linked the gospel account of the transfiguration with
1 Thess. 4:17. See 'The Divine Names', in *Pseudo-Dionysius: The Complete Works*, tr.
C. Luibheid (London: SPCK, 1987), p. 52.
See also *ST* 3a q. 45 a. 2 ad. 3, where Thomas reads the splendour of Christ's body on
Mt Tabor as a sign of believers' future state.

through the Spirit-led life. We have now, as 'sons of light' (5:5), a principle of the future's shape. For just as Christ is the true light and reveals himself as such to the three disciples on Mt Tabor, so at his coming in dazzling brightness, God will reveal just how much he wills our bodily transformation, something he had already signalled at the transfiguration:

> He will come again with His body, as I have learned, in such form as He was seen by His disciples on the mountain, as He showed Himself for that moment when His deity overpowered His carnality.[119]

Precision is important here about the kind of parallels drawn. Whether the light we have now as children awaiting full maturity is the radiance of Christ's glory *reflected* in our being or whether it is the energy of Christ moving within us is of less importance than stating categorically that Christ's glory and that glory which *we* both share in and anticipate are not to be ontologically confused. Eastern Orthodox thinking has always been careful to distinguish between the 'essence' and 'energy' of the God who reveals himself in Christ. Our unity with God, made possible by God in Christ incarnate, is never confused with this unique and unrepeatable hypostatic union. God's energies provide the basis for our mystical experience, but we do not in any way approach the essence of God. Pulling close to the light revealed in Christ, we become participants in the light and 'of' it, united with its forward expansion, but not in any way confused with its uncreated essence:

> He who participates in the divine energy, himself becomes, to some extent, light; he is united to the light; and by that light he sees in full awareness all that remains hidden to those who have not this grace . . . for the pure in heart see God . . . who, being light, dwells in them and reveals Himself to those who love Him.[120]

This life lived out in the light, straining towards the uncreated and transformative light of the parousia, is distinguished by its constancy of prayer. In the history of the church, and especially those with strong monastic traditions, Paul's injunction to pray 'ceaselessly' (ἀδιαλείπτως, 1 Thess. 5:17) has provoked a rich stream of thought. Although some have read

---

[119] Gregory Nazianzen, 'St Gregory Nazianzen's Letter to Cledonius', translated in McGuckin, *St. Cyril*, p. 393.

[120] Gregory of Palamas, 'Homily on the Presentation of the Holy Virgin in the Temple'. Cited in and translated by Lossky, *Mystical Theology*, p. 224.

Paul's injunction in the strictest literal sense, in the sense of 'saying prayers',[121] as early as Origen the Fathers recognised that the only way to read Paul's injunction was by uniting

> prayer with the deeds required and right deeds with prayer. For the only way we can accept the command to 'pray constantly' as referring to a real possibility is by saying that the entire life of the saint taken as a whole is a single great prayer. What is customarily called prayer is, then, a part of this prayer.[122]

In its mystical sense prayer is the ascent of the individual to God, the rising up of the whole person into the presence of God. 'We supplicate with this continual supplication not to convince God, for he acts always spontaneously, nor to draw him to us, for he is everywhere, but to lift ourselves up towards him.'[123] Prayer is the spiritual approach to God, of which our glorification at the parousia is the final stage. Set in such a key, prayer is not purely a vocal exercise as some have erroneously thought, but an active and ceaseless participation within God's vision and work. As Kallistos Ware articulates, praying 'ceaselessly' is 'not so much an activity as a state'.[124] The mainstream of Eastern monasticism has therefore understood Paul's injunction as a call to take on an implicit state of prayer, a call 'to be prayer' in everything we do, driven by a continual wonder at God. This assumption of prayer within the total being of the loving individual before God is, as Kallistos Ware points out, a road of discipline and faith in God's grace.[125] Being in a state of continual prayer – 'being prayer' – is not something that comes automatically or cheaply. Integrating the state of prayer, as communion within God and ascent to God, within our whole selves (body, soul and spirit) and within *all* that we do is ultimately a question of faithful discipleship, a responsibility open to all Christians and not just a spiritual élite:

> Sacred Scripture never commands us to do what is impossible. The Apostle himself recited Psalms, read Scripture, and served others, yet he prayed without ceasing. Continual prayer means

---

[121] The fourth- and fifth-century monastic movement of Syria and the Near East – the Messalians – interpreted Paul's injunction quite literally, and prayed vocally to the exclusion of everything else.

[122] Origen, 'On Prayer', XII.2, in *Origen*, tr. R. Greer (London: SPCK, 1979).

[123] Palamas, *Triads*, II.i.30. Cited in J. Meyendorff, *A Study of Gregory Palamas*, tr. G. Lawrence (London: The Faith Press, 1964), p. 141.

[124] K. Ware, 'Pray Without Ceasing', in *The Inner Kingdom* (Crestwood: Saint Vladimir's Seminary Press, 2000), p. 81.

[125] *Ibid.*, p. 84.

keeping the soul attentive to God with great reverence and love,
constantly hoping in him. It means entrusting ourselves to him
in everything that happens, whether in things we do or in events
that occur.[126]

The state of constant prayer becomes, in this perspective, a drive towards
union with God,[127] a future in which we are promised being 'with Jesus
forever' (4:17). The emphasis of constant prayer is not so much on vocal
words directed to God (although that clearly has an important role) as on
a ceaseless enjoyment of the life of God within one's own life, a deep
sense that one is being taken up into the reality of God.[128] Moreover, we
would want to add the proviso that 'being prayer' is not grasped in full
now, but must await the final consummation of the parousia. Just as we
have within us the light of God now, but at the end will shine with light
in all our being, so too at the end will we *be* what we practise now –
ceaseless prayer.

4.4   The 'dead in Christ'

Paul's desire is that the Thessalonian Christians should see no separation
between the biologically dead and alive, because in dying 'for us' Christ
enables both the dead and the living to live with him (5:10). In this context
Paul's assertion that the believer's relationship with Christ survives death
is not surprising. If God 'raised Jesus from the dead' (1:10), it seems apt
that Paul declares to the church that is also 'in God the Father' (1:1) –
i.e. the same God who raised Jesus – that their dead are 'in Christ'
(4:16).

The image of 'the dead in Christ' will occupy our attention in this
section. It is much more than a synonym for 'dead Christians'. Paul, it
is true, uses the phrase 'in Christ' in a number of ways, not all of them
conveying a sense of mystical participation,[129] but in this instance there
can be little dispute that it means much more than what we understand
by the term 'Christian'. There are two principal reasons why we can

---

[126] Maximus the Confessor, *Liber Asceticus*, no. 25. *PG* 90:929D; 932A. Cited and
translated in I. Hausherr, *The Name of Jesus*, tr. C. Cummings (Kalamazoo: Cistercian
Press, 1978), p. 137.

[127] Palamas, *Triads*, II.iii.35.

[128] D. Stăniloae, *Prayer and Holiness*, tr. Sisters of the Love of God (Oxford: Sisters of
the Love of God Press, 1982), p. 10.

[129] Apart from the mystical-locative sense 'in Christ' enjoys in 1 Thess. 4:16, Paul can
deploy 'in Christ' in an instrumental sense, with the meaning that Christ is the instrument of God's salvific will. One example is Rom. 3:24, 'the redemption that is in Christ
Jesus'.

say that 'in Christ' means much more than 'Christian'. First, it is surely significant that the phrase is always linked to claims of Jesus' Messiahship or Lordship. Thus although we find Paul using 'in Christ', 'in Christ Jesus' or 'in the Lord', *never* in the *Hauptbriefe* do we find the phrase 'in Jesus'. Secondly, the paralleling of the phrase ἐν τῷ Ἀδάμ with ἐν τῷ Χριστῷ in 1 Cor. 15:22 would suggest a juxtaposing of two different spheres of power and dominion. There is much more depth within this phrase than 'dead Christian' would allow. Nevertheless, it should equally be noted that I am agnostic about whether or not Paul *intended* his 'in Christ' to convey the realism I sense, having much more conviction that it can legitimately be theologically exegeted in this way, as words pointing towards a salvific reality.

Close reading suggests that it is significant that the text does not refer to 'the dead who were in Christ', but instead to a *present* reality running across the temporal interruption of death. The text clearly refers to the dead *who are* in Christ, an interpretative move supported by 5:9–10, where both the dead and living are caught up within the saving dominion of 'the Lord Jesus Christ'. Death presents no barrier to the Lordship of the One who 'died and rose', for in himself he has broken through death's boundary, and has the capacity now to embrace both the dead and living. These three words – νεκροὶ ἐν Χριστῷ – thus present the paradox of faith in Christ: although dead we continue to be saved by the force that is our salvation, for we remain alive to the outworking of God's saving resurrection.

To talk of 'the dead in Christ' is highly risky. On the one hand, 'the dead in Christ' is clearly metaphorical in some way, in the sense that our language cannot entirely correspond to the transcendent reality it is trying to depict. Since our union with Christ is an operation of God, through the activity of the Holy Spirit,[130] we should be looking for recognition that there is no neat division between our language and full perception. Although there is no tidy correspondence between our language and the reality which it is trying to evoke, we can say that 'the dead in Christ' *is* pointing to something that is really true. The dead *really are* in Christ, though we should not confuse that reality with the language under which we labour. Here we meet the paradox of eschatological faith – the dead really are in Christ, though this is not a reality which our language can capture or contain. In this sense the language

---

[130] Cf. 1 Cor. 1:30, where Paul indicates that God is the 'source' of their life 'in Christ' (ἐξ αὐτοῦ δὲ ὑμεῖς ἐστε ἐν Χριστῷ Ἰησοῦ).

of Scriptural revelation is the revelation of eschatological mystery, not clarity. Within the very language itself is *hidden* a reality which, although we may unfold and unravel it, we cannot expect to possess fully in understanding.

The use of 'in Christ' is shorthand and a pointer to the mystical reality of where the dead are now: those who have died believing in the saving work of Christ Jesus are still within the fold of his grace, and will rise from the dead to meet with all who have died after them. This is akin to passages where Paul talks of Christ living in him (Gal. 2:20), language which, although it points to something that is ultimately true, is not verifiable in any crude physical sense. Clearly there would be no physical tests we could apply to affirm whether or not Christ is 'in' somebody, or we are 'in' Christ, but that does not in any sense make them untrue statements of a reality. The reality that such language is pointing to is therefore the participation of ourselves and our futures in the saving works of God in Christ. Living in Christ, and with Christ living within us, we no longer lead a created life, but rather the eternal life of God who dwelt within Jesus.[131] What is happening to those 'in Christ' is the communication to us of the life Christ possessed and enjoyed by virtue of his divine union. The pattern of God in Christ's suffering life, death and triumphant resurrection is now open to all, 'in Christ': 'I have been crucified with Christ; and it is no longer I who live, but it is Christ who lives in me' (Gal. 2:19–20).

Christ's grace (explored above in the 'for us' formula) and our faith meeting, Christ passes his dominion over death to all those 'in' him. United to Christ's death 'for us', being 'in Christ' is faith's appropriation of all that Christ has achieved 'for us', as Calvin powerfully recognised:

> as long as Christ remains outside of us, and we are separated from him, all that he has suffered and done for the salvation of the human race remains useless and of no value for us . . . all that he possesses is nothing to us until we grow into one body with him.[132]

---

[131] Palamas, *Triads*, III.i.35. So Meyendorff, *Gregory Palamas*, p. 182, on Palamas' soteriology links our salvation 'in Christ' indissolubly with the hypostatic union as the ontological root of our deification. It is important to clarify, however, that Eastern Christianity has always been aware that there is only one, unrepeatable hypostasis. Whilst the incarnation has set up the renewed possibility of a reciprocity between God and humanity, there is *never* any suggestion in Eastern Christian thought of a mingling of the essence of divine and human natures.

[132] Calvin, *Institutes*, III.i.1.

Eastern Christianity's understanding of the synergy between God's grace and our faith might help here in exploring the relationship between Christ and those united to him, in life or death. The benefits of his divine power are transferred to the humanity of the 'dead in Christ', yet with no suggestion that the one becomes the other. What happens in the synergistic movement is not so much the equal cooperation of God and humanity as partners as the meeting of our will to be saved with God's redeeming love.[133] The classical hypostatic images which communicate union without confusion are clearly relevant to understanding our union 'in Christ'. The union of the 'dead in Christ' with the risen Christ is like the relationship between a flame and a wick,[134] or between the heat and sharpness of a searing sword.[135] Just as there are in these instances two distinct operations and yet one effect, so too 'in Christ' are the effects of Christ's union with the Word communicated to us without confusion. Whilst never becoming ontologically confused with Christ, his effects are fully communicated to us.

To die 'in Christ' is therefore to enter into a movement and dynamic of grace initiated by God in Christ. In a Rahnerian sense it is to make a supreme decision of freedom, allowing ourselves to be defined by the mysterious boundlessness of Christ and his future, taking the choice in freedom to allow our lives to reach their point of consummation in Christ's grace. Dying in Christ, we enter the realm of 'the dead in Christ', becoming in death what we chose to be and align ourselves with during our life. Our lives and our deaths, in Christ, are thus radically interwoven, just as Christ's death was filled with the life of God. To be dead in Christ is to be caught up within the saving work of Christ, open to his grace and assured of a conformity to the pattern of Jesus' life, death and resurrection. God in Christ dying for us becomes himself the boundary of the death that bounds us, and so we dying in Christ bring all that our deaths signify and represent into a point of connection with this life-saving force. Dying 'in Christ' as an act of faith is a statement that God remains as God the Healer and Redeemer in the very face of death, that God in Christ has now invaded and defeated the threat of death.

---

[133] Williams, *The Ground of Union*, p. 133.

[134] Gregory of Nyssa, 'An Address on Religious Instruction', §10.

[135] John Damascene, 'Exposition of the Orthodox Faith', III.xv. The image of a burning-hot sword, which acquires both the property of a searing heat and a cutting edge in union, without there being any change in either property, was a favourite Patristic motif. See Maximus the Confessor, 'Difficulty 5', in Louth, *Maximus*, p. 178.

4.5   The 'sleeping' Christians

Commentators are keen on noting Paul's metaphor for the dead in 4:13: they are 'sleeping' (κοιμώμενος), not dead.[136] For some, Paul is here deploying a euphemism for death, akin to the contemporary 'passing on'.[137] Charles Wanamaker notes that the idiom, in its Greek and Hebrew deployment, conveyed no presuppositions of an afterlife.[138] Rather than relying on the word's pre-history in Hebrew usage, there may be potential in concentrating upon its literary context. Fruitfully, Martin Luther observes that in 4:14, Paul does not use the same verb to refer to Christ's own death (ἀπέθανεν).[139] It is worth exploring the underlying logic evident within 4:13–14, as noted by Luther. The Thessalonian Christians are not to grieve, 'for' (γάρ) those who believe that Christ 'died and rose' must see that the 'dead in Christ' (4:16) are in actual fact sleeping (κοιμωμένων). Christ died, but those who die *in him* now sleep, because the death and resurrection of Christ 'in this way' (οὕτως) point to our conformity with this act of rising to new life.[140]

As it is for 'the others' (οἱ λοιποί, 4:13), our death is therefore a tangible end to something physical. But there is hope for those who die 'in Christ' because Christian death has close parallels with sleep.[141] On the one hand, there is in both sleep and death a dumbing of the senses,[142] but on the other, both in 'sleep' and with 'dying in Christ' there is the expectation that we shall wake again 'refreshed and restored'.[143] Just as Christ rises out of the darkness of hell and into the dawn of a new day, so his rising at first light points forward to the glory awaiting our bodies' redemption on the 'Day of the Lord'.[144] Christ's own resurrection at daybreak was,

---

[136] Best, *A Commentary*, p. 185, rigorously maintains that in Paul's usage the term has no reference to an 'intermediate state'. What I am building here upon Paul's use of the word 'sleeping' might appear to have no justification in the sense that Paul intended. Nevertheless, as throughout this study, my role is less that of a 'curator' and more that of exploring the text's polysemy and meaning through time.

[137] E.g. Richard, *First and Second Thessalonians*, p. 226.

[138] C. A. Wanamaker, *The Epistles to the Thessalonians* (NIGTC; Grand Rapids: Eerdmans, 1990), p. 167.

[139] M. Luther, 'Two Funeral Sermons, 1532', in *Luther's Works*, vol. LI, ed. and tr. F. W. Doberstein (Philadelphia: Muhlenberg Press, 1959), p. 233.

[140] One would not want to stretch this too far, for it is clear that in the sense that Jesus was resurrected, his death too had slumber-like qualities. What Luther points to, correctly, I think, is the transformation open to all believers. In dying and rising, Christ transforms our death into something from which we shall awake.

[141] *CD* III/2, pp. 638–9.   [142] Luther, 'Two Funeral Sermons', p. 239.

[143] *Lectio* IV.II.93; Duffy, *Commentary*, p. 35.   [144] Cf. *ST* 3a q. 53 a. 2 ad. 3.

in every way, a proleptic pledge of the redemption awaiting our bodies as we awake from our sleep.

At the very least we can concur with Barth when he notes how strikingly peaceful the image of believers 'falling asleep' is, a peace which is itself an image of the reconciliation delivered by God in Christ going ahead and dying 'for us'. If we can assume that Paul was picking up and adopting an early Christian term for Christian death (which would appear to be corroborated by the use of the aorist passive ἐκοιμήθη in Acts 7:60), the word denotes a notable pacificity, a conviction that death itself is now embraced within God's peace.[145] Death, having passed through the life of God in Christ, has been deprived of its grip over us, and our state of dormition symbolises our patient anticipation of death's final defeat. After all, as Chrysostom encouraged us to realise, if the dead are awaiting their resurrection, and the hope of a fuller life, then it is right to displace death with talk of sleep.[146]

4.6   The consummation of the world in God's grace

Towards the end of 1 Thess. 4:13–18 Paul turns to a number of fantastic images in his portrayal of the victory and consummation of God's grace over death: there will be a shout of command, God's trumpet will sound,[147] archangels will cry out, Christ will descend from heaven (where he reigns), the dead and the living will be 'caught up', and both will rise to a meeting with Jesus in the clouds (4:16–17). Properly used, these symbols and images of the victory of Christ's communion over death should be constantly exerting us to know more of God's transcendent will *through them*. Awareness that these images do not *in themselves* depict reality, and yet a reality is depicted through them, is intrinsic

---

[145] *CD* III/2, p. 639.

[146] John Chrysostom, *In. Haebr.*, Hom. 17:2; *PG* 63:129. Cited in and translated by J. Meyendorff, *Byzantine Theology: Historical Trends and Doctrinal Themes* (2nd edn; New York: Fordham University Press, 1983), p. 162.

[147] As Thomas' commentary (*Lectio* IV.II.99) witnesses, Christian tradition commonly understood the 'shout of command' as a reference to Jn. 5:28. Cyril of Alexandria, *Commentary on the Gospel According to St John*, VII (on Jn. 11:43–4), understands this resurrection call in line with Jesus' command to Lazarus to come out of the cave (Jn. 11:43), and Paul's reference to the 'trumpet of God' in line with the Feast of the Tabernacles: 'Celebrate it as "a memorial of trumpets" (Lev. 23:24). For when human bodies are about to be set up again, as tabernacles, and every man's soul is about to take to itself its own bodily habitation in a way as yet unknown, the masterful command will be previously proclaimed, and the signal of the resurrection will sound forth, even the "the trump of God" (1 Thess. 4:16), as it is said. As a type therefore of this, in the case of Lazarus Christ uttered a great and audible cry.'

to a knowledge of God's mystery attuned to apophaticism. In vocabulary familiar to practitioners of apophaticism, our reading must be disciplined by the dazzling darkness of these bright yet necessarily opaque images.

As we read this beguiling mixture of imagery 'around Christ', it becomes clear that the key image is the representation of us ascending and Christ descending (once again) to meet us. Reference should be made here to our climactic understanding of Jesus' death 'for us' (section 3.3), most fully understood as a 'wondrous exchange'. Just as God in Christ initiated the salvific process of restoration by 'coming down' or 'descending' to our level, so we are assured that our future is of 'rising up' and fully enjoying in our bodily selves the life of God.[148] The images which the text employs – the Lord will descend (καταβήσεται) from heaven, the dead will rise (ἀναστήσονται) and the dead and the living will be caught up together to meet Jesus in the clouds – point towards the whole reality and triumph of the incarnational drama: God in Christ descending to our level, to raise us up to his level.[149] The triumphant conclusion of this process of salvation, finally manifest at Jesus' parousia, is its own microcosm of the cosmic reconciling exchange: he descends to meet us and we rise up to his level. Jesus coming down from heaven symbolises that which is true of his incarnation: that he is *both* the One who comes down from his Godhead and eternally the One who lifts us up out of our present existence and into the potential of life with God for ever (4:17). Only at the parousia is this divine plan complete, for only then do we 'body and soul and spirit' live with Jesus eternally:

> the Lord, putting on the body, became man, so we men are deified by the Word as being taken to Him through His flesh.[150]

There is always the risk of saying too much about eschatology and our end 'in Christ'. It is important to outline what we can and cannot say the resurrection of the whole of our dead selves represents in the saving will of God in Christ. The resurrection of our bodies is the triumphant

---

[148] So Cyril of Alexandria, *On the Unity of Christ*, p. 64.

[149] A common strand in Byzantine and Orthodox thought, e.g. Maximus the Confessor, 'Ad Thalassium 22', in *On the Cosmic Mystery of Jesus Christ: Selected Writings from St Maximus the Confessor*, tr. P. M. Blowers and R. L. Wilken (Crestwood: Saint Vladimir's Seminary Press, 2003), pp. 115–18.

[150] Athanasius, 'Four Discourses against the Arians', III.xxvi.34. Deification, vital to Eastern Patristic soteriology, is most linked with the interpretation of 2 Peter 1:4 (and Ps. 82:6), and less with the Pauline texts. However, Breck, 'Divine Initiative', p. 119, tentatively links Paul's Christ-mysticism in 1 Thess. 4:16 with 'participation in divine life' and hence with *theōsis*.

conclusion to the reconciling exchange revealed by God in Christ. Our bodies are something *desired* by God, for from creation, via the whole drama of incarnation and through to our bodily resurrection, bodies are revealed both as something which God uses and something in which he takes delight. The parousia is the triumphant conclusion of our grace-filled return to God, the necessary final chapter of the resurrection by which God desires to live with us in harmony and for eternity (4:17).

While it is not for us to predict the 'how' of the transformation of our selves before God, it *is* the legitimate role of theology to explore how the parousia acts as an attestation of the God whose purpose for humanity *will* reach consummation. Just as God in Christ offers all the promise of his life-giving power, so we in Christ take on and adopt and become all that God himself is in Christ.[151] To be 'in Christ' is therefore to have made an eschatological decision, that our futures are somehow more than just with God but, mystically, located with*in* God. What will be revealed with the consummation of God's grace is what we have begun to know 'in Christ', his story becoming our story. Like Christ we shall burn and arise with the eternal life-giving force of God himself, and living with Jesus 'forever' (4:17) we shall be clothed in the blessings of eternal life which God has always enjoyed. Just as God is eternal – living in a mysterious commingling of past, present and future – so we shall be eternal, and as we live with Jesus in this state, the reconciling exchange will have reached its triumphant conclusion.

Talk of eschatology is therefore located within a curious paradox, a constant balancing out of the necessarily hidden quality of the future in its very futurity and the confidence that in Christ the nature and shape of our future together are revealed to a certain extent.[152] While eschatology must, of necessity, remain aloof from any tendency to enclose or confine it,[153] Christian theology is in the position of insisting that the principle of the world's end – God in Christ – has been and is already tightly interwoven into the form of the world. The incarnation, in its essential act of filling humanity with the mystery of divinity and so fusing the two, cuts across any system which insists upon the immanence of eschatology increasing in inverse proportion to eschatology's transcendence. Christian eschatology, the world's end in the God who revealed Christ, cannot be wholly transcendent because Christ has already pulled God's will and his

---

[151] Hooker, 'Interchange and Atonement', 476.

[152] K. Rahner, 'Christianity and the "New Man"', in *Theological Investigations*, vol. V, tr. K.-H. Kruger (London: Darton, Longman and Todd, 1966), p. 135.

[153] K. Rahner, 'Immanent and Transcendent Consummation of the World', in *Theological Investigations*, vol. X, tr. D. Bourke (London: Darton, Longman and Todd, 1973), p. 278.

world closer together, rather as the dead and the alive already share a state of living 'in Christ'. Christian eschatological existence is thus defined by the curious reality that we are:

> living in time by that which is beyond time; living by that which is not yet come, but which we already know and possess.[154]

But to retain the paradoxical element to eschatology, just as soon as we think that we can discern the principle at work in the world's consummation, we must recommit ourselves to the utter transcendence of the world's future. No room can be afforded for anything that looks like 'evolutionary' eschatology,[155] anything that smacks of our progress or advance. Any linear model of eschatology, behaviour that submits eschatology to predictability, assimilation or closure, needs to be reminded that the end, coming 'like a thief in the night' (5:2), is always a future in God's hands. An eschatology which takes account of that will properly place more emphasis on the experience of its transcendence than on our ability to deduce its movement.

The promise of the second coming is that we will become gloriously and finally what we are in the process of becoming in the life of the Spirit. What we decided in favour of and grew into in the shape of our freedom in time will be ours in the full fruit of eternity, to adopt a distinctly Rahnerian outlook. When we cross over from our time into God's time as eternity, the future that was always God's is revealed as eternally valid and enduring, where everything we have reached for in life attains its definitive status. As we rise into the life and communion of the triune God, what we were in part and in shadows we shall become in full. Only at this stage will symbols and likenesses rest. For now, though, we have little choice but to continue with our images until, as Gregory of Nyssa assures us,

> that moment when we shall be taught the mystery of the Resurrection by the reality of it . . . [for] every calculation that tries to arrive conjecturally at the future state will be reduced to nothingness by the object of our hopes, when it comes upon us.[156]

---

[154] A. Schmemann, 'Liturgy and Eschatology', in *Liturgy and Tradition: Theological Reflections of Alexander Schmemann*, ed. T. Fisch (Crestwood: Saint Vladimir's Seminary Press, 1990), p. 95.

[155] K. Rahner, 'A Fragmentary Aspect of a Theological Evaluation of the Concept of the Future', in *Theological Investigations*, vol. X, tr. D. Bourke (London: Darton, Longman and Todd, 1973), p. 236.

[156] Gregory of Nyssa, 'On the Soul and Resurrection', in *NPNF²* V, tr. W. Moore and H. A. Wilson (Edinburgh: T. & T. Clark, 1892), p. 464.

Excursus 3 – a note on 1 Thess. 5:1–11

The ambiguity of the Greek in 1 Thess. 5:1–11 does not add to the lucidity of the metaphors deployed by Paul in these verses. The verb γρηγορέω (5:10) can be translated either as 'to be awake' or 'to be alive', and in the same verse, the verb καθεύδω can be translated as 'to be asleep' or 'to be dead'. In the previous verses Paul had counselled against the danger of being found sleeping when Jesus returns (5:6). The Thessalonian Christians must be found 'sober and alert'. It is unlikely, however, that Paul is still deploying this metaphor in this verse. He is not incorporating the futures of the 'awake' and the dead, but in a reversion to the concerns of 1 Thess. 4:13–18 is encouraging the Thessalonians to see that both the dead and the living have an assured future 'together' and with Christ.

Those who dissent from the majority opinion that καθεύδωμεν is another euphemism for 'death' as in 1 Thess. 4:13 (κοιμάομαι) make much of the fact that these are not the same verbs. T. R. Edgar exhaustively lists other New Testament uses of καθεύδω and argues that as with those examples, here it must also refer to a lack of vigilance.[157] But, failing to understand that the central message of 1 Thessalonians is Christ's defeat of the community-rending effects of death (hence the emphasis in 1 Thess. 4:15, 17 on the corporate aspect of the resurrection), Edgar is distracted by the different metaphors, and does not see that no matter how these two verbs are used in the rest of the New Testament, *here* they are being used to return to Paul's message of consolation – your loved ones who have died have not been cast out of the sphere of Christ's power. Moreover, Edgar pays scant attention to the theological logic of 5:9–10: Jesus died 'for us' *so that* whether 'we are dead or alive we might live with him'.

---

[157] T. R. Edgar, 'The Meaning of "Sleep" in 1 Thessalonians 5:10', *JETS* 22 (1979), 345–9.

CONCLUSION

In concluding this study, three tasks must be undertaken. First, it is worth reminding ourselves of the hermeneutical journey undertaken. Secondly, we must reflect on the integrity of Part III's conversational mode of interpretation. Thirdly, some departing images need to be offered through which and with which our theological exegesis might be best seen.

1   The hermeneutical journey travelled

The study began with a critique of hitherto dominant historical-critical readings of 1 Thessalonians. For James Dunn, offering a general defence of historical criticism, the Biblical text is 'first and foremost' a historical text,[1] witnessing chiefly to a historically grounded communication. Dunn offers no consideration on how, free from the distracting concern with history and origins, the truth of Scripture resides within the rich field of meaning it creates. Similarly, for Karl Donfried the theology of 1 Thessalonians is only ever a meaning that originally *served* a situation lying in an event behind the text. In Donfried's reading of 1 Thessalonians, to understand the text's historical origins is to grasp its theological message. Both Dunn and Donfried reveal the dominance of historicist tendencies within New Testament studies, the assumption that to understand a text is equivalent to grasping its origins.

Historical-critical readings, it was then argued, are hampered by a restricted notion of meaning and truth; by an assumption that fixes the language of Scripture into a restrictively reflective relationship between text and original context; and by a misreading of Scripture's quality of 'witness'. All these claims were advanced in relation to specific examples of scholarship on 1 Thessalonians. The majority of the scholars examined remain fascinated with the historical Paul, with his personal religious and social context, and with the context in which he evangelised and taught.

[1] Dunn, 'Historical Text', p. 346.

In a very limited sense there is a legitimacy to these projects, insofar as the Bible is clearly at one level a historical document and can be studied just as one would study any other ancient document. Revelation, as Barth reminds us, has to occur in the particularity of our time.[2] It is, however, the particular responsibility of theologians to point out that an inappropriate fixation with the authority of origins bypasses what fascinated and transfixed Paul – the transfiguration of the world by virtue of the divine–human encounter that is God in Christ – and so the fact that Paul's language receives its impulse from this reality.

Historicist scholarship, as identified in this book, places excessive emphasis on an always putative authorial intention, and invests too much authority in the origins of Biblical texts. Historical criticism therefore misses what is most enduring and engaging about the language of Scripture – its constant ability to set in motion a panoply of meaning, a depth released in and through the time of its reading community, the church. The notion of revelation developed in chapter 1 – as an eschatological momentum experienced in and through the church – heightened our critique of the historicist tendency to dismiss the harvest of Scriptural meaning accumulated through time.

The intention of Part II was precisely to reap (only some of) the benefits of 1 Thessalonians' very particular harvest of meaning. Therefore, after the severe limitations of the historical-critical project were identified, elements of the inexhaustible content within 1 Thessalonians were extracted and *displayed*. The pre-modern commentaries of Thomas Aquinas and John Calvin were studied not as historical curiosities, or as a polite nod to quaint reading practices, but precisely to re-examine marginalised reading strategies. Fresh perspectives on the infinite content within 1 Thessalonians were additionally acquired. Attention was thus directed to both Thomas' and Calvin's *mode* of reading and the *results* of their reading.

In Thomas' commentary, in particular on 1 Thess. 4:13f., Christ acts as a 'hermeneutical axis',[3] the figure around whom Paul's causal way of thinking is to be understood. Linking eschatology to Christology, and both of these to the text, Thomas allows Christ's resurrection itself to be understood anew as a dynamic, active power. This commitment in linking (instrumental) Christology to the text was an insight whose steps we would endeavour to follow in Part III. In relation to his exegetical

[2] *CD* I/2, p. 50.

[3] P. M. Blowers, 'Theology as Integrative, Visionary, Pastoral: The Legacy of Maximus the Confessor', *Pro Ecclesia* 2 (1993), 219.

practice it is clear that Thomas was committed to the logic of Scripture, as demonstrated in the richness of his canonically driven exegesis. In Thomas' exegesis, proper attention is given to the providence of God, as the ultimate author and power behind Scripture. Finally, Thomas' commitment to Paul as the author of 1 Thessalonians is evident in his intricate and sustained division of the text, a method which is a discipline in reading very closely what is actually there in the text, reading what the text is saying in reality.

To turn to Calvin, it is apparent that his much-vaunted 'spiritual sobriety' played its part in his reluctance to embrace the amplitude of a canonically led conversation.[4] Calvin stands at the crossroads between pre-modernity and modernity: his preference for 'spiritual sobriety',[5] his evident reluctance to expose 1 Thessalonians to the medley of its wider canonical context, and his marshalling of philological and lexical apparatus in pursuit of Paul's 'meaning' all have clear resonances with the historical-critical drive that developed after Calvin.[6] Calvin insisted that it is *individually* possible to acquire the single, true sense of the author's meaning, quite independently of the support offered by the collective memory of tradition. This has obvious links with subsequent fateful developments in which a fixation with historical context takes on the role of a rampart against Scripture's wealth of meaning, for in many forms of historical criticism it is *assumed* that only determined historical-critical attention can free us from the impositions of dogma. Although Calvin is certainly pre-modern insofar as he expected to find in his interpretation a deeper understanding of Christ, some of his methods are undoubtedly preludes to future developments. There is, as we had cause to note frequently, a noticeably tense aspect to Calvin's exegetical methods, and he reads very much as one on the cusp of modernity.

Calvin's contribution to the reading of 1 Thessalonians is his determination to read the whole of the letter in an eschatological vein. Where Thomas lavishes his attention on the causality indicated by Paul in 1 Thess. 4:13f., Calvin's attention to Paul is evidenced by his reading of the whole of the letter through eschatological lenses. In chapter 5, I was especially keen to shadow Calvin's balancing out of the future and already-present aspects of his eschatology and his determination to exhibit this perspective throughout his exegesis of 1 Thessalonians.

Notwithstanding the stated misgivings in relation to aspects of Calvin's methodological bequest, it is apparent that the hermeneutical stances of both Thomas and Calvin challenge historical critics to rethink what it is

---

[4] *Comm. 1 Thess. 5:6.*   [5] *Comm. 1 Thess. 5:6.*   [6] *Comm. 1 Thess. 4:13.*

to listen intently to Paul. For those like Krister Stendahl, fidelity to Paul is achieved by putting a maximal distance between ourselves and the historical Paul,[7] and supposing that we can recover an authorial intention as a truth that comes from nowhere. For historical critics the 'otherness' of Paul is always a historical distance,[8] and *not* what he is actually saying in its captivating depth. Both Thomas and Calvin listen carefully to the Paul of 1 Thessalonians. Calvin reads 1 Thessalonians shaped by a vision which creatively switches between the end's current out-working and its transcendence. Thomas pays studied attention to Paul's teaching in 1 Thess. 4:14, and demonstrates the potential of using Christ as an exegetical pivot, the figure around whom Paul's witness can be divined. For both Thomas and Calvin, 1 Thessalonians is a text through which God is addressing us, a text whose ultimate centre is the divine initiative of grace. Thomas' and Calvin's patient engagement with the text (in contrast to the disengagement so easily practised by historical critics) is a reminder that at the centre of the text, and at the heart of Christianity, is the mystery of the divine–human encounter in Christ.

This supreme mystery, miraculously witnessed to in the frailty of Biblical words, is what we attempted to wrestle with, explore and encounter in the self-consciously Christ-ruled reading of Part III. Taking our cue from both Thomas and Calvin, we explored the redemptive imagery of the text, guided by the notion that Scripture is a symbol of the miraculous divine–human encounter revealed in Christ.

In chapter 5 the work of the one who 'died for us' and whose grace continues to transfigure the world was explored by virtue of a fluid conversation with the text, Fathers and selected theologians from across the Christian tradition. We prepared ourselves hermeneutically by turning to the work of Karl Rahner and his seminal essay 'The Hermeneutics of Eschatological Assertions'. For Karl Rahner there is a radical truth stretching across the experience of the Thessalonians and for those now who dare to place their hope in God's eschatological vision, for eschatology remains always, in all places, the forward expansion of Christ's grace experienced in the present. Anything that is said eschatologically, at any time, always emanates from the experience of Christ's grace and 'derives from the assertion about the salvific action of God in his grace on actual man'.[9] Rahner's hermeneutical manifesto helped us imagine an interpretation of 1 Thessalonians, with its obvious eschatological themes, as a momentum *participating* in the activity of eschatological grace.

---

[7] E.g. Stendahl, 'The Bible as Classic', 9.
[8] Dunn, 'Historical Text', p. 358.   [9] Rahner, 'The Hermeneutics', p. 338.

After due attention was paid to the integrity of Paul's contribution, and the extent to which 1 Thessalonians can be read as pointing to the unity of God in Christ's saving action, the richness of the text was expounded to help us understand the central, and striking, claim of 1 Thess. 4:14, namely the resurrection of the dead, and the linking of that resurrection with Christ's resurrection. A three-fold interpretation of the apostolic claim that Jesus died 'for us' (5:10) was deployed: that Jesus' death is a demonstration of God's radically *complete* grace; that Jesus' death discloses God's radical *love*; and that the death of the Son ignites God's radical *exchange*. It was this final image of Jesus' death as a reconciling exchange which most adequately prepared us for the final section of chapter 5. Here, the argument that a commitment to images offers the best hope of wrestling with Paul's teaching in 1 Thess. 4:14 was consolidated.

Numerous images within the text were explored. First, a theme of transfiguration within the text was discerned, a transformation witnessed in the triad of faith, hope and 'God-taught' love (4:9). This theme of transfiguration was extended in our second grouping of images: light (5:5) and continual prayer (5:17). A close connection between the light of Jesus' transfiguration, the light of which we are now and the light of the parousia was argued for and demonstrated. Thirdly, the image of the 'dead in Christ' (4:16) was explored in its mystical depth, and it was argued that it was possible to read this phrase as meaning much more than merely 'dead Christians'. Fourthly, the reference to the 'sleeping' (4:13) Christians was investigated as a symbol of our anticipation of death's climactic defeat. Finally, the image of the parousia itself was examined (4:16–17); its symbolism of Christ descending and Christians ascending was read as a fitting microcosm of the wondrous exchange God reveals in Christ. Returning to the hermeneutical themes of the opening section of this chapter, I contended that eschatological existence is a perennially precipitous affair, a balancing out of the future's necessary obscurity and yet present immanence.

2   The integrity of our hermeneutical conversation

One of the striking features of Part III was the hermeneutical conversation I attempted to construct and maintain. Such a conversation was foreshadowed in chapter 1, where I cited David Tracy's dictum that 'neither interpreter nor text but the common subject matter takes over in genuine conversation'.[10] Building on Part II, Part III's implicit challenge

---

[10] Tracy, 'Is a Hermeneutics of Religion Possible?', p. 124.

to dominant assumptions within the New Testament guild was that loyalty to Paul is to encounter *what* he is attempting to communicate, and in that cause to enter into conversation with Paul's witness.

The question of our particular conversation's integrity is paramount. There can be no escaping the fact that although we are committed to the text's liveliness, a liveliness communicated through the church's ruminative reading of 1 Thessalonians and of the whole canon, it is I as the author of this book who have convened this conversation, and it is I who decided when to give voice to certain traditions, when to draw upon certain perspectives, and when not to draw upon other interpretative insights. In such a scenario there is always the risk or temptation for me to conceal what I am *really interested* in saying and concluding, and in that pursuit raising aloft 'conversation' as an alluring, if ultimately deceptive, chimera.

In the final chapter there always loomed this danger of a closed discourse under the mask of a genuine dialogue. Nevertheless, it is important to recall that the vocation of theology is to articulate a conversation gripped by its subject matter, tolerant of its necessary provisionality, faithful to Scripture's generative capacity, and correspondingly empowered to seek those appropriate spaces and silences in which a renewing, transformative voice might speak. Such a conversation will indeed be doomed to futility or the error of our ways of thinking if it does not retain a liturgical quality, a commitment to balancing out the language we use about God, and the language we turn back towards God. Only this doxological element of theological discourse can hope to secure its integrity.[11]

In the final chapter, whilst acutely aware of the self-delusion that we were having a fluid conversation with the text, we nevertheless held out the hope that a conversation with the text's witness *is* possible if attention is paid to the crafting of its (the conversation's) integrity. Such integrity is best demonstrated by a genuinely open-ended quality, an awareness that there could always be a response, or a text, or a refinement, or a watchful silence that could suggest new possibilities of understanding. In the end, a conversation's resistance to determinacy or closure is the best guide as to its integrity.[12]

As Rowan Williams notes in his seminal essay 'Theological Integrity', it is the inescapable burden of theological language (precisely because of its subject matter) to hover on the edge of tumbling into a totalising mindset. It is precisely because of this danger that theological language,

---

[11] R. Williams, 'Theological Integrity', in *On Christian Theology*, p. 7.
[12] *Ibid.*, p. 5.

of which the final chapter is a player, must remain responsive to the practices of prayer, penitence and praise.[13]

3   Some departing images in relation to theological exegesis

Aside from these reflections on the contribution and potential of interpretation understood as conversation, there are two further images that aid thought on the style of exegesis explored in Part III.

Our probing of the *images* of redemption within 1 Thessalonians suggests that the book has developed a certain 'iconic' understanding of Scriptural language. There is certainly precedence in Christian tradition for discerning parallels between icons and the words of Scripture:

> What the word transmits through the ear, that painting silently shows through the image and by these two means, mutually accompanying one another . . . we receive knowledge of one and the same thing.[14]

Both Scripture and the icons of Orthodox devotion are images and representations of the divine truth experienced and encountered, whilst always remaining ineffable and transcendent. Although there is a close connection between the reality indicated by both Scripture and the icon (the insight of faith is precisely to discern this interweaving of God's will and the world), the image of the icon always remains distinct and separate in nature from the reality which it indicates.[15] Just as with the icon, so too in Scripture have we been aware of the acute difference between the form and content of Scriptural pronouncements.

Both the icon and the Scriptural text, moreover, are invitations to participate in the inexhaustible grace of God's divine–human encounter, and both are bearers of an infinite depth of meaning and understanding, precisely and only because of what they witness to and signify. Both, read

---

[13] Another issue needing urgent *theological* consideration is the question of the *mis-readings* of Scripture's infinite content, and the devastating effects this has had (and does have) on its victims. In relation to our study the interpretation history of 1 Thess. 2:14–16 is highly pertinent. It is to be hoped that one of the outcomes of the recent emphasis on the *Wirkungsgeschichte* of the Bible might be an increase in truthful and penitent confession on the part of the church for damaging readings of Scripture. What is clear is that remorse is a corporate act, a painful recognition on the part of the church of our fellowship with past sinful readers of the Bible, and an equal identification with the countless groups and individuals who have been damaged by these very same readings.

[14] Acts of the VIIth Ecumenical Council, Act 6. Cited and translated in L. Ouspensky, 'The Meaning and Language of Icons', in L. Ouspensky and V. Lossky, *The Meaning of Icons*, tr. G. E. H. Palmer and E. Kadloubovsky (Crestwood: SVSP, 1982), p. 30.

[15] Ouspensky, 'The Meaning', p. 32.

in the light of what they are willing us to encounter, resist any notion of an exhaustive or definitive interpretation. So too, in both the icon and the Scriptural text there is a bare exterior form (a two-dimensional depiction or some squiggles on a page) with which we must engage prior to entering into the depth of its reference. Pivotal to the Scriptural images of redemption explored in Part III and to the use of icons in Eastern Christianity is the notion that we are primarily being invited to participate in the world they propose we imagine.

Attentive readers of both the Scriptural text and icons discern a world being proposed by the imagination of faith. In the 'inverse perspective' of the icon and the divine–human transformation witnessed to in the frailty of the Bible's words, the attentive reader 'stands, as it were, at the start of a pathway . . . which unfolds itself before him in all its immensity'.[16] If we apprehend Scripture's address, Paul's language is of less interest for what it reveals of his own age, and of far more interest as the communication of an apostle whose very words are transfigured by their content.[17] The spatial prepositions employed here bring out the contrasts in relation to historical critics. Where historical critics talk of getting *behind* the text, as if its origins were theologically crucial or the most interesting thing we could say about the text, an attempt has been made here to see *into* the depths of 1 Thessalonians, and so to press the text (and indeed ourselves) *forwards* into an irrepressibly ruminative process.

A second image also aids reflection on the adopted style of Part III. The kind of expansive reading we advocated could be seen to enjoy parallels with Gregory of Nyssa's influential articulation of *epectasis*: the constant, ceaseless straining forwards into yet deeper spiritual truths and experiences. This conception of exegesis, as something capable of an inexhaustible fullness, is predicated on the basis of the text's content and reference, which, being divine, is infinite.[18]

Theological exegesis, with this understanding of the text, will always be seeking new meanings in which it can temporarily take root, whilst nurturing an expanding network of understanding. In this economy, spiritually attentive readers will constantly be aware of the provisionality of their insights into the text, and will insistently be searching for what is yet deeper and more illuminative. Precisely because theological exegesis is committed to the depth of 1 Thessalonians, it is set on an ever-expanding

---

[16] *Ibid.*, p. 41.

[17] D. Stăniloae, 'Revelation through Acts, Words and Images', in *Theology and the Church*, p. 111.

[18] Gregory of Nyssa, *The Life of Moses*, §236, tr. A. J. Malherbe and E. Ferguson (New York: Paulist Press, 1978).

path of fullness, seeking to know ever more though the text and nourished on this quest by the truths it has already glimpsed.[19]

Set on such a course, where the imagination of the world proposed by Scripture is always overtaking us, we are properly gripped, subdued and inspired by the *mira profunditas* of Scripture itself, and in our hold on meaning there is always the possibility of yet more depth.[20] To be possessed by this depth of Scripture is to be gripped by a restlessness, for spiritually shaped exegesis is bound only by the infinite nature of God.[21]

Proposing a reading of Scripture open to its spiritual wealth runs counter to much of the disengaged, fragmented and atomised style of current theological study. That contemporary theology no longer enjoys a mutually critical and refining relationship with spirituality needs little demonstration. A pathology of theology's dismemberment is quite outside the scope of this concluding sketch, save to say that this entire study has been partly motivated by dismay at the loss of what Paul Blowers terms (in discussing Maximus the Confessor) an 'integrative vision',[22] a conviction that theological rigour, Biblical attention, spiritual nourishment and pastoral relevance can *only* stand together.

Contemporary theological study, with its departments within departments and its appropriate professional society for each of these sub-disciplines, has proven remarkably adept at breaking up, but noticeably reluctant to consider how these disciplines contribute to a collective wisdom. In an intellectual context where prayerful, spiritual reflection is likely to be treated with much suspicion (as if personal involvement with God and the intellect were competitive in relationship), theology needs to be reminded that it is at heart talk about *God* not merely proposed as an intellectual idea, but encountered and recognised as a dynamic mystery. In our call for a restored integrative approach to Biblical study, there is therefore an appeal to combine the skills of the intellect with the mystical and spiritual content of theological utterances.

These images with which we have allusively concluded – Scripture as an 'icon' and Scripture as a bottomless well of meaning for spiritually alert readers – remain as images. They remind us that at the heart of all theological endeavour there resides a divine mystery humbly received with delight and wonder. The reading of 1 Thessalonians proposed in this book has striven, in a modest way, to demonstrate the viability

---

[19] *Ibid.*, §226.

[20] See Gilbert of Stanford, *In Cant. Prol.* Cited and translated in H. De Lubac, *Medieval Exegesis. Volume I: The Four Senses of Scripture*, tr. M. Sebanc (Edinburgh: T. & T. Clark, 1998), pp. 75–6.

[21] Gregory of Nyssa, *Life of Moses*, §239.   [22] Blowers, 'Theology as Integrative'.

and potential of reading the Bible attentive to precisely this generative centre. All theology which attempts to convey this mystery with a sense of exhilaration must constantly shield itself from idolatrous tendencies, and so by way of final conclusion, Paul's dictum provides a worthy antidote to the theologian's verbosity:

> Anyone who claims to know something does not yet have the necessary knowledge.   (1 Cor. 8:2)

BIBLIOGRAPHY

1 Classical authors

Aristotle, *On the Soul, Parva Naturalia, On Breath*, tr. W. S. Hett (LCL vol. 288;
London: Heinemann, 1935).
On Interpretation, tr. J. T. Oesterle (Milwaukee: Marquette University Press,
1962).

2 Patristics

Athanasius, 'Four Discourses against the Arians', tr. J. H. Newman, in P. Schaff
and H. Wace, eds., *NPNF*² IV, revd A. Robertson (Edinburgh: T. & T. Clark,
1891), pp. 303–447.
'On the Incarnation of the Word', tr. A. Robertson, in *NPNF*² IV (Edinburgh:
T. & T. Clark, 1891), pp. 31–67.
'Ad Adelphium', tr. A. Robertson, in *NPNF*² IV (Edinburgh: T. & T. Clark,
1891), pp. 575–8.
Augustine 'On the Trinity', in *Basic Writings of Saint Augustine*, vol. II, tr. A. W.
Haddan, ed. W. J. Oates, revd W. G. T. Shedd (New York: Random House,
1948), pp. 665–878.
'Eight Questions of Dulcitius', in *Saint Augustine: Treatises on Various Sub-
jects*, ed. R. J. Deferrari, tr. M. S. Muldowney et al. (FOC 16; Washington:
Catholic University of America Press, 1952), pp. 427–66.
Letter 199, in *Saint Augustine. Letters: Volume IV (165–203)*, tr. W.
Parsons (FOC 30; Washington: Catholic University of America Press, 1977),
pp. 356–401.
The City of God against the Pagans, tr. R. W. Dyson (Cambridge: Cambridge
University Press, 1998).
Cyril of Alexandria, *On the Unity of Christ*, tr. J. A. McGuckin (Crestwood: Saint
Vladimir's Seminary Press, 1995).
Commentary on the Gospel According to S. John, various translators, members
of the English Church (London: Walter Smith, 1885).
John Damascene, 'Homily on the Transfiguration of Our Lord Jesus Christ by
Saint John of Damascus', tr. H. L. Weatherby, *GOTR* 32 (1987), 1–29.
'Exposition of the Orthodox Faith', tr. S. D. F. Salmond, in *NPNF*² IX
(Edinburgh: T. & T. Clark, 1898), pp. 1–101.
Pseudo-Dionysius, the Areopagite, *Pseudo-Dionysius: The Complete Works*, tr.
C. Luibheid (London: Society for Promoting Christian Knowledge, 1987).

Maximus the Confessor, *On the Cosmic Mystery of Jesus Christ: Selected Writings from St Maximus the Confessor*, tr. P. M. Blowers and R. L. Wilken (Crestwood: Saint Vladimir's Seminary Press, 2003).

Gregory Nazianzen, 'Select Orations', tr. C. G. Browne and J. E. Swallow, in *NPNF*[2] VII (Edinburgh: T. & T. Clark, 1893), pp. 203–434.

Gregory Nyssen, *The Catechetical Oration*, tr. J. H. Srawley (London: Society for Promoting Christian Knowledge, 1917).

'An Address on Religious Instruction', in *Christology of the Later Fathers*, tr. and ed. E. R. Hardy in collaboration with C. C. Richardson (London: Student Christian Movement, 1954), pp. 268–325.

The Life of Moses, tr. A. J. Malherbe and E. Ferguson (New York: Paulist Press, 1978).

'Against Eunomius', tr. W. Moore and H. A. Wilson, in *NPNF*[2] V (Edinburgh: T. & T. Clark, 1892), pp. 33–239.

'On the Soul and Resurrection', tr. W. Moore and H. A. Wilson, in *NPNF*[2] V (Edinburgh: T. & T. Clark, 1892), pp. 430–68.

Origen, 'On Prayer,' in *Origen*, tr. R. Greer (London: Society for Promoting Christian Knowledge, 1979), pp. 81–170.

Gregory Palamas, *The Triads*, tr. N. Gendle (New York: Paulist Press, 1983).

3   Thomas Aquinas

(i)   Primary sources

Super Evangelium S. Ioannis Lectura, ed. P. R. Cai (Turin: Marietti, 1952).

Super Epistolas S. Pauli Lectura, vol. II, ed. P. R. Cai (Turin: Marietti, 1953).

(ii)   Translations

The *'Summa Theologica' of St. Thomas Aquinas. Third Part (Supplement)*, *QQ LXIX–LXXXVI*, tr. Fathers of the English Dominican Province (London: Burns Oates and Washbourne, 1921).

Compendium of Theology, tr. C. Vollert (St Louis: Herder, 1962).

Summa Theologiae, vols. I–LX, ed. T. Gilby and T. C. O'Brien, various translators (London/New York: Blackfriars, 1964–73).

Commentary on Saint Paul's Epistle to the Ephesians, tr. M. L. Lamb (Aquinas Scripture Series; Albany: Magi Books, 1966).

Commentary on Saint Paul's First Letter to the Thessalonians, tr. M. Duffy (Aquinas Scripture Series; Albany: Magi Books, 1969).

Commentary on the Gospel of St. John, vol. I, tr. F. R. Larcher (Aquinas Scripture Series; Albany: Magi Books, 1980).

Commentary on the Metaphysics of Aristotle, tr. J. P. Rowan (Chicago: Henry Regnery Company, 1961).

4   Medieval theology

(i)   Primary sources

Peter Lombard, *In Omnes D. Pauli Apoſt. Epiſtolas Collectanea* (Paris, 1537).

(ii) Translations

Anselm of Canterbury, 'Why God Became Man', in *A Scholastic Miscellany: Anselm to Ockham*, ed. and tr. E. R. Fairweather (London: Student Christian Movement, 1956), pp. 100–83.

5 John Calvin

(i) Primary sources

Ioannis Calvini Opera quae Supersunt Omnia (vol. LII, being part of the *Corpus Reformatorum*), ed. W. Baum, E. Cunitz and E. Reuss (Brunsvigae: C. A. Schwetscke, 1863–1900).

(ii) Translations

Institutes of the Christian Religion, tr. F. L. Battles, ed. J. T. McNeill (Philadelphia: Westminster Press, 1960).
Commentaries of John Calvin (Edinburgh: Calvin Translation Society): *Commentary on the Book of Psalms* (vol. I), tr. J. Anderson, 1845; *Commentaries on the Book of Genesis* (vol. I), tr. J. King, 1847; *Commentaries on the Prophet Ezekiel* (vol. I), tr. T. Myers, 1849; *Commentaries on the Four Last Books of Moses* (vol. I), tr. C. W. Bingham, 1852; *Commentary on the Prophet Isaiah* (vol. III), tr. W. Pringle, 1852; *Commentaries on the Book of the Prophet Jeremiah and the Lamentations* (vol. V), tr. J. Owen, 1855.
Calvin's Commentaries, ed. D. W. Torrance and T. F. Torrance (Edinburgh: Saint Andrew Press/Oliver and Boyd): *The Gospel According to St John 1–10*, tr. T. H. L. Parker, 1959; *The First Epistle of Paul the Apostle to the Corinthians*, tr. J. W. Fraser, 1960; *The Epistles of Paul the Apostle to the Romans and to the Thessalonians*, tr. R. Mackenzie, 1961; *The Epistle of Paul the Apostle to the Hebrews and the First and Second Epistles of St. Peter*, tr. W. B. Johnston, 1963; *The Second Epistle of Paul the Apostle to the Corinthians and the Epistles to Timothy, Titus and Philemon*, tr. T. A. Smail, 1964; *The Epistles of Paul the Apostle to the Galatians, Ephesians, Philippians and Colossians*, tr. T. H. L. Parker, 1965; *A Harmony of the Gospels: Matthew, Mark and Luke* (vol. I), tr. A. W. Morrison, 1972.
'Psychopannychia', in *Tracts and Treatises in Defence of the Reformed Faith*, vol. III, tr. H. Beveridge, ed. T. F. Torrance (Edinburgh: Oliver and Boyd, 1958), pp. 413–90.
'Calvin's Reply to Sadoleto', in *A Reformation Debate: Sadoleto's Letter to the Genevans and Calvin's Reply*, tr. H. Beveridge, ed. J. C. Olin (New York: Harper and Row, 1966), pp. 49–94.

6 Martin Luther

(i) Translation

'Two Funeral Sermons, 1532', in *Luther's Works*, vol. LI, ed. and tr. F. W. Doberstein (Philadelphia: Muhlenberg Press, 1959), pp. 231–55.

7   **Karl Rahner**

(i)   Monographs

On the Theology of Death, tr. C. H. Henkey (Freiburg: Herder, 1961).
Foundations of Christian Faith, tr. W. V. Dych (London: Darton, Longman and Todd, 1978).
I Remember, tr. H. D. Egan (London: Student Christian Movement, 1985).

(ii)   Articles from Theological Investigations

There are various translators for this series published in London by Darton, Longman and Todd and in Baltimore by Helicon Press (1961–92) from the German original, *Schriften zur Theologie* (Einsiedeln: Benziger, 1954–84). Dates in parentheses are the dates of publication in English translation.
'Current Problems in Christology', *TI* I, pp. 149–200 (1961).
'The Resurrection of the Body', *TI* II, pp. 203–16 (1963).
'The Hermeneutics of Eschatological Assertions', *TI* IV, pp. 323–46 (1966).
'The Life of the Dead', *TI* IV, pp. 347–54 (1966).
'Thoughts on the Possibility of Belief Today', *TI* V, pp. 3–22 (1966).
'Christianity and the "New Man"', *TI* V, pp. 135–53 (1966).
'On Christian Dying', *TI* VII, pp. 285–93 (1971).
'Ideas for a Theology of Childhood', *TI* VIII, pp. 33–50 (1971).
'Christian Humanism', *TI* IX, pp. 187–204 (1972).
'A Fragmentary Aspect of a Theological Evaluation of the Concept of the Future', *TI* X, pp. 235–41 (1973).
'Immanent and Transcendent Consummation of the World', *TI* X, pp. 273–89 (1973).
'Theological Observations on the Concept of Time', *TI* XI, pp. 288–308 (1974).
'The Question of the Future', *TI* XII, pp. 181–201 (1974).
'Jesus' Resurrection', *TI* XVII, pp. 16–23 (1981).
'The Body in the Order of Salvation', *TI* XVII, pp. 71–89 (1981).
'The Death of Jesus and the Closure of Revelation', *TI* XVIII, pp. 132–42 (1983).
'Christian Dying', *TI* XVIII, pp. 226–56 (1983).

8   **Secondary literature**

Abraham, W. J., *Divine Revelation and the Limits of Historical Criticism* (Oxford: Oxford University Press, 1982).
Adam, A. K. A., *Making Sense of New Testament Theology: 'Modern' Problems and Prospects* (Macon: Mercer University Press, 1995).
Aertsen, J. A., 'Aquinas's Philosophy in its Historical Setting', in N. Kretzmann and E. Stump, eds., *The Cambridge Companion to Aquinas* (Cambridge: Cambridge University Press, 1993), pp. 12–37.
Albertson, J. S., 'Instrumental Causality in St. Thomas', *New Scholasticism* 28 (1954), 409–35.
Allchin, A. M., *Participation in God: A Forgotten Strand in Anglican Tradition* (London: Darton, Longman and Todd, 1988).
Anderson, R. S., *Theology, Death and Dying* (Oxford: Basil Blackwell, 1986).
Astley, J., 'Revelation Revisited', *Theology* 83 (1980), 339–46.

Aulén, G., *Christus Victor*, tr. A. G. Hebert (London: Society for Promoting Christian Knowledge, 1931).

Baglow, C. T., *'Modus et Forma': A New Approach to the Exegesis of Saint Thomas with an Application to the* Lectura super Epistolam ad Ephesios (Rome: Editrice Pontificio Istituto Biblico, 2002).

Baillie, J., *The Idea of Revelation in Recent Thought* (New York: Columbia University Press, 1956).

Baldner, S., 'The Use of Scripture for the Refutation of Error according to St. Thomas Aquinas', in D. V. Stump et al., eds., *Hamartia: The Concept of Error in the Western Tradition* (New York: Edwin Mellen Press, 1983), pp. 149–69.

Barclay, J. M. G., 'Thessalonica and Corinth: Social Contrasts in Pauline Christianity', *JSNT* 47 (1992), 49–72.

'Conflict in Thessalonica', *CBQ* 55 (1993), 512–30.

'Paul among Diaspora Jews: Anomaly or Apostate?', *JSNT* 60 (1995), 89–120.

Barr, J., 'Allegory and Historicism', *JSOT* 69 (1996), 105–20.

The Concept of Biblical Theology: An Old Testament Perspective (London: Student Christian Movement, 1999).

Barth, K., *The Epistle to the Romans*, tr. E. C. Hoskyns (2nd edn; Oxford: Oxford University Press, 1933).

The Resurrection of the Dead, tr. H. J. Stenning (London: Hodder and Stoughton, 1933).

'Revelation', in *God in Action: Theological Addresses*, tr. E. G. Homrighausen and K. J. Ernst (Edinburgh: T. & T. Clark, 1936), pp. 3–19.

'Revelation', tr. J. O. Cobham and R. J. C. Gutteridge, in J. Baillie and H. Martin, eds., *Revelation* (London: Faber and Faber, 1937), pp. 41–81.

'The Christian Understanding of Revelation', in *Against the Stream: Shorter Post-War Writings 1946–52*, tr. S. Godman, ed. R. G. Smith (London: Student Christian Movement, 1954), pp. 203–40.

Christ and Adam: Man and Humanity in Romans 5, tr. T. A. Smail (*SJT* Occasional Papers No. 5; Edinburgh: Oliver and Boyd, 1956).

Church Dogmatics, various translators, eds. G. W. Bromiley and T. F. Torrance (Edinburgh: T. & T. Clark, 1956–69), vols. I/1, I/2, III/2, IV/1.

The Word of God and the Word of Man, tr. D. Horton (New York: Harper & Row, 1957).

'The Humanity of God', in *The Humanity of God*, tr. J. Newton Thomas (London: Collins, 1961), pp. 33–64.

'Rudolf Bultmann – An Attempt to Understand Him', tr. R. H. Fuller, in H.-W. Bartsch, ed., *Kerygma and Myth: A Theological Debate*, vol. II (London: Society for Promoting Christian Knowledge, 1962), pp. 83–132.

Evangelical Theology, tr. G. Foley (London: Weidenfeld and Nicolson, 1963).

The Göttingen Dogmatics: Instruction in the Christian Religion, vol. I, tr. G. W. Bromiley, ed. H. Reiffen (Grand Rapids: Eerdmans, 1991).

The Theology of John Calvin, tr. G. W. Bromiley (Grand Rapids: Eerdmans, 1995).

Epistle to the Philippians, tr. J. W. Leitch (Louisville: Westminster John Knox Press, 2002).

Barthes, R., 'The Death of the Author', in *Image-Music-Text*, tr. S. Heath (London: Fontana Press, 1977), pp. 142–8.

Barton, J., 'Historical-Critical Approaches', in J. Barton, ed., *The Cambridge Companion to Biblical Interpretation* (Cambridge: Cambridge University Press, 1998), pp. 9–20.

Barton, S. C., 'New Testament Interpretation as Performance', *SJT* 52 (1999), 179–208.

Bassler, J. M., ed., *Pauline Theology, Volume I: Thessalonians, Philippians, Galatians and Philemon* (Minneapolis: Fortress Press, 1991).

'Peace in All Ways: Theology in the Thessalonian Letters', in J. M. Bassler, ed., *Pauline Theology, Volume I: Thessalonians, Philippians, Galatians and Philemon* (Minneapolis: Fortress Press, 1991), pp. 71–85.

Battenhouse, R. W., 'The Doctrine of Man in Calvin and in Renaissance Platonism', *Journal of the History of Ideas* 9 (1948), 447–71.

Battles, F. L., 'Calvin's Humanistic Education', in R. Benedetto, ed., *Interpreting John Calvin* (Grand Rapids: Baker Books, 1996), pp. 47–64.

Berkouwer, G. C., *Holy Scripture*, tr. J. B. Rogers (Grand Rapids: Eerdmans, 1975).

Best, E. A., *One Body in Christ: A Study of the Relationship of the Church to Christ in the Epistles of the Apostle Paul* (London: Society for Promoting Christian Knowledge, 1955).

A Commentary on the First and Second Epistles to the Thessalonians (BNTC; London: A. & C. Black, 1972).

Bietenhard, H., 'The Millennial Hope in the Early Church', *SJT* 6 (1953), 12–30.

Black, C. C., 'St. Thomas' Commentary on the Johannine Prologue: Some Reflections on its Character and Implications', *CBQ* 48 (1986), 681–98.

Blanchette, O., 'Saint Cyril of Alexandria's Idea of the Redemption', *Sciences Ecclésiastiques* 16 (1964), 455–80.

Blondel, M., 'History and Dogma', in *The Letter on Apologetics, and History and Dogma*, tr. A. Dru and I. Trethowan (London: Harvill Press, 1964).

Blowers, P. M., *Exegesis and Spiritual Pedagogy in Maximus the Confessor: An Investigation of the 'Quaestiones ad Thalassium'* (Notre Dame: University of Notre Dame Press, 1991).

'Theology as Integrative, Visionary, Pastoral: The Legacy of Maximus the Confessor', *Pro Ecclesia* 2 (1993), 216–30.

'The Passion of Jesus Christ in Maximus the Confessor: A Reconsideration', in M. F. Wiles and E. J. Yarnold, eds., *SP* 37 (Leuven: Peeters, 2001), pp. 361–77.

'The World in the Mirror of Holy Scripture: Maximus the Confessor's Short Hermeneutical Treatise in *Ambiguum ad Joannem 37*', in P. M. Blowers et al., eds., *In Dominico Eloquio – In Lordly Eloquence: Essays on Patristic Exegesis in Honor of Robert Louis Wilken* (Grand Rapids: Eerdmans, 2002), pp. 408–26.

Blumberg, H. 'The Problem of Immortality in Avicenna, Maimonides and St. Thomas Aquinas', in J. I. Dienstag, ed., *Eschatology in Maimonidean Thought: Messianism, Resurrection and the World to Come* (New York: Ktav Publishing House, 1983), pp. 76–96.

Bockmuehl, M., 'A Commentator's Approach to the "Effective History" of Philippians', *JSNT* 60 (1995), 57–88.

'"To Be or Not to Be": The Possible Futures of New Testament Scholarship', *SJT* 51 (1998), 271–306.

Boff, C., 'Hermeneutics: Constitution of Theological Pertinency', in R. S. Sugirtharajah, ed., *Voices from the Margin: Interpreting the Bible in the Third World* (London: Society for Promoting Christian Knowledge, 1991), pp. 9–36.

Bonhoeffer, D., *Christology*, tr. J. Bowden (London: Collins, 1966).

Bouwsma, W. J., 'Calvin and the Renaissance Crisis of Knowing', *CTJ* 17 (1982), 190–211.

   John Calvin: A Sixteenth Century Portrait (New York: Oxford University Press, 1988).

   'Calvinism as Renaissance Artifact', in T. George, ed., *Calvin and the Church: A Prism for Reform* (Louisville: Westminster John Knox Press, 1990), pp. 28–41.

Boyle, J. F., 'St Thomas Aquinas and Sacred Scripture', *Pro Ecclesia* 4 (1995), 92–104.

Breck, J., 'Divine Initiative: Salvation in Orthodox Theology', in J. Meyendorff and R. Tobias, eds., *Salvation in Christ: A Lutheran–Orthodox Dialogue* (Minneapolis: Augsburg Press, 1992), pp. 105–20.

Breen, Q., *John Calvin: A Study in French Humanism* (2nd edn; Hamden: Archon Books, 1968).

Bria, I., 'The Creative Vision of D. Stăniloae: An Introduction to his Theological Thought', *Ecumenical Review* 33 (1981), 53–9.

Brown, D., *The Divine Trinity* (London: Duckworth, 1985).

   'Did Revelation Cease?', in A. G. Padgett, ed., *Reason and the Christian Religion: Essays in Honour of Richard Swinburne* (Oxford: Clarendon Press, 1994), pp. 121–41.

   Tradition and Imagination: Revelation and Change (Oxford: Oxford University Press, 1999).

   Discipleship and Imagination: Christian Tradition and Truth (Oxford: Oxford University Press, 2000).

Brown, R. M., '"Tradition" as a Problem for Protestants', *USQR* 16 (1961), 197–221.

Bruce, F. F., *1 and 2 Thessalonians* (WBC; Waco: Word Books, 1982).

Buehrer, R. L., 'John Calvin's Humanistic Approach to Church History' (Unpublished Ph.D. Thesis, University of Washington, 1974).

Bulgakov, S., 'The Church as Tradition', in *The Orthodox Church*, tr. E. S. Cram (London: The Centenary Press, 1935), pp. 18–47.

   'Revelation', tr. D. F. Clarke and X. Braikevitch, in J. Baillie and H. Martin, eds., *Revelation* (London: Faber and Faber, 1937), pp. 125–80.

Bultmann, R., *Theology of the New Testament*, vol. I, tr. K. Grobel (London: Student Christian Movement, 1965).

Burke, S., *The Death and Return of the Author: Criticism and Subjectivity in Barthes, Foucault and Derrida* (2nd edn; Edinburgh: Edinburgh University Press, 1998).

Burnett, R. E., *Karl Barth's Theological Exegesis* (Tübingen: Mohr Siebeck, 2001).

Callan, C. J., 'The Bible in the *Summa Theologica* of St. Thomas Aquinas', *CBQ* 9 (1947), 33–47.

Chadwick, H., 'Eucharist and Christology in the Nestorian Controversy', *JTS* NS 2 (1951), 145–64.

Chamberas, P. A., 'The Transfiguration of Christ: A Study in the Patristic Exegesis of Scripture', *SVTQ* 14 (1970), 48–65.

Chenu, M. D., *Toward Understanding St. Thomas*, tr. A.-M. Landry and D. Hughes (Chicago: Henry Regnery Press, 1964).

Childs, B. S., 'Interpretation in Faith: The Theological Responsibility of an Old Testament Commentary', *Interpretation* 18 (1964), 432–49.

Biblical Theology in Crisis (Philadelphia: Westminster Press, 1970).

'The *Sensus Literalis* of Scripture: An Ancient and Modern Problem', in H. Doner, R. Hanhart and R. Smend, eds., *Beiträge zur Alttestamentlichen Theologie: Festschrift für Walther Zimmerli zum 70. Geburtstag* (Göttingen: Vandenhoeck and Ruprecht, 1977), pp. 80–93.

'Reclaiming the Bible for Christian Theology', in C. E. Braaten and R. W. Jenson, eds., *Reclaiming the Bible for the Church* (Edinburgh: T. & T. Clark, 1995) pp. 1–17.

'Toward Recovering Biblical Exegesis', *Pro Ecclesia* 6 (1997), 16–26.

Compier, D. H., 'The Independent Pupil: Calvin's Transformation of Erasmus' Theological Hermeneutics', *WTJ* 54 (1992), 217–33.

Congar, Y. M., *Tradition and Traditions*, tr. M. Naseby and T. Rainborough (London: Burns and Oates, 1966).

Cooper, C., 'Chiliasts and the Chiliasts', *RTR* 29 (1970), 11–21.

Copeland, R., 'Rhetoric and the Politics of the Literal Sense in Medieval Literary Theory: Aquinas, Wyclif, and the Lollards', in P. Boitani and A. Torti, eds., *Interpretation: Medieval and Modern* (Cambridge: D. S. Brewer, 1993), pp. 1–23.

Cousar, C. B., *A Theology of the Cross: The Death of Jesus in the Pauline Letters* (Minneapolis: Fortress Press, 1990).

Crotty, N., 'The Redemptive Role of Christ's Resurrection', *The Thomist* 25 (1962), 54–106.

Crouzel, H., *Origen*, tr. A. S. Worrall (Edinburgh: T. & T. Clark, 1989).

Crowley, P. G., '*Instrumentum Divinitatis* in Thomas Aquinas: Recovering the Divinity of Christ', *TS* 52 (1991), 451–75.

Cullmann, O., *Immortality of the Soul or Resurrection of the Dead? The Witness of the New Testament* (London: Epworth Press, 1958).

Daley, B. E., *The Hope of the Early Church: A Handbook of Patristic Eschatology* (Cambridge: Cambridge University Press, 1991).

Dalferth, I. U., 'Karl Barth's Eschatological Realism', in S. W. Sykes, ed., *Karl Barth: Centenary Essays* (Cambridge: Cambridge University Press, 1989), pp. 14–45.

'Christ Died for Us: Reflections on the Sacrificial Language of Salvation', in S. W. Sykes, ed., *Sacrifice and Redemption: Durham Essays in Theology* (Cambridge: Cambridge University Press, 1991), pp. 299–325.

Daniélou, J., *From Glory to Glory: Texts from Gregory of Nyssa's Mystical Writings*, selection and introduction J. Daniélou, tr. H. Musurillo (London: John Murray, 1962).

Davies, P. R., *Whose Bible is it Anyway?* (JSOTSup 204; Sheffield: Sheffield Academic Press, 1995).

Davies, R. E., 'Calvin', in *The Problem of Authority in the Continental Reformers* (London: Epworth Press, 1946), pp. 93–153.

De Vos, C. S., *Church and Community Conflicts: The Relationships of the Thessalonian, Corinthian, and Philippian Churches with their Wider Civic Communities* (SBLDS 168; Atlanta: Scholars Press, 1999).

Dibelius, M., *An die Thessalonicher I, II; An die Philipper* (Tübingen: J. C. B. Mohr, 1937).

Dobbs-Weinstein, I., 'Medieval Biblical Commentary and Philosophical Inquiry as Exemplified in the Thought of Moses Maimonides and St. Thomas Aquinas', in E. L. Ormsby, ed., *Moses Maimonides and his Time* (Washington: Catholic University of America Press, 1989), pp. 101–20.

Donfried, K. P., 'The Cults of Thessalonica and the Thessalonian Correspondence', *NTS* 31 (1985), 336–356.

'The Theology of 1 Thessalonians', in K. P. Donfried and I. H. Marshall, *The Theology of the Shorter Pauline Letters* (Cambridge: Cambridge University Press, 1993), pp. 1–79.

'The Assembly of the Thessalonians: Reflections on the Ecclesiology of the Earliest Christian Letter', in R. Kampling and T. Soding, eds., *Ekklesiologie des Neuen Testaments: Für Karl Kertelge* (Freiburg: Herder, 1996), pp. 390–408.

Paul, Thessalonica, and Early Christianity (London: T. & T. Clark, 2002).

Donfried, K. P. and Beutler, J., eds., *The Thessalonians Debate: Methodological Discord or Methodological Synthesis?* (Grand Rapids: Eerdmans, 2000).

Dowey, E. A., *The Knowledge of God in Calvin's Theology* (expanded edition; Grand Rapids: Eerdmans, 1994).

Dratsellas, C., 'Questions on Christology of St Cyril of Alexandria' (*sic*), *Abba Salama* 6 (1975), 203–32.

Dunn, J. D. G., 'Paul's Understanding of the Death of Jesus as Sacrifice', in S. W. Sykes, ed., *Sacrifice and Redemption: Durham Essays in Theology* (Cambridge: Cambridge University Press, 1991), pp. 35–56.

'Historical Text as Historical Text: Some Basic Hermeneutical Reflections in Relation to the New Testament', in J. Davies, G. Harvey and W. G. E. Watson, eds., *Words Remembered, Texts Renewed: Essays in Honour of J. F. A. Sawyer* (JSOTSup 195; Sheffield: Sheffield Academic Press, 1995), pp. 340–59.

'The Bible in the Church', in D. F. Ford and D. L. Stamps, eds., *Essentials of Christian Community: Essays for Daniel W. Hardy* (Edinburgh: T. & T. Clark, 1996), pp. 117–30.

Eagleton, T., *Literary Theory: An Introduction* (2nd edn; Oxford: Blackwell, 1996).

Eco, U., 'Between Author and Text', in U. Eco, ed. S. Collini, *Interpretation and Overinterpretation* (Cambridge: Cambridge University Press, 1992), pp. 67–88.

Edgar, T. R., 'The Meaning of "Sleep" in 1 Thessalonians 5:10', *JETS* 22 (1979), 345–9.

Edson, C., 'Cults of Thessalonica', *HTR* 41 (1948), 153–204.

Elders, L. J., 'Aquinas on Holy Scripture as the Medium of Divine Revelation', in L. J. Elders, ed., *La doctrine de la révélation divine de saint Thomas d'Aquin* (Vatican: Pontificia Accademia di S. Tommaso e di religione Cattolica, 1990), pp. 132–52.

Engel, M. P., *John Calvin's Perspectival Anthropology* (Atlanta: Scholars Press, 1988).

Eschmann, I. T., 'A Catalogue of St Thomas' Work', tr. L. K. Shook, in E. Gilson, *The Christian Philosophy of St Thomas Aquinas* (London: Victor Gollancz, 1957), pp. 381–437.

Farrar, F. W., 'Calvin as an Expositor', *The Expositor* 7 (2nd series, 1884), 426–44.

Fee, G. D., 'St Paul and the Incarnation: A Reassessment of the Data', in S. T. Davis, D. Kendall and G. O'Collins, eds., *The Incarnation: An Interdisciplinary Symposium on the Incarnation of the Son of God* (Oxford: Oxford University Press, 2002), pp. 62–92.

Fitzmyer, J. A., 'Reconciliation in Pauline Theology', in J. W. Flanagan and A. W. Robinson, eds., *No Famine in the Land: Studies in Honor of John L. McKenzie* (Claremont: Scholars Press, 1975), pp. 155–77.

Florovsky, G., 'The Lamb of God', *SJT* 4 (1951), 13–28.

'On the Tree of the Cross', *SVSQ* 1 (1953), 11–34.

Bible, Church, Tradition. Collected Works, vol. I (Belmont: Nordland, 1972).

Forstman, H. J., *Word and Spirit: Calvin's Doctrine of Biblical Authority* (Stanford: Stanford University Press, 1962).

'Coherence and Incoherence in the Theology of John Calvin', in J. H. Leith, ed., *Calvin Studies III* (Davidson: Davidson College, 1986), pp. 47–62.

Fowl, S. E., *Engaging Scripture: A Model for Theological Interpretation* (Oxford: Blackwell, 1998).

Frame, J. E., *A Critical and Exegetical Commentary on the Epistles of St Paul to the Thessalonians* (ICC; Edinburgh: T. & T. Clark, 1912).

Froehlich, K., 'Church History and the Bible', in M. S. Burrows and P. Rorem, eds., *Biblical Hermeneutics in Historical Perspective: Studies in Honor of Karlfried Froehlich on his Sixtieth Birthday* (Grand Rapids: Eerdmans, 1991), pp. 1–15.

'Which Paul? Observations on the Image of the Apostle in the History of Biblical Exegesis', in B. Nassif, ed., *New Perspectives on Historical Theology: Essays in Memory of John Meyendorff* (Grand Rapids: Eerdmans, 1996), pp. 279–99.

'Aquinas, Thomas', in D. M. McKim, ed., *Historical Handbook of Major Biblical Interpreters* (Downers Grove: Inter-Varsity Press, 1998), pp. 85–91.

Fullerton, K., 'The Reformation Principle of Exegesis and the Initial Breakdown of the Theory of Predictive Prophecy: Calvin', in *Prophecy and Authority: A Study in the History of the Doctrine and Interpretation of Scripture* (New York: Macmillan, 1919), pp. 133–64.

Gadamer, H.-G., *Truth and Method*, tr. W. Glen-Doepel (London: Sheed and Ward, 1975).

'The Universality of the Hermeneutical Problem', in *Philosophical Hermeneutics*, tr. D. E. Linge (Berkeley: University of California Press, 1976), pp. 3–17.

Gamble, R. C., 'Calvin's Theological Method: Word and Spirit, A Case Study', in R. V. Schnuckner, ed., *Calviniana: Ideas and Influence of John Calvin* (Kirksville: Sixteenth Century Journal Publishers Inc., 1988), pp. 63–75.

'*Brevitas et Facilitas*: Toward an Understanding of Calvin's Hermeneutic', in R. C. Gamble, ed., *Calvin and Hermeneutics* (New York: Garland Press, 1992), pp. 33–49.

'Exposition and Method in Calvin', in R. C. Gamble, ed., *Calvin and Hermeneutics* (New York: Garland Press, 1992), pp. 51–63.

Gaventa, B. R., *First and Second Thessalonians* (Interpretation; Louisville: John Knox Press, 1998).

Geenan, G., 'The Council of Chalcedon in the Theology of St. Thomas', in the Staff of *The Thomist*, ed., *From an Abundant Spring: The Walter Farrell Memorial Volume of The Thomist* (New York: P. J. Kennedy & Sons, 1952), pp. 172–217.

Gerrish, B. A., 'The Word of God and the Word of Scripture: Luther and Calvin on Biblical Authority', in *The Old Protestantism and the New: Essays on the Reformation Heritage* (Edinburgh: T. & T. Clark, 1992), pp. 51–68.

Gillette, G., 'The Glory of Christ's Second Coming in Augustine's *Enarrationes in Psalmos*', in E. A. Livingstone, ed., *SP* 33 (Leuven: Peeters Press, 1997), pp. 88–93.

Gilson, E., *History of Christian Philosophy in the Middle Ages* (London: Sheed and Ward, 1955).

Grayston, K., *Dying, We Live: A New Enquiry into the Death of Christ in the New Testament* (London: Darton, Longman and Todd, 1990).

Green, J. B., 'Modernity, History and the Theological Interpretation of the Bible', *SJT* 54 (2001), 308–29.

Greene-McCreight, K., 'Ad Litteram: Understandings of the Plain Sense of Scripture in the Exegesis of Augustine, Calvin and Barth of Genesis 1–3' (Unpublished Ph.D. Thesis, Yale University, 1994).

Greer, R., *Broken Lights and Mended Lives: Theology and Common Life in the Early Church* (University Park: Pennsylvania State University Press, 1986).

Gunton, C., *A Brief Theology of Revelation* (Edinburgh: T. & T. Clark, 1995).

Hall, B., *John Calvin: Humanist and Theologian* (London: The Historical Association, 1956).

'Calvin and Biblical Humanism', in R. C. Gamble, ed., *Influences upon Calvin and Discussion of the 1559 Institutes* (New York: Garland Press, 1992), pp. 55–69.

Hansen, G. W., 'Rhetorical Criticism', in G. F. Hawthorne, R. P. Martin and D. G. Reid, eds., *Dictionary of Paul and his Letters* (Downers Grove: Inter-Varsity Press, 1993), pp. 822–6.

Hanson, R. P. C., *Allegory and Event: A Study of the Sources and Significance of Origen's Interpretation of Scripture* (London: Student Christian Movement, 1959).

Harbison, E. H., 'Calvin', in *The Christian Scholar in the Age of the Reformation* (New York: Charles Scribner's Sons, 1956), pp. 137–64.

'Calvin's Sense of History', in *Christianity and History* (Princeton: Princeton University Press, 1964), pp. 270–88.

Harrison, J. R., 'Paul and the Imperial Gospel at Thessaloniki', *JSNT* 25 (2002), 71–96.

Harrison, N. V., 'Word as Icon in Greek Patristic Theology', *Sobornost* 10 (1988), 38–49.

'Theosis as Salvation: An Orthodox Perspective', *Pro Ecclesia* 6 (1997), 429–43.

Hart, T., 'Humankind in Christ and Christ in Humankind: Salvation as Participation in our Substitute in the Theology of John Calvin', *SJT* 42 (1989), 67–84.

Hausherr, I., *The Name of Jesus*, tr. C. Cummings (Kalamazoo: Cistercian Publications, 1978).

Hazlett, W. I. P., 'Calvin's Latin Preface to his Proposed French Edition of Chrysostom's Homilies: Translation and Commentary', in J. Kirk, ed., *Humanism and Reform: The Church in Europe, England, and Scotland, 1400–1643* (Oxford: Blackwell, 1991), pp. 129–50.

Healy, N. M., *Thomas Aquinas: Theologian of the Christian Life* (Aldershot: Ashgate, 2003).

Hendrix, H. L., 'Thessalonicans Honor Romans' (Unpublished Th.D. dissertation, Harvard University, 1984).

'Archaeology and Eschatology at Thessalonica', in B. A. Pearson, ed., *The Future of Early Christianity: Essays in Honor of Helmut Koester* (Minneapolis: Fortress Press, 1991), pp. 107–18.

Hengel, M., *The Atonement: The Origins of the Doctrine in the New Testament*, tr. J. Bowden (London: SCM, 1981).

Henle, R. J., *Saint Thomas and Platonism: A Study of the Plato and Platonici Texts in the Writings of Saint Thomas* (The Hague: Martinus Nijhoff, 1956).

Hill, C. E., *Regnum Caelorum: Patterns of Future Hope in Early Christianity* (Oxford: Clarendon Press, 1992).

Holtz, T., 'On the Background of 1 Thessalonians 2:1–12', in K. P. Donfried and J. Beutler, eds., *The Thessalonians Debate: Methodological Discord or Methodological Synthesis?* (Grand Rapids: Eerdmans, 2000), pp. 69–80.

Holwerda, D. E., 'Eschatology and History: A Look at Calvin's Eschatological Vision', in R. C. Gamble, ed., *Calvin's Theology, Theology Proper, Eschatology* (New York: Garland Publishing, 1992), pp. 130–59.

Hooker, M. D., 'Interchange in Christ', *JTS* NS 22 (1971), 349–61.

'Interchange and Atonement', *BJRL* 60 (1978), 462–81.

'Interchange and Suffering', in W. Horbury and B. McNeil, eds., *Suffering and Martyrdom in the New Testament: Studies Presented to G. M. Styler by the Cambridge New Testament Seminar* (Cambridge: Cambridge University Press, 1981), pp. 70–83.

'Chalcedon and the New Testament', in S. Coakley and D. Pailin, eds., *The Making and Remaking of Christian Doctrine: Essays in Honour of Maurice Wiles* (Oxford: Clarendon Press, 1993), pp. 73–93.

Horsley, R. A., ed., *Paul and Empire: Religion and Power in Roman Imperial Society* (Harrisburg: Trinity Press International, 1997).

ed., *Paul and Politics: Ekklesia, Israel, Imperium, Interpretation* (Harrisburg: Trinity Press International, 2000).

Howard, J. E., 'The New Historicism in Renaissance Studies', *ELR* 16 (1986), 13–43.

Hughes, F. W., 'The Rhetoric of 1 Thessalonians', in R. F. Collins, ed., *The Thessalonian Correspondence* (Leuven: Leuven University Press, 1990), pp. 94–116.

Hultgren, A. J., *Christ and his Benefits: Christology and Redemption in the New Testament* (Philadelphia: Fortress Press, 1987).

Hunsinger, G., 'Karl Barth's Christology: Its Basic Chalcedonian Character', in J. Webster, ed., *The Cambridge Companion to Karl Barth* (Cambridge: Cambridge University Press, 2000), pp. 127–42.

Hurd, J. C., 'Paul Ahead of his Time: 1 Thess. 2:13–16', in P. Richardson and D. Granskou, eds., *Anti-Judaism in Early Christianity* (Ontario: Canadian Corporation for Studies in Religion, 1986), pp. 21–36.

Iggers, G. G., 'Historicism: The History and Meaning of the Term', *Journal of the History of Ideas* 56 (1995), 129–52.

Jeanrond, W., 'Karl Barth's Hermeneutics', in N. Biggar, ed., *Reckoning with Barth: Essays in Commemoration of the Centenary of Karl Barth's Birth* (London: Mowbray, 1988), pp. 80–97.

'Theology in the Context of Pluralism and Postmodernity: David Tracy's Theological Method', in D. Jasper, ed., *Postmodernism, Literature and the Future of Theology* (Basingstoke: Macmillan, 1993), pp. 143–63.

Jenson, R. W., 'The Religious Power of Scripture', *SJT* 52 (1999), 89–105.

Jewett, R., *The Thessalonian Correspondence: Pauline Rhetoric and Millenarian Piety* (Minneapolis: Fortress Press, 1986).

Johnson, J. F., 'Biblical Authority and Scholastic Theology', in J. D. Hannah, ed., *Inerrancy and the Church* (Chicago: Moody Press, 1984), pp. 67–97.

Johnson, L. T., *The Real Jesus: The Misguided Quest for the Historical Jesus and the Truth of the Traditional Gospels* (New York: HarperCollins, 1996).

'Imagining the World Scripture Imagines', *MT* 14 (1998), 165–80.

Johnson, M. F., 'Another Look at the Plurality of the Literal Sense', *Medieval Philosophy and Theology* 2 (1992), 117–41.

Jordan, M. D., 'Theological Exegesis and Aquinas's Treatise "against the Greeks"', *CH* 56 (1987), 445–56.

Jowett, B., 'On the Interpretation of Scripture', in *Essays and Reviews* (London: Longman, Green, Longman and Roberts, 1861), pp. 330–433.

Jülicher, A., 'A Modern Interpreter of Paul', tr. K. R. Crim, in J. M. Robinson, ed., *The Beginnings of Dialectic Theology*, vol. I (Richmond: John Knox Press, 1968), pp. 72–81.

Jüngel, E., 'Theology as Metacriticism: Toward a Hermeneutic of Theological Exegesis', in *Karl Barth: A Theological Legacy*, tr. G. E. Paul (Philadelphia: Westminster Press, 1986), pp. 70–82.

Jurgensen, H., 'Awaiting the Return of Christ: A Re-Examination of 1 Thessalonians 4:13–5:11 from a Pentecostal Perspective', *JPT* 4 (1994), 81–113.

Käsemann, E., 'The Saving Significance of the Death of Jesus in Paul', in *Perspectives on Paul*, tr. M. Kohl (London: Society for Promoting Christian Knowledge, 1969), pp. 32–59.

'Some Thoughts on the Theme "The Doctrine of Reconciliation in the New Testament"', tr. C. E. Carlston and R. P. Scharlemann, in J. M. Robinson, ed., *The Future of our Religious Past: Essays in Honour of Rudolf Bultmann* (London: SCM, 1971), pp. 49–64.

Keating, D. A., 'Divinization in Cyril: The Appropriation of Divine Life', in T. G. Weinandy and D. A. Keating, eds., *The Theology of St Cyril of Alexandria: A Critical Appreciation* (London: T. & T. Clark, 2003), pp. 149–85.

Kelley, D. R., *Foundations of Modern Historical Scholarship: Language, Law, and History in the French Renaissance* (New York: Columbia University Press, 1970).

Kennedy, R. G., 'Thomas Aquinas and the Literal Sense of Sacred Scripture' (Unpublished Ph.D. Thesis, University of Notre Dame, 1985).

Khiok-Khng, Y., 'A Political Reading of Paul's Eschatology in I and II Thessalonians', *AJT* 12 (1998), 77–88.

Kierkegaard, S., 'Of the Difference between a Genius and an Apostle', in *The Present Age and Two Minor Ethico-Religious Treatises*, tr. A. Dru and W. Lowrie (London: Oxford University Press, 1940), pp. 137–63.

Koen, L., *The Saving Passion: Incarnational and Soteriological Thought in Cyril of Alexandria's Commentary on the Gospel According to St. John* (Uppsala: Acta Universitatis Upsaliensis, 1991).

Koester, H., 'From Paul's Eschatology to the Apocalyptic Schemata of 2 Thessalonians', in R. F. Collins, ed., *The Thessalonian Correspondence* (Leuven: Leuven University Press, 1990), pp. 441–58.

Kramer, W., *Christ, Lord, Son of God*, tr. B. Hardy (London: Student Christian Movement, 1966).

Kraus, H.-J., 'Calvin's Exegetical Principles', in R. C. Gamble, ed., *Calvin and Hermeneutics* (New York: Garland Publishing, 1992), pp. 2–12.

LaCapra, D., 'Rethinking Intellectual History and Reading Texts', in *Rethinking Intellectual History: Texts, Contexts, Language* (Ithaca: Cornell University Press, 1983), pp. 23–71.

Lamb, M. L., 'Introduction', in Thomas Aquinas, *Commentary on Saint Paul's Epistle to the Ephesians*, tr. M. L. Lamb (Albany: Magi Books, 1966), pp. 1–36.

Lane, A. N. S., 'Calvin's Use of the Fathers and the Medievals', *CTJ* 16 (1981), 149–205.

Lash, N., 'Interpretation and Imagination,' in M. Goulder, ed., *Incarnation and Myth: The Debate Continued* (London: Student Christian Movement, 1979), pp. 19–26.

'What Might Martyrdom Mean?', *Ex Auditu* 1 (1985), 14–24.

'The Church in the State We're In', in L. G. Jones and J. J. Buckley, eds., *Spirituality and Social Embodiment* (Oxford: Blackwell, 1997), pp. 121–37.

Lassen, E., 'The Use of the Father Image in Imperial Propaganda and 1 Corinthians 4:14–21', *TB* 42 (1991), 127–36.

Lee, D. E. and Beck, R. N., 'The Meaning of "Historicism"', *American Historical Review* 59 (1954), 568–77.

Leget, C., *Living with God: Thomas Aquinas on the Relation between Life on Earth and 'Life' after Death* (Leuven: Peeters, 1997).

Lindbeck, G., *The Nature of Doctrine – Religion and Theology in a Postliberal Age* (Philadelphia: Westminster Press, 1984).

'Barth and Textuality', *Theology Today* 43 (1986), 361–76.

'The Story-Shaped Church: Critical Exegesis and Theological Interpretation', in G. Green, ed., *Scriptural Authority and Narrative Interpretation* (Philadelphia: Fortress Press, 1987), pp. 161–78.

'Scripture, Consensus and Community', *This World* 23 (1988), 5–24.

'The Search for Habitable Texts', *Daedalus* 117 (1988), 153–6.

'The Church's Mission to a Postmodern Culture', in F. B. Burnham, ed., *Postmodern Theology: Christian Faith in a Pluralist World* (San Francisco: Harper and Row, 1989), pp. 37–55.

Linder, R. D., 'Calvinism and Humanism: The First Generation', *CH* 44 (1975), 167–81.

Lohfink, G., *Death is not the Final Word*, tr. R. J. Cunningham (Chicago: Franciscan Herald Press, 1977).

Longenecker, R. N., 'The Nature of Paul's Early Eschatology', *NTS* 31 (1985), 85–95.

Lossky, V., *The Image and Likeness of God*, various translators, ed. J. H. Erickson and T. E. Bird (London: Mowbrays, 1974).

The Mystical Theology of the Eastern Church, various translators (Crestwood: Saint Vladimir's Seminary Press, 1976).

Loughlin, G., 'Using Scripture: Community and Letterality', in J. Davies, G. Harvey and W. G. E. Watson, eds., *Words Remembered, Texts Renewed: Essays in Honour of John F. A. Sawyer* (JSOTSup 195; Sheffield: Sheffield Academic Press, 1995), pp. 321–39.

Telling God's Story: Bible, Church and Narrative Theology (Cambridge: Cambridge University Press, 1996).

'The Basis and Authority of Doctrine', in C. E. Gunton, ed., *The Cambridge Companion to Christian Doctrine* (Cambridge: Cambridge University Press, 1997), pp. 41–64.

Louth, A., *Theology and Spirituality* (revised edn; Oxford: Sisters of the Love of God Press, 1978).

Discerning the Mystery: An Essay on the Nature of Theology (Oxford: Clarendon Press, 1983).

Maximus the Confessor (London: Routledge, 1996).

'The Orthodox Dogmatic Theology of Dumitru Stăniloae', *MT* 13 (1997), 253–67.

St John Damascene: Tradition and Originality in Byzantine Theology (Oxford: Oxford University Press, 2002).

Lubac, H. De, *Medieval Exegesis. Volume I: The Four Senses of Scripture*, tr. M. Sebanc (Edinburgh: T. & T. Clark, 1998).

Ludlow, M., *Universal Salvation: Eschatology in the Thought of Gregory of Nyssa and Karl Rahner* (Oxford: Oxford University Press, 2000).

Luz, U., *Matthew 1–7: A Commentary*, tr. W. C. Linss (Edinburgh: T. & T. Clark, 1990).

Matthew in History: Interpretation, Influence, and Effects (Minneapolis: Fortress Press, 1994).

'The Disciples in the Gospel According to Matthew', tr. R. Morgan, in G. Stanton, ed., *The Interpretation of Matthew* (Edinburgh: T. & T. Clark, 1995), pp. 115–48.

McCormack, B. L., 'Historical Criticism and Dogmatic Interest in Karl Barth's Theological Exegesis of the New Testament', in M. S. Burrows and P. Rorem, eds., *Biblical Hermeneutics in Historical Perspective: Studies in Honor of Karlfried Froehlich on his Sixtieth Birthday* (Grand Rapids: Eerdmans, 1991), pp. 322–38.

Karl Barth's Critically Realistic Dialectical Theology: Its Genesis and Development 1909–36 (Oxford: Clarendon Press, 1995).

'The Significance of Karl Barth's Theological Exegesis of Philippians', in Karl Barth, *Epistle to the Philippians*, tr. J. W. Leitch (Louisville: Westminster John Knox Press, 2002), pp. v–xxv.

McDermot, B. O., 'The Bonds of Freedom', in L. J. O'Donovan, ed., *A World of Grace: An Introduction to the Themes and Foundations of Karl Rahner's Theology* (New York: Seabury Press, 1980), pp. 50–63.

McGrath, A., *The Intellectual Origins of the European Reformation* (Oxford: Blackwell, 1987).

McGuckin, J. A., *The Transfiguration of Christ in Scripture and Tradition* (Lewiston: Edwin Mellen Press, 1986).

'The Patristic Exegesis of the Transfiguration', in E. A. Livingstone, ed., *SP* 17 (Leuven: Peeters Press, 1989), pp. 335–41.

St. Cyril of Alexandria: The Christological Controversy, its History, Theology, and Texts (Leiden: E. J. Brill, 1994).

Standing in God's Holy Fire: The Byzantine Tradition (London: Darton, Longman and Todd, 2001).

McGuckin, T., 'Saint Thomas Aquinas and Theological Exegesis of Sacred Scripture', *New Blackfriars* 73 (1993), 197–213.

McIntosh, M. A., *Mystical Theology: The Integrity of Spirituality and Theology* (Oxford: Blackwell, 1998).

McIntyre, J., *The Shape of Soteriology: Studies in the Doctrine of the Death of Christ* (Edinburgh: T. & T. Clark, 1992).

McKee, E. A., 'Exegesis, Theology, and Development in Calvin's *Institutio*: A Methodological Suggestion', in E. A. McKee and B. G. Armstrong, eds., *Probing the Reformed Tradition* (Louisville: Westminster John Knox Press, 1989), pp. 154–72.

'Some Reflections on Relating Calvin's Exegesis and Theology', in M. S. Burrows and P. Rorem, eds., *Biblical Hermeneutics in Historical Perspective: Studies in Honor of Karlfried Froehlich on his Sixtieth Birthday* (Grand Rapids: Eerdmans, 1991), pp. 213–26.

McKinion, S. A., *Words, Imagery, and the Mystery of Christ: A Reconstruction of Cyril of Alexandria's Christology* (Leiden: E. J. Brill, 2000).

McNally, R. E., 'Medieval Exegesis', *TS* 22 (1961), 445–54.

Malherbe, A. J., '"Gentle as a Nurse": The Cynic Background to I Thess ii', *NovT* 12 (1970), 203–17.

'Exhortation in First Thessalonians', *NovT* 25 (1983), 238–56.

'Paul – Hellenistic Philosopher or Christian Pastor?', in *Paul and the Popular Philosophers* (Minneapolis: Fortress Press, 1989), pp. 67–79.

'"Pastoral Care" in the Thessalonian Church', *NTS* 36 (1990), 375–91.

'God's New Family in Thessalonica', in L. M. White and D. L. Yarbrough, eds., *The Social World of the First Christians: Essays in Honor of Wayne A. Meeks* (Minneapolis: Fortress Press, 1995), pp. 116–25.

'Conversion to Paul's Gospel', in A. J. Malherbe, F. W. Norris and J. W. Thompson, eds., *The Early Church in its Context: Essays in Honor of Everett Ferguson* (Leiden: E. J. Brill, 1998), pp. 230–44.

The Letter to the Thessalonians: A New Translation with Introduction and Commentary (AB; New York: Doubleday, 2000).

Mann, N., 'The Origins of Humanism', in J. Kraye, ed., *The Cambridge Companion to Renaissance Humanism* (Cambridge: Cambridge University Press, 1996), pp. 1–19.

Mantzaridis, G. I., *The Deification of Man: St Gregory Palamas and the Ortho-dox Tradition*, tr. L. Sherrard (Crestwood: Saint Vladimir's Seminary Press, 1984).

'Spiritual Life in Palamism', in J. Raitt, ed., *Christian Spirituality: High Middle Ages and Reformation* (New York: Crossroad, 1987), pp. 208–22.

Marshall, B. D., *Christology in Conflict: The Identity of a Saviour in Rahner and Barth* (Oxford: Basil Blackwell, 1987).

Marshall, I. H., 'Pauline Theology and the Thessalonian Correspondence', in M. D. Hooker and S. G. Wilson, eds., *Paul and Paulinism: Essays in Hon-our of C. K. Barrett* (London: Society for Promoting Christian Knowledge, 1982), pp. 173–83.

Martin, R. P., *Reconciliation: A Study of Paul's Theology* (London: Marshall, Morgan and Scott, 1981).

Mascall, E. L., *Theology and the Gospel of Christ* (London: Society for Promoting Christian Knowledge, 1977).

Maurer, A., *St Thomas and Historicity* (Milwaukee: Marquette University Press, 1979).

Mearns, C. L., 'Early Eschatological Development in Paul: The Evidence of I and II Thessalonians', *NTS* 27 (1980–1), 137–57.

Merk, O., '1 Thessalonians 2:1–12: An Exegetical Study', in K. P. Donfried and J. Beutler, eds., *The Thessalonians Debate: Methodological Discord or Methodological Synthesis?* (Grand Rapids: Eerdmans, 2000), pp. 89–113.

Meyendorff, J., *A Study of Gregory Palamas*, tr. G. Lawrence (London: The Faith Press, 1964).

Christ in Eastern Christian Thought, tr. Y. Dubois (Crestwood: Saint Vladimir's Seminary Press, 1975).

'Foreword', in Dumitru Stăniloae, *Theology and the Church*, tr. R. Barringer (Crestwood: Saint Vladimir's Seminary Press, 1980), pp. 7–9.

Byzantine Theology: Historical Trends and Doctrinal Themes (2nd edn; New York: Fordham University Press, 1983).

'Christ's Humanity: The Paschal Mystery', *SVTQ* 31 (1987), 5–40.

Meyer, H., *The Philosophy of St. Thomas Aquinas*, tr. F. Eckhoff (St Louis: Herder, 1946).

Miguez Bonino, J., 'Hermeneutics, Truth, and Praxis', in *Doing Theology in a Revolutionary Situation* (Philadelphia: Fortress Press, 1975), pp. 86–105.

Milbank, J., 'The Conflict of the Faculties: Theology and the Economy of the Sciences', in M. T. Nation and S. Wells, ed., *Faithfulness and Fortitude: In Conversation with the Theological Ethics of Stanley Hauerwas* (Edinburgh: T. & T. Clark, 2000), pp. 39–57.

Miller, C., *The Gift of the World: An Introduction to the Theology of Dumitru Stăniloae* (Edinburgh: T. & T. Clark, 2000).

Milligan, G., *St Paul's Epistles to the Thessalonians: The Greek Text with an Introduction and Notes* (London: Macmillan, 1908).

Mitchell, B. and Wiles, M., 'Does Christianity need a Revelation? A Discussion', *Theology* 83 (1980), 103–14.

Mitchell, M. M., *The Heavenly Trumpet: John Chrysostom and the Art of Pauline Interpretation* (Louisville: Westminster John Knox Press, 2002).

Moberly, R. W. L., *The Bible, Theology and Faith: A Study of Abraham and Jesus* (Cambridge: Cambridge University Press, 2000).

Moltmann, J., 'Christian Hope: Messianic or Transcendent? A Theological Discussion with Joachim of Fiore and Thomas Aquinas', tr. M. D. Meeks, *Horizons* 12 (1985), 328–48.

Moo, D. J., *The Epistle to the Romans* (NICNT; Grand Rapids: Eerdmans, 1996).

Morgan, R., 'Expansion and Criticism in the Christian Tradition', in R. Morgan and M. Pye, eds., *The Cardinal Meaning: Essays in Comparative Hermeneutics, Buddhism and Christianity* (The Hague: Mouton Press, 1973), pp. 59–101.

The Nature of New Testament Theology (London: Student Christian Movement, 1973).

'The Historical Jesus and the Theology of the New Testament', in L. D. Hurst and N. T. Wright, eds., *The Glory of Christ in the New Testament: Studies in Christology in Memory of George Bradford Caird* (Oxford: Clarendon Press, 1987), pp. 187–206.

'Historicism', in R. J. Coggins and J. L. Houlden, eds., *A Dictionary of Biblical Interpretation* (London: Student Christian Movement, 1990), pp. 290–1.

Romans (Sheffield: Sheffield Academic Press, 1995).

Morris, L., *The First and Second Epistles to the Thessalonians* (NICNT; revised edn; Grand Rapids: Eerdmans, 1991).

Moule, C. F. D., *The Origins of Christology* (Cambridge: Cambridge University Press, 1977).

Myung, J. A., 'The Influences on Calvin's Hermeneutics and the Development of his Method', *Hervormde Teologiese Studies* 55 (1999), 228–39.

Muller, R. A. and Thompson, J. L., 'The Significance of Pre-critical Exegesis: Retrospect and Prospect', in R. A. Muller and J. L. Thompson, eds., *Biblical Interpretation in the Era of the Reformation: Essays Presented to David C. Steinmetz in Honor of his Sixtieth Birthday* (Grand Rapids: Eerdmans, 1996), pp. 335–45.

Nicole, R., 'John Calvin and Inerrancy', *JETS* 25 (1982), 425–42.

Oberman, H. O., 'Initia Calvini: The Matrix of Calvin's Reformation', in W. H. Neuser, ed., *Calvinus Sacrae Scripturae Professor* (Grand Rapids: Eerdmans, 1994), pp. 113–54.

Ollenburger, B. C., 'Biblical Theology: Situating the Discipline', in J. T. Butler, E. W. Conrad and B. C. Ollenburger, eds., *Understanding the Word: Essays in Honor of Bernard W. Anderson* (JSOTSup 37; Sheffield: Sheffield Academic Press, 1985), pp. 37–62.

'What Krister Stendahl "Meant" – A Normative Critique of "Descriptive Biblical Theology"', *HBT* 8 (1986), 61–98.

O'Loughlin, T., 'Christ and the Scriptures: The Chasm between Modern and Pre-modern Exegesis', *The Month* 31 (1998), 475–85.

O'Meara, T. F., *Thomas Aquinas – Theologian* (Notre Dame: University of Notre Dame Press, 1997).

Oort, J. Van, 'John Calvin and the Church Fathers', in I. Backus, ed., *The Reception of the Church Fathers in the West*, vol. II (Leiden: E. J. Brill, 1997), pp. 661–700.

Ouspensky, L., 'The Meaning and Language of Icons', in L. Ouspensky and V. Lossky, *The Meaning of Icons*, tr. G. E. H. Palmer and E. Kadloubovsky (Crestwood: Saint Vladimir's Seminary Press, 1982), pp. 23–49.

Packer, J. I., 'John Calvin and the Inerrancy of Holy Scripture', in J. D. Hannah, ed., *Inerrancy and the Church* (Chicago: Moody Press, 1984), pp. 143–88.

Pailin, D., 'Incarnation as a Continuing Reality', *RS* 6 (1970), 303–27.

Parker, T. H. L., *Calvin's New Testament Commentaries* (London: SCM, 1971).

'Calvin the Biblical Expositor', in R. C. Gamble, ed., *Calvin and Hermeneutics* (New York: Garland Press, 1992), pp. 65–73.

Partee, C., 'The Soul in Plato, Platonism, and Calvin', *SJT* 22 (1969), 278–95.

'Soul and Body in Anthropology', in *Calvin and Classical Philosophy* (Leiden: E. J. Brill, 1977), pp. 51–65.

Payton, J. R., 'History as Rhetorical Weapon: Christian Humanism in Calvin's Reply to Sadoleto, 1539', in R. C. Gamble, ed., *Calvin's Early Writings and Ministry* (New York: Garland Press, 1992), pp. 208–44.

Pearson, B. A., '1 Thessalonians 2:13–16: A Deutero-Pauline Interpretation', *HTR* 64 (1971), 79–94.

Persson, P. E., *Sacra Doctrina: Reason and Revelation in Aquinas*, tr. R. Mackenzie (Oxford: Basil Blackwell, 1970).

Pesch, O. M., 'Paul as Professor of Theology: The Image of the Apostle in St Thomas' Theology', *The Thomist* 38 (1974), 584–605.

Phan, P. C., *Eternity in Time: A Study of Karl Rahner's Eschatology* (Selinsgrove: Susquehanna University Press, 1988).

Pitkin, B., *What Pure Eyes Could See: Calvin's Doctrine of Faith in its Exegetical Context* (Oxford: Oxford University Press, 1999).

Pope, H., *St Thomas Aquinas as an Interpreter of Holy Scripture* (Oxford: Basil Blackwell, 1924).

Potts, M., 'Aquinas, Hell and the Resurrection of the Damned', *Faith and Philosophy* 15 (1998), 341–51.

Principe, W. H., 'Thomas Aquinas' Principles for Interpretation of Patristic Texts', *Studies in Medieval Culture* 8 (1978), 111–21.

Provence, T. E., 'The Sovereign Subject Matter: Hermeneutics in the *Church Dogmatics*', in D. K. McKim, ed., *A Guide to Contemporary Hermeneutics: Major Trends in Biblical Interpretation* (Grand Rapids: Eerdmans, 1986), pp. 241–62.

Prust, R. C., 'Was Calvin a Biblical Literalist?', *SJT* 20 (1967), 312–28.

Puckett, D. L., *John Calvin's Exegesis of the Old Testament* (Louisville: Westminster John Knox Press, 1995).

Quistorp, H., *Calvin's Doctrine of the Last Things*, tr. H. Knight (London: Lutterworth Press, 1955).

Räisänen, H., *Beyond New Testament Theology: A Story and Programme* (London: Student Christian Movement, 1990).

'The Effective "History" of the Bible: A Challenge to Biblical Scholarship', *SJT* 45 (1992), 303–24.

'The New Testament in Theology', in P. Byrne and L. Houlden, eds., *Companion Encyclopedia of Theology* (London: Routledge, 1995), pp. 122–41.

'Comparative Religion, Theology and New Testament Exegesis', *Studia Theologica* 52 (1998), 116–29.

'Biblical Critics in the Global Village', in H. Räisänen et al., *Reading the Bible in the Global Village* (Atlanta: SBL, 2000), pp. 9–28.

Rice, E. F., 'The Humanist Idea of Christian Antiquity: Lefèvre d'Etaples and his Circle', *Studies in the Renaissance* 9 (1961), 126–41.

Richard, E. J., 'Early Pauline Thought: An Analysis of 1 Thessalonians', in J. M. Bassler, ed., *Pauline Theology, Volume I: Thessalonians, Philippians, Galatians, Philemon* (Minneapolis: Fortress Press, 1991), pp. 39–51.

First and Second Thessalonians (SP; Collegeville: Liturgical Press, 1995).

Riches, J. K., 'A Future for New Testament Theology?', *Literature and Theology* 8 (1994), 343–53.

'Theological Interpretation of the New Testament and the History of Religions – Some Reflections in the Light of Galatians 5:17', in A. Y. Collins and M. M. Mitchell, eds., *Antiquity and Humanity: Essays on Ancient Religion and Philosophy – Presented to Hans Dieter Betz on His 70th Birthday* (Tübingen: Mohr Siebeck, 2001), pp. 245–62.

Ricoeur, P., *Interpretation Theory: Discourse and the Surplus of Meaning* (Fort Worth: Texas Christian University Press, 1976).

'Toward a Hermeneutic of the Idea of Revelation', in *Essays in Biblical Interpretation*, ed. L. S. Mudge (London: Society for Promoting Christian Knowledge, 1981), pp. 73–118.

'Response to Josef Blank', in H. Küng and D. Tracy, eds., *Paradigm Change in Theology: A Symposium for the Future* (Edinburgh: T. & T. Clark, 1989), pp. 283–6.

Robinson, J. A. T., *The Body: A Study in Pauline Theology* (London: Student Christian Movement, 1957).

Rodgers, R., 'An Introduction to the Anabaptists', *EQ* 54 (1982), 36–45.

Rogers, E. F., Jr, *Thomas Aquinas and Karl Barth: Sacred Doctrine and the Natural Knowledge of God* (Notre Dame: University of Notre Dame Press, 1995).

'How the Virtues of an Interpreter Presuppose and Perfect Hermeneutics: The Case of Thomas Aquinas', *JR* 76 (1996), 64–81.

Rogich, D., 'Homily 34 of Saint Gregory Palamas', *GOTR* 33 (1988), 135–66.

Rossouw, H. W., 'Calvin's Hermeneutics of Holy Scripture', no editor cited, *Calvinus Reformatur: His Contribution to Theology, Church and Society* (Potchefstroom: Potchefstroom University for Christian Higher Education, 1982), pp. 149–80.

Rousseau, M. F., 'Elements of a Thomistic Philosophy of Death', *The Thomist* 43 (1979), 581–602.

Russell, N., '"Partakers of the Divine Nature" (2 Peter 1:4) in the Byzantine Tradition', in J. Chrysostomides, ed., *Kathegetria: Essays Presented to Joan Hussey for her 80th Birthday* (Camberley: Porphyrogenitus, 1988), pp. 51–67.

Cyril of Alexandria (London: Routledge, 2000).

Russo, G., 'Rahner and Palamas: A Unity of Grace', *SVTQ* 32 (1988), 157–80.

Sabra, G., *Thomas Aquinas' Vision of the Church: Fundamentals of an Ecumenical Ecclesiology* (Mainz: Matthias-Grünewald-Verlag, 1987).

Sanders, E. P., *Paul and Palestinian Judaism: A Comparison of Patterns of Religion* (London: Student Christian Movement, 1977).

Sandys-Wunsch, J. and Eldredge, L., 'J. P. Gabler and the Distinction between Biblical Studies and Dogmatic Theology: Translation, Commentary and Discussion of his Originality', *SJT* 33 (1980), 133–58.

Sanks, T. H., 'David Tracy's Theological Project: An Overview and Some Implications', *TS* 54 (1993), 698–727.

Schaff, P., 'Calvin as a Commentator', *Presbyterian and Reformed Review* 3 (1892), 462–9.

Schmemann, A., 'Liturgy and Eschatology', in *Liturgy and Tradition: Theological Reflections of Alexander Schmemann*, ed. T. Fisch (Crestwood: Saint Vladimir's Seminary Press, 1990), pp. 89–100.

Schmithals, W., *Paul and the Gnostics*, tr. J. E. Steely (Nashville: Abingdon Press, 1972).

Scholl, H., 'Karl Barth as Interpreter of Calvin's *Psychopannychia*', tr. E. J. Furcha, in W. H. Neuser and B. G. Armstrong, eds., *Calvinus Sincerioris Religionis Vindex* (Kirksville: Sixteenth Century Publishing Inc., 1997), pp. 291–308.

Schweitzer, A., *The Mysticism of Paul the Apostle*, tr. W. Montgomery (London: A. & C. Black, 1931).

Schweizer, E., 'Dying and Rising with Christ', *NTS* 14 (1967), 1–14.

Seifrid, M. A., 'In Christ', in G. F. Hawthorne, R. P. Martin and D. G. Reid, eds., *Dictionary of Paul and his Letters* (Downers Grove: Inter-Varsity Press, 1993), pp. 433–6.

Shanley, B. J., 'Eternal Knowledge of the Temporal in Aquinas', *American Catholic Philosophical Quarterly* 17 (1997), 197–224.

Sheets, J., 'The Scriptural Dimension of St. Thomas', *American Ecclesiastical Review* 144 (1961), 154–73.

Shepphard, G. T., 'Between Reformation and Modern Commentary: The Perception of the Scope of Biblical Books', in G. T. Shepphard, ed., *A Commentary – Galatians, William Perkins* (New York: Pilgrim Press, 1989), pp. xlviii–lxxvii.

Sherrard, P., 'On Death and Dying: A Christian Approach', in *Christianity: Lineaments of a Sacred Tradition* (Edinburgh: T. & T. Clark, 1998), pp. 180–99.

Sherwood, Y., *A Biblical Text and its Afterlives: The Survival of Jonah in Western Culture* (Cambridge: Cambridge University Press, 2000).

Smalley, B. S., *The Study of the Bible in the Middle Ages* (Oxford: Blackwell, 1952).

The Gospels in the Schools (London: Hambledon Press, 1985).

Smeeton, D. D., 'Calvin's Conflict with the Anabaptists', *EQ* 54 (1982), 46–54.

Smith, A., *Comfort One Another – Reconstructing the Rhetoric and Audience of 1 Thessalonians* (Louisville: Westminster John Knox Press, 1995).

Smith, J. W., 'Suffering Impassibly: Christ's Passion in Cyril of Alexandria's Soteriology', *Pro Ecclesia* 11 (2002), 463–83.

Stăniloae, D., *Theology and the Church*, tr. R. Barringer (Crestwood: SVSP, 1980).

Prayer and Holiness, tr. Sisters of the Love of God (Oxford: Sisters of the Love of God Press, 1982).

'The Mystery of the Church', no tr., in G. Limouris, ed., *Church, Kingdom, World: The Church as Mystery and Prophetic Sign* (Geneva: World Council of Churches, 1986), pp. 50–7.

The Experience of God. Orthodox Dogmatic Theology. Volume I: Revelation and Knowledge of the Triune God, tr. and ed. I. Ionita and R. Barringer (Brookline: Holy Cross Orthodox Press, 1994).

Eternity and Time, tr. D. Allchin (Oxford: Sisters of the Love of God Press, 2001).

Stanley, D. M., *Christ's Resurrection in Pauline Soteriology* (Rome: Editrice Pontificio Instituto Biblico, 1961).

Stanton, G., 'Presuppositions of New Testament Criticism', in I. H. Marshall, ed., *New Testament Interpretation: Essays on Principles and Methods* (Carlisle: Paternoster Press, 1977), pp. 60–71.

Steinmetz, D. C., 'The Superiority of Pre-Critical Exegesis', *Theology Today* 37 (1980), 27–38.

'Luther and Calvin on Church and Tradition', *Michigan Germanic Studies* 10 (1984), 98–111.

Stendahl, K., 'Biblical Theology, Contemporary', in G. A. Buttrick et al., eds., *The Interpreter's Dictionary of the Bible* (New York: Abingdon Press, 1962), pp. 418–32.

'Method in the Study of Biblical Theology', in J. P. Hyatt, ed., *The Bible in Modern Scholarship* (London: Carey Kingsgate Press, 1965), pp. 196–209.

Paul among Jews and Gentiles and Other Essays (Minneapolis: Fortress Press, 1976).

'The Bible as Classic and the Bible as Holy Scripture', *JBL* 103 (1984), 3–10.

'Biblical Theology, Contemporary', in H. Räisänen et al., eds., *Reading the Bible in the Global Village* (Atlanta: SBL, 2000), pp. 67–106.

'Dethroning Biblical Imperialism in Theology', in H. Räisänen et al., eds., *Reading the Bible in the Global Village* (Atlanta: SBL, 2000), pp. 61–66.

Still, T., *Conflict at Thessalonica: A Pauline Church and its Neighbours* (JSNTSup 183; Sheffield: Sheffield Academic Press, 1999).

Stout, J., 'What is the Meaning of a Text?', *NLH* 14 (1982), 1–12.

'The Relativity of Interpretation', *The Monist* 69 (1986), 103–18.

Stuhlmacher, P., 'On Pauline Christology', in *Reconciliation, Law and Righteousness: Essays in Biblical Theology*, tr. E. Kalin (Philadelphia: Fortress Press, 1986), pp. 169–81.

Stump, E., 'Biblical Commentary and Philosophy', in N. Kretzmann and E. Stump, eds., *The Cambridge Companion to Aquinas* (Cambridge: Cambridge University Press, 1993), pp. 252–68.

'Revelation and Biblical Exegesis: Augustine, Aquinas and Swinburne', in A. Padgett, ed., *Reason and the Christian Religion: Essays in Honour of Richard Swinburne* (Oxford: Clarendon Press, 1994), pp. 161–97.

Swinburne, R., *Revelation: From Metaphor to Analogy* (Oxford: Clarendon Press, 1992).

Tannehill, R. C., *Dying and Rising with Christ: A Study in Pauline Theology* (Berlin: Verlag Alfred Töpelmann, 1967).

Tanner, K., *Jesus, Humanity and the Trinity: A Brief Systematic Theology* (Edinburgh: T. & T. Clark, 2001).

Tarazi, P. N., *1 Thessalonians: A Commentary* (Crestwood: Saint Vladimir's Seminary Press, 1982).

Tavard, G. H., *The Starting Point of Calvin's Theology* (Grand Rapids: Eerdmans, 2000).

Thiselton, A. C., *New Horizons in Hermeneutics* (London: HarperCollins, 1992).

The First Epistle to the Corinthians: A Commentary on the Greek Text (NIGTC; Grand Rapids: Eerdmans, 2000).

Thompson, B., 'Calvin', in *Humanists and Reformers: A History of the Renaissance and Reformation* (Grand Rapids: Eerdmans, 1996), pp. 471–502.

Thunberg, L., *Man and the Cosmos: The Vision of St. Maximus the Confessor* (Crestwood: Saint Vladimir's Seminary Press, 1985).

Torrance, T. F., *Kingdom and Church: A Study in the Theology of the Reformation* (Edinburgh: Oliver and Boyd, 1956).

'The Eschatology of the Reformation', in T. F. Torrance and J. K. S. Reid, eds., *Eschatology* (*SJT* Occasional Papers No. 2; Edinburgh: Oliver and Boyd, 1957), pp. 36–62.

'Scientific Hermeneutics According to St. Thomas Aquinas', *JTS* NS 13 (1962), 259–89.

'The Mind of Christ in Worship: The Problem of Apollinarianism in the Liturgy', in *Theology in Reconciliation* (London: Geoffrey Chapman, 1975), pp. 139–214.

The Hermeneutics of John Calvin (Edinburgh: T. & T. Clark, 1988).

'The Incarnate Saviour', in *The Trinitarian Faith: The Evangelical Theology of the Ancient Catholic Church* (Edinburgh: T. & T. Clark, 1988), pp. 146–90.

Karl Barth: Biblical and Evangelical Theologian (Edinburgh: T. & T. Clark, 1990).

Divine Meaning: Studies in Patristic Hermeneutics (Edinburgh: T. & T. Clark, 1995).

Torrell, J.-P., *Saint Thomas Aquinas, Volume I: The Person and his Work*, tr. R. Royal (Washington: Catholic University of America Press, 1996).

Tracy, D., *The Analogical Imagination: Christian Theology and the Culture of Pluralism* (London: Student Christian Movement, 1981).

'Creativity in the Interpretation of Religion: The Question of Radical Pluralism', *NLH* 15 (1984), 289–309.

'Is a Hermeneutics of Religion Possible?', in L. S. Rouner, ed., *Religious Pluralism* (Notre Dame: University of Notre Dame Press, 1984), pp. 116–29.

Plurality and Ambiguity (London: Student Christian Movement, 1987).

'The Uneasy Alliance Reconceived: Catholic Theological Method, Modernity, and Postmodernity', *TS* 50 (1989), 548–70.

Trites, A. A., 'The Transfiguration in the Theology of Luke: Some Redactional Links', in L. D. Hurst and N. T. Wright, eds., *The Glory of Christ in the New Testament: Studies in Christology in Memory of George Bradford Caird* (Oxford: Clarendon Press, 1987), pp. 71–81.

Tugwell, S., *Albert and Thomas: Selected Writings*, tr. and ed. S. Tugwell (New York: Paulist Press, 1988).

'Introduction', in *Albert and Thomas: Selected Writings*, tr. and ed. S. Tugwell (New York: Paulist Press, 1988), pp. 201–351.

Turner, H. E. W., *The Patristic Doctrine of Redemption* (London: Mowbray, 1952).

Tyrrell, G., *Christianity at the Cross-Roads* (London: Longmans, 1913).

Valkenberg, W. G. B. M., 'Readers of Scripture and Hearers of the Word in the Medieval Church', *Concilium* 1 (1991), 47–57.

Words of the Living God: Place and Function of Holy Scripture in the Theology of St. Thomas Aquinas (Leuven: Peeters, 2000).

Vass, G. T., '*Secundum Illud Apostoli*': *A Study of the Use of Biblical Auctoritas in the Systematic Theology of Thomas Aquinas* (Rome: Pontificia Universitas Gregoriana, 1962).

Vickers, M. J., 'Hellenistic Thessaloniki', *Journal of Hellenic Studies* 92 (1972), 156–70.

Vos, J. S., 'On the Background of 1 Thessalonians 2:1–12: A Response to Traugott Holtz', in K. P. Donfried and J. Beutler, eds., *The Thessalonians Debate: Methodological Discord or Methodological Synthesis?* (Grand Rapids: Eerdmans, 2000), pp. 81–8.

Walchenbach, J. R., 'John Calvin as Biblical Commentator: An Investigation into Calvin's Use of John Chrysostom as an Exegetical Tutor' (Unpublished Ph.D. Thesis, University of Pittsburgh, 1974).

Walton, S., 'What has Aristotle to Do with Paul? Rhetorical Criticism and 1 Thessalonians', *TB* 46 (1995), 229–50.

Wanamaker, C. A., *The Epistles to the Thessalonians* (NIGTC; Grand Rapids: Eerdmans, 1990).

Ware, K., 'God Hidden and Revealed: The Apophatic Way and the Essence–Energies Distinction,' *Eastern Churches Review* 7 (1975), 125–36.

 The Inner Kingdom (Crestwood: Saint Vladimir's Seminary Press, 2000).

Watson, D. F., 'Paul's Appropriation of Apocalyptic Discourse – The Rhetorical Strategy of 1 Thessalonians', in G. Carey and L. G. Bloomquist, eds., *Vision and Persuasion: Rhetorical Dimensions of Apocalyptic Discourses* (St Louis: Chalice Press, 1999), pp. 61–79.

Watson, F., *Text, Church and World: Biblical Interpretation in Theological Perspective* (Edinburgh: T. & T. Clark, 1994).

 'Is Revelation an "Event"?', *MT* 10 (1994), 383–99.

 'Bible, Theology and the University: A Response to Philip Davies', *JSOT* 71 (1996), 3–16.

 Text and Truth: Redefining Biblical Theology (Edinburgh: T. & T. Clark, 1997).

 'The Bible', in J. B. Webster, ed., *The Cambridge Companion to Karl Barth* (Cambridge: Cambridge University Press, 2000), pp. 57–71.

 'Barth's *Philippians* as Theological Exegesis', in Karl Barth, *Epistle to the Philippians*, tr. J. W. Leitch (Louisville: Westminster John Knox Press, 2002), pp. xxvi–li.

Weaver, D., 'From Paul to Augustine: Romans 5:12 in Early Christian Exegesis', *SVTQ* 27 (1983), 187–206.

 'The Exegesis of Romans 5:12 among the Greek Fathers and its Implication for the Doctrine of Original Sin: The 5th–12th Centuries', *SVTQ* 29 (1985), 133–59 and continued in *SVTQ* 29 (1985), 231–57.

Weber, O., *Foundations of Dogmatics*, vol. I, tr. D. L. Guder (Grand Rapids: Eerdmans, 1981).

Webster, J., 'Locality and Catholicity: Reflections on Theology and the Church', *SJT* 45 (1992), 1–17.

 'Hermeneutics in Modern Theology: Some Doctrinal Reflections', *SJT* 51 (1998), 307–41.

 'Eschatology, Anthropology and Postmodernity', *International Journal of Systematic Theology* 2 (2000), 13–28.

 Word and Church: Essays in Christian Dogmatics (Edinburgh: T. & T. Clark, 2001).

Wedderburn, A. J. M., 'Some Observations on Paul's Use of the Phrases "In Christ" and "With Christ"', *JSNT* 25 (1985), 83–97.

Weima, J. A. D., 'An Apology for the Apologetic Function of 1 Thessalonians 2:1–12', *JSNT* 68 (1997), 73–99.

'The Function of 1 Thessalonians 2:1–12 and the Use of Rhetorical Criticism', in K. P. Donfried and J. Beutler, eds., *The Thessalonians Debate: Methodological Discord or Methodological Synthesis?* (Grand Rapids: Eerdmans, 2000), pp. 114–31.

Weinandy, T. G., *In the Likeness of Sinful Flesh: An Essay on the Humanity of Christ* (Edinburgh: T. & T. Clark, 1993).

Weisheipl, J. A., *Friar Thomas d'Aquino: His Life, Thought and Work* (New York: Doubleday and Company, 1974).

'The Meaning of *Sacra Doctrina* in *Summa Theologiae* I q.1', *The Thomist* 38 (1974), 49–80.

'The Johannine Commentary of Friar Thomas', *CH* 45 (1975), 185–95.

Wendel, F., *Calvin: The Origins and Development of his Religious Thought*, tr. P. Mairet (London: Collins, 1963).

Wengst, K., *Pax Romana and the Peace of Jesus Christ*, tr. J. Bowden (London: SCM, 1987).

Wharton, J. A., 'Karl Barth as Exegete and his Influence on Biblical Interpretation', *USQR* 28 (1972), 5–13.

Wickham, L. R., 'Symbols of the Incarnation in Cyril of Alexandria', in M. Schmidt and C. F. Geyer, eds., *Typus, Symbol, Allegorie bei den Östlichen Vätern und ihren Parallelen im Mittelalter* (Regensburg: Verlag Friedrich Puslet, 1982), pp. 41–53.

Wiles, M. F., *The Divine Apostle: The Interpretation of St Paul's Apostles in the Early Church* (Cambridge: Cambridge University Press, 1967).

Wilken, R. L., 'Exegesis and the History of Theology: Reflections on the Adam-Christ Typology in Cyril of Alexandria', *CH* 35 (1966), 139–56.

'St Cyril of Alexandria: The Mystery of Christ in the Bible', *Pro Ecclesia* 4 (1995), 454–78.

'St Cyril of Alexandria: Biblical Expositor', *Coptic Church Review* 19 (1998), 30–41.

Williams, A. N., *The Ground of Union: Deification in Aquinas and Palamas* (New York: Oxford University Press, 1999).

Williams, G. H., 'Calvin and the Radical Reformation', in *The Radical Reformation* (London: Weidenfeld and Nicholson, 1962), pp. 580–614.

Williams, R., 'The Philosophical Structures of Palamism', *Eastern Churches Review* 9 (1977), 27–44.

'Poetic and Religious Imagination', *Theology* 80 (1977), 178–87.

Resurrection (London: Darton, Longman and Todd, 1982).

Open to Judgement (London: Darton, Longman and Todd, 1994).

'The Body's Grace', in C. Hefling, ed., *Our Selves, Our Souls and Bodies: Sexuality and the Household of God* (Cambridge: Cowley Publications, 1996), pp. 58–68.

Lost Icons: Reflections on Cultural Bereavement (Edinburgh: T. & T. Clark, 2000).

On Christian Theology (Oxford: Blackwell, 2000).

Wink, W., *The Bible in Human Transformation* (Philadelphia: Fortress Press, 1973).

Winslow, D. F., *The Dynamics of Salvation: A Study in Gregory of Nazianzus* (Cambridge: Philadelphia Patristic Foundation, 1979).

Wright, N. T., *The Climax of the Covenant: Christ and the Law in Pauline Theology* (Edinburgh: T. & T. Clark, 1991).

'Gospel and Theology in Galatians', in L. A. Jervis and P. Richardson, eds., *Gospel in Paul: Studies on Corinthians, Galatians and Romans for Richard N. Longenecker* (JSNTSup 108; Sheffield: Academic Press, 1994), pp. 222–39.

'Paul's Gospel and Caesar's Empire', in R. A. Horsley, ed., *Paul and Politics: Ekklesia, Imperium, Interpretation* (Harrisburg: Trinity Press International, 2000), pp. 160–83.

Wyneken, K. H., 'Calvin and Anabaptism', in R. C. Gamble, ed., *Calvin's Opponents* (New York: Garland Publishing, 1992), pp. 2–13.

Yarbro Collins, A., 'Fundamentalist Interpretation of Biblical Symbols', in M. J. Selvidge, ed., *Fundamentalism Today: What Makes it So Attractive?* (Elgin: Brethren Press, 1984), pp. 107–14.

Yeago, D. S., 'Jesus of Nazareth and Cosmic Redemption: The Relevance of St Maximus the Confessor', *MT* 12 (1996), 163–93.

'The New Testament and the Nicene Dogma: A Contribution to the Recovery of Theological Exegesis', in S. E. Fowl, ed., *The Theological Interpretation of Scripture: Classic and Contemporary Readings* (Oxford: Blackwell, 1997), pp. 87–100.

Young, F. M., 'A Reconsideration of Alexandrian Christology', *JECH* 22 (1971), 103–14.

Sacrifice and the Death of Christ (London: Society for Promoting Christian Knowledge, 1975).

Zachman, R. C., 'Gathering Meaning from the Context: Calvin's Exegetical Method', *JR* 82 (2000), 1–26.

INDEX OF BIBLICAL REFERENCES

INDEX OF AUTHORS

INDEX OF SUBJECTS